AMERICAN DUDE RANCH

The *William F. Cody*
Series on the History and
Culture of the American West

AMERICAN DUDE RANCH

A TOUCH OF THE COWBOY AND THE THRILL OF THE WEST

LYNN DOWNEY

UNIVERSITY OF OKLAHOMA PRESS : NORMAN

Buffalo Bill Center of the West sponsorship of The William F. Cody Series on the History and Culture of the American West is generously funded by the Geraldine W. & Robert J. Dellenback Foundation, Inc.

Library of Congress Cataloging-in-Publication Data

Names: Downey, Lynn, 1954– author.
Title: American dude ranch : a touch of the cowboy and the thrill of the West / Lynn Downey.
Description: Norman : University of Oklahoma Press, [2022] | Series: The William F. Cody series on the history and culture of the American West ; volume 8 | Includes bibliographical references. | Summary: "Provides a history of the dude ranch that includes an examination of its connections to American cultural touchstones such as film, literature, clothing, food, race relations, and the role of women"—Provided by publisher.
Identifiers: LCCN 2021031892 | ISBN 978-0-8061-8022-9 (paperback)
Subjects: LCSH: Dude ranches—United States.
Classification: LCC GV198.95 .D69 2022 | DDC 796.56—dc23
LC record available at https://lccn.loc.gov/2021031892

American Dude Ranch: A Touch of the Cowboy and the Thrill of the West is Volume 8 in The William F. Cody Series on the History and Culture of the American West

The paper in this book meets the guidelines for permanence and durability of the Committee on Production Guidelines for Book Longevity of the Council on Library Resources, Inc. ∞

Copyright © 2022 by the University of Oklahoma Press, Norman, Publishing Division of the University. Manufactured in the U.S.A.

All rights reserved. No part of this publication may be reproduced, stored in a retrieval system, or transmitted, in any form or by any means, electronic, mechanical, photocopying, recording, or otherwise—except as permitted under Section 107 or 108 of the United States Copyright Act—without the prior written permission of the University of Oklahoma Press. To request permission to reproduce selections from this book, write to Permissions, University of Oklahoma Press, 2800 Venture Drive, Norman, OK 73069, or email rights.oupress@ou.edu.

For my parents

Harvey Orion Downey Jr.
1925–2005

Evadne Lee Pickering
1928–1985

Contents

Series Editors' Foreword	ix
Preface	xi
Acknowledgments	xvii
Chapter 1	1
Chapter 2	12
Chapter 3	24
Chapter 4	35
Chapter 5	46
Chapter 6	58
Chapter 7	70
Chapter 8	82
Chapter 9	123
Chapter 10	137
Chapter 11	149
Chapter 12	160
Chapter 13	171
Chapter 14	183
Epilogue	196
Appendix: The Dude Ranchers' Association	201
Notes	205
Bibliography	213
Index	219

Series Editors' Foreword

Like many well-to-do easterners in the 1880s, Theodore Roosevelt came west for the first time to hunt bison in the Dakota Badlands. Soon after the young "dude" from New York purchased a horse and invested in a cattle ranch. Only two years later, Owen Wister, a fellow Harvard graduate and a friend of Roosevelt's, completed his first hunting trip to Wyoming and drew upon his experiences to write *The Virginian* (1902), which is considered the first successful western novel. Early in his career, Buffalo Bill guided royal figures such as the Grand Duke Alexis and prominent entrepreneurs such as Winston Churchill's grandfather Leonard Jerome, who could afford such extravagances, on extensive tours of the West. Collectively through their writings, Wister and Roosevelt translated their direct experiences primarily to upper- and middle-class Americans and Europeans, many of whom visited the West in style, while a select few chose to enjoy more rugged experiences. The dramatic reenactments of western adventures presented by Buffalo Bill's Wild West show expanded that audience to include lower-middle- and working-class families who embraced the popular interpretation of the American West.

The popular appeal of the rugged lifestyle in the American West that Roosevelt called the "strenuous life" drew many visitors who wanted to experience more than scenery, preferring instead to inhabit the role of the increasingly iconic cowboy. Howard Eaton, one of Roosevelt's Dakota neighbors, noted the increase in visitors to his ranch and realized he could make more money hosting "dudes" than chasing cattle. In 1904 he established Eatons' Ranch, the first official dude ranch in Wolf, Wyoming. Toward the end of his life, Buffalo Bill also transformed his beloved TE Ranch in Wyoming to accommodate tourists. Lynn Downey's *American Dude Ranch* provides a broad social and cultural history of this phenomenon and the diverse community drawn to these ranches for the chance to live out their dreams of playing cowboy for a week or more. Downey explores how dude ranches, both within and without the American West, broadly influenced American culture and transnational perceptions of the romanticized western mythology.

Downey's account shows how the dude ranching experience influenced mainstream American popular culture, literary works, and consumer products. Hollywood stars such as Gary Cooper, Bella Lugosi, and Elvis enjoyed staying and working at various dude ranches. The isolated setting of dude ranches also inspired authors, including Ernest Hemingway, who worked on his manuscripts while recreating in Wyoming, and scriptwriter Herman Mankiewicz, who wrote portions of *Citizen Kane* at a California dude ranch. Downey also notes how the popularity of dude ranching influenced western clothing styles (or very little clothing, as in the case of Sally Rand's nudist ranch). The strenuous lifestyle on these ranches even led many consumers to embrace a pain-relieving liniment rub for horses, developed in 1892 by W. F. Young, Inc., of Massachusetts, which was ultimately reformulated and rebranded for human use as Absorbine Jr.

While Downey focuses on traditional tourists and the well-known divorce ranches in Nevada, she also brings long-overdue attention to the western-themed resorts that served African American and Jewish guests, as well as the ways that some resort ranches employed and catered to the LGBT community. Downey demonstrates that this unique experience, in the same vein as Buffalo Bill's Wild West exhibitions and other popularizers of western lore, inspired and touched a diverse population, from the dude ranchers and wranglers to many kinds of dudes from all around the world.

Jeremy Johnston
Frank Christianson
Douglas Seefeldt

Preface

In June 2006 I hopped into a blue Saturn sedan loaded with luggage, bags of snacks, a pile of books and maps, and a tablet of Mad Libs. The car belonged to my childhood friend Kay, a professor at the State University of New York in Fredonia, near Buffalo. She was starting a year-long sabbatical and had decided to spend it in the San Francisco Bay Area where we'd grown up together and where her family (and I) still lived. She wanted to drive out to California and invited me to come along, so I flew east to join her.

Picture it: two women in their mid-fifties, driving a clunky car with a SUNY sticker on the bumper and classical music blaring from the CD player. Thelma and Louise we weren't. But we were westerners and historians, and we made sure our trip through the upper Midwest, Badlands, Tetons, and Great Basin hit as many heritage high spots as possible.

About halfway through our road trip we took a wildlife-filled drive through Bighorn National Forest and started out of the mountains toward Cody, Wyoming, our next stop. Just before the road veered down a steep hill toward the flatlands, we noticed a couple of cars stopped in front of a cattle guard, so we pulled up behind them. There were also some pickup trucks parked on the side of the road. We then saw a weathered middle-aged man walk up to the first car, say something to the people inside, and make his way to us. He wore a red-and-white-striped western shirt, battered cowboy hat, well-worn jeans, and scuffed, calf-colored boots. I was at the wheel that day, and I rolled down the window as he approached.

He touched his hat and said, "Hello, ladies. Sorry for the delay, but we're driving some cattle up into the mountains for the summer and we have to use the road for about another half hour."

Kay asked him, "Do you have any help at the other end?"

"Well, we had a couple of dudes with us, but they took off to have some lunch. I've got some men down there at the bottom."

We laughed, as he seemed amused about the dudes, rather than irritated. A few minutes later a line of brown and black steers trotted toward us. They seemed to know where they were going and skirted the cattle guard as they headed onto a mountain path. The flow slowed down after about twenty minutes, and the cowboy waved to those of us in our cars, motioning that we could now drive down the hill. We met a few bovine stragglers as we went around a bend, but they scooted away from us. When we cleared the mountain, we could see the endless sky and glorious landscape of the Bighorn Basin.

We also saw two young, mounted cowboys who were keeping watch at the other end of the operation. I drove slowly past them and we waved our thanks through the open car window. They touched their hats, and their leather saddles creaked as they bowed in our direction. At that moment Kay and I—mature intellectuals old enough to be grandmothers—turned into giggly, blushing teenagers. We leaned out the window, squealed "Thank you!" and blushed even more when the cowboys smiled, their tanned faces crinkling.

The rest of our trip was like a live-action western postcard: Yellowstone, the Tetons, a sliver of Idaho, and the long, lovely Nevada desert. The coffee got better the farther west we went (a diner in Winnemucca was the high point), and we made it to the Bay Area tired but triumphant.

Our adventures stayed with me for a long time, especially the cowboys and the cattle drive. I'd heard people use the word "dude" to mean a tenderfoot, of course—that is, someone who isn't a cowboy but wants to be. However, I didn't expect a "real" cowboy to call someone a dude and mean it without irony or ridicule.

I was intrigued but also a little embarrassed.

Because I was also a dude.

More accurately, I was a "dudine," the clumsy feminine form of the word. Even though there were actual cowboys in my family, I was afraid of horses. During the 1960s, one of my uncles raised quarter horses in a working-class suburb east of San Francisco, and two of my cousins were bulldoggers and calf ropers on the rodeo circuit. I have a photo of my first time on Ginger, one of my uncle's horses, when I was about three, and even in the small black-and-white snapshot you can see how uneasy I was. I look a little happier as an eleven-year-old in a trail ride photo, taken on a family vacation at California's Trinity Lake, but it would be nearly forty years before I got on a horse again. Although many a dudine sat well in a saddle, I was not one of them.

As I grew up and came to love the history of the West, I sometimes asked myself, "How can I call myself a westerner and not be horsey?" I eventually decided that my career as an archivist of western history collections and the books I wrote on the same subject—work that came from a deep love of my home region—absolved me. Not only that, in 1989 I was hired as the first historian for Levi Strauss & Co. in San Francisco, a company with impeccable western credentials.

I ran into the word "dude" a lot when I started working at LS&Co. I was in charge of the firm's archives, and among its many treasures was a folder of 1930s clothing catalogs for something called "Dude Ranch Duds." Many pieces of this clothing were also in the archives: satin shirts in bright colors with piping in contrasting shades, side-zip gabardine riding pants for women, and plaid shirts for both sexes in fine, soft flannel.

Thanks to films and television shows, I was under the impression that dude ranches had the same reputation as the word "dude" itself: something not quite legitimate, a place where people pretended to be cowboys in clothing no real cowboy would be seen in, and where they were figures of fun. I accepted the conventional wisdom about dudes, though every time I handled the "duds" in the LS&Co. archives I knew there had to be more to the story.

I found it in the small Arizona town of Wickenburg.

Located about fifty miles northwest of Phoenix, Wickenburg started life as a mining camp, but locals and out-of-towners began to open dude ranches in the area around World War I, and by the end of the 1940s vacationers had nearly ten ranches to choose from.

I first went to Wickenburg in 2003 to do research on a pair of old Levi's jeans that a miner had purchased there in 1917. The folks at the Desert Caballeros Western Museum welcomed me and helped me find what I needed, and I fell in love with the desert and the town itself. I met people doing all kinds of work, including running dude ranches. When I decided to write a book about Wickenburg's history, I thought it would be a good idea to stay at one of them.

Five days at the Flying E Ranch changed my entire perspective on what a dude ranch is.

Far from being a place where wobbly tourists bounced on horses and wore citified, fancy clothing, the ranch was filled with people who'd been coming there for years, who were serious horsemen and horsewomen, who wore old jeans and dirt-encrusted boots on twice-daily rides, and who were so comfortable it was as if they were in their own home. The longtime managers were locals who had grown up on horses themselves, and I knew the cowboy shirts they wore were from their closets and weren't a costume.

No one made fun of me as I struggled onto a horse for my first trail ride since 1965, led by a wrangler who was also a poet and who made a few stops along the way to declaim the occasional verse. Everyone answered my questions about history and dude ranch life with interest and enthusiasm, and I left the Flying E feeling as though I'd discovered a new country.

A few years later I organized a press tour for Levi Strauss & Co. at another Wickenburg ranch, the Rancho de los Caballeros. More upscale but no less authentic, Los Cab offered a dozen fashion editors a variety of western activities to choose from. I gave interviews about how LS&Co. created the first jeans for women in 1934 so that eastern ladies would have something sturdy and feminine to wear on dude ranches.

Both of these experiences upended my thinking about the dude ranch and its place in western history, and my fascination grew. I began to collect postcards, matchbooks, pamphlets, magazine articles, posters, paper dolls, memoirs, and bandannas, turning the walls of my home office into a sort of dude's gallery.

I also started to read books about the history of western tourism and often encountered the snarky, antidude attitude I'd seen in TV shows and movies. But some authors saw the dude ranch as a legitimate response to the romantic notions about the West that are sometimes submerged in American culture but never really go away.

I discovered that as early as the 1920s, cities like Cody, Wyoming; Bandera, Texas; and Victorville, California—as well as Wickenburg—billed themselves as the "Dude Ranch Capital of America," or the "Dude Ranch Capital of the World." States that had no dude ranches at all regularly featured stories in regional newspapers about the Bar B C, the Remuda Ranch, the OTO, and others, which operated from Jackson Hole to Tucson. Why was it so important to be the Dude Ranch Capital of anything? Why did dude ranches capture the public imagination in places they didn't exist?

I continued my reading, and I also studied the archives in the McCracken Research Library at the Buffalo Bill Center of the West in Cody, as well as the collections of the American Heritage Center at the University of Wyoming in Laramie. I ordered scads of digital material from Montana State University in Bozeman, and I hired a friend in Helena to do research for me at the Montana Historical Society. I wanted to know how and why dude ranching got started, and how ranches (and their owners) have changed as society, vacation habits, and attitudes about the West have changed. I wondered what kind of people started dude ranches, and why they stuck with them.

I also wanted to follow dude ranching's path through American culture. The dude ranch has influenced movies and TV, books, music, clothing, the role of women, even how we eat. Anti-Semitism, LGBTQ history, comic strips, the *Green Book*, and the origin of the word "dude" itself are also part of the story. And above all is a nostalgia for the iconic cowboy. How did this happen?

This book is the result of my research and obsessive collecting. In my wanderings I found a richer—and sometimes funnier—story than I expected. However contested and complicated, western history is one of America's national origin stories that we turn to in times of cultural upheaval and national nervousness. Dude ranches provide a tangible link to this imagined, but no less important past, and the persistence and popularity of dude ranching demonstrates how important this link still is. For 140 years dude ranches have given visitors from all over the world a touch of the cowboy and the thrill of the West. This book tells their story.

A note to the reader: the long history of dude ranching includes a couple of themes that are not in the book. The first is the decades-long relationship between dude ranchers and the federal government, which has wavered back and forth between cooperation and conflict. The second is the opinion of early ranchers regarding the importance of wildlife and wilderness conservation, as well as environmental stewardship in general. These two subjects alone could fill a book and are well documented in works by Lawrence Borne, Joel Bernstein, and Hudson Kensel, which can be found in the bibliography.

Except for writing about the histories of the founding dude ranches of the late nineteenth and early twentieth centuries, I do not discuss the many ranches still in business today. Every dude ranch has a fascinating story, and writing about all of them could fill a whole book (and would be an interesting read). But for those who are interested, there are quite a few books out there about the history of individual ranches.

So, to the dude ranchers I've spent time with and to those I hope to meet, this book is about all of you and your place in the history of the West.

Acknowledgments

Writing acknowledgments is one of my favorite parts of being an author. I get to thank a list of lovely people and give well-deserved kudos to my fellow archivists and the extraordinary places they work.

When you write about the West, there are two repositories you absolutely must visit: the McCracken Research Library at the Buffalo Bill Center of the West in Cody, Wyoming, and the American Heritage Center at the University of Wyoming in Laramie. I was lucky enough to go to both places when doing the research for this book, thanks to a resident fellowship from the McCracken Library and a travel grant from the American Heritage Center. Over two separate trips and some follow-up emails, the staff members of these institutions helped me pull from their collections the stories and images that are at the heart of this book.

I would like to thank Mary Robinson, Housel Director at the McCracken Research Library, and staff members Samantha Harper, Karen Preis, Karen Roles, and Eric Rossborough for their tireless pulling of boxes, deep knowledge of their collections, and patient answers to my many questions. I am especially grateful to Mary Robinson, who indulged me on my birthday by letting me hold a signed photo of Annie Oakley, whose birthday I share. Buffalo Bill Center of the West historian Jeremy Johnston's research on the links between Cody and California philanthropist Phoebe Hearst helped me add a great story to my narrative. And thanks also to Terry Harley for helping me navigate the fellowship paperwork.

Ginny Kilander and Vicki Glantz at the American Heritage Center were almost as enthusiastic about my project as I was. They and the center's knowledgeable staff suggested avenues of research I had not considered, and my book is the better for it. While I was in Laramie, my life was also enriched by the kindness of Mark Jones and Kori Wilkinson, Amanda Smith, and Jenne Lee Sanford, a story I tell in the epilogue.

Three amazing women graciously dropped what they were doing to give me interviews about their lives and experiences: Dolly Turner, former dude ranch owner; Colleen Chisman, dude ranch wrangler and all-around employee; and Bryce Albright, executive director of the Dude Ranchers' Association. Bryce also patiently answered my many questions along the way, and she and former DRA executive director Colleen Hodson let me muscle my way into the organization's 2020 annual meeting to give a talk about dude ranch history.

John Johnson of Helena, Montana, dug deep into the collections of the Montana Historical Society to find dude ranch materials for me and also read a draft of the manuscript. I would like to thank his wife, my childhood friend Shawnee Farnham, for her patience as John and I talked about dudes for the many months I worked on this book.

While at the Montana Historical Society, John found Molly Wilson's 1946 letters from the Bones Brothers Ranch. These documents helped me find Molly's daughter, Lucy Murphy, who gave me the great privilege of telling her mother's story.

Lynne Lugosi Sparks, granddaughter of Bela Lugosi, was equally generous in allowing me to add a little-known tale about her grandfather to my book.

Patricia A. Billingsley discovered the diary of Philip Cummings and generously shared its contents and her own insights with me.

Dr. Eric Gonzaba, assistant professor in the Department of American Studies at California State University, Fullerton, gave me much-needed insight into the LGBTQ history of the West. If you don't already follow him on Twitter, you should.

Sherry Monahan cleared up the mystery of "Dude Soda."

My friends and colleagues Tracey Panek and Laura O'Hara of the Levi Strauss & Co. Archives cheerfully indulged my requests for images and documents. Seeing the historical materials again brought back many happy memories.

Thanks also to my tireless first readers, advisers, and cheerleaders: Patti Elkin, Jennifer Gunn, Jill Hunting, Roger Peterson, Jeff Spielberg, and Mark Yateman.

Don Silverek's digital scanning skills made the historical photos shine. And Laurel Anderton's elegant editing made my prose do the same.

I am also thankful for the following people and institutions: Gary Barnhart, Montana State University; Lauren Goss, Special Collections and University Archives, University of Oregon; Joshua Rowley, David M. Rubenstein Rare

Book and Manuscript Library, Duke University; Laura E. Rocke, Special Collections and University Archives, University of Nevada, Reno; University of Iowa Libraries; Houghton Library, Harvard University; and Yale Collection of Western Americana, Beinecke Rare Book and Manuscript Library.

Finally, I am deeply grateful for the friends and family members who have been listening to me talk about dude ranching during the years I spent researching and writing this book. I never saw your eyes glaze over. That means everything to an author.

Chapter 1

On an early summer day in 1915 a suntanned, middle-aged man named Howard Eaton walked into the downtown Pittsburgh office of novelist and mystery writer Mary Roberts Rinehart. Originally from Pittsburgh himself, he now lived in Wolf, Wyoming, where he and his brothers owned something called a "dude ranch." Eaton was also the most well-known hunting and packing guide in the region, and he was organizing a big horseback trip into newly opened Glacier National Park that July. He hoped that Rinehart and her physician husband would join the group; Eaton was a savvy self-promoter and knew that having the famous writer along would be good for business.

Dr. Rinehart loved the idea because his wife needed a distraction. She had gone overseas to work as a correspondent in the early months of World War I. After returning from Europe, she fell into a depression brought about by what she had seen over there, by too much hard work on her writing, and by the death of a beloved uncle.

Rinehart reluctantly agreed to come along, and the group—which included famed western artist Charles M. Russell—met up at the Eaton ranch before setting out on the trail. The experience changed her life. After the Glacier trip she and her family spent many seasons at Eatons,' and around 1925 she started publishing articles about dude ranches: what they were, what you did there, what you wore there, how well-suited they were for women tourists. She always held up Howard Eaton's place as the best example of its kind, and there was a good reason for this, which Rinehart knew well and rarely failed to mention.

Eatons' was America's first dude ranch.

The Eaton brothers began their operation informally and watched it turn into the model for an established industry. They and their fellow westerners hosted visitors at ranches and camps in the first place because many cultural trails had come together in the mid-nineteenth century. The first of these was the lure of hunting in the Rocky Mountain West, popularized by members of the English aristocracy.

Stories about vast herds of game in the wilds of Wyoming and Montana made their way to England in the 1850s, and men like famed hunter Sir John Watts Garland trekked to the Rockies in the years after the Civil War. Garland built camps and a small lodge that he returned to off and on for years, an idea that other men copied for themselves and their friends. The Irish Earl of Dunraven was another entranced visiting hunter who showed up in the early 1870s. Buffalo Bill Cody and Texas Jack Omohundro, also a scout like his friend Cody, led Dunraven's party on a month-long elk hunt. The earl also built a lodge (as well as a cattle ranch) as his base of operations in Estes Park, Colorado.

Hunters continued to stream into the Rocky Mountain West. So did a few intrepid tourists like English-born Isabella Bird, who paid locals near Estes Park for a place to stay and greasy, fly-specked food to eat in the days before she became a celebrity in 1873 for climbing Longs Peak. The description of Bird's privations in her 1879 book, *A Lady's Life in the Rocky Mountains*, did nothing to discourage people from traveling to Colorado.

This publicity brought more attention to the region and fueled a growing interest in the West beyond its reputation for excellent elk, deer, and antelope hunting. In 1872 the US government opened Yellowstone National Park, and people flocked there to see the geysers and spectacular mountain scenery they'd heard about. A decade later President Chester A. Arthur decided to take a trip West. Accompanied by generals Phil Sheridan and William T. Sherman, Arthur went to Fort Washakie, Wyoming, in 1883 and joined a waiting pack train. The party went up the Wind River, then to Jackson Hole, and on to Yellowstone. Newspapers across the country followed his progress and reported on the strange story of a party of "Texas cowboys" who planned to kidnap the president and hold him for ransom, later described as a typical western "yarn."[1]

Both the descriptions of Yellowstone's wonders and the short-term excitement of cowboy depredations made the West look both enticing and slightly dangerous, a combination guaranteed to inspire a certain kind of traveler. But while hunting tales and presidential pack trains brought a few dollars to locals who had spare rooms in their cabins for passing visitors, one more historical trail was needed before the dude ranch could be conceived.

You can't have a ranch without cattle.

The cattle business as we know it began in the years after the Civil War, showing strongest in Kansas, Nebraska, Wyoming, Montana, Colorado, the Dakotas, and Texas as railroads snaked across the country. Cattle drives spurred herds to railheads across the West, and big livestock firms took in investors who saw how profitable the cattle business was. Some of them were the British hunting enthusiasts who already had comfortable lodges, such as the Irish Dunraven. Another, Moreton Frewen, built a huge ranch on the Powder River, a waterway that straddles the Montana-Wyoming border. He was a charming host who loved visitors, and some of the friends who came to stay at his ranch bought properties themselves.

These early ranchers were happy to give lodging to the strangers who were passing by, on their way to either hunt or simply take in the local scenery. But generosity was expensive, so Frewen and others began to charge their visitors money, trade them fresh meat for the use of a horse, or barter other valuable commodities to cover costs.

The good times ended in the winter of 1886–87, when unprecedented winter blizzards and plummeting temperatures broke the industry's back by killing off whole herds of livestock, a horror called the "Big Die-Up." People still needed beef, and the business didn't disappear completely, but the days of big cattle drives were over. Small outfits also suffered and were often in worse condition than bigger ones. Some went under, others hung in until conditions got better, and some prospered because they had other sources of income.

Enter the Eaton brothers.

The family, which counted nine children, lived in Pittsburgh, and Howard was born there in 1851, followed by Willis in 1852, and Alden in 1859. Howard chafed at life in Pennsylvania and lit out for the West when he was just seventeen, working for a time in Omaha, followed by some months at sea, and then a return home. In 1879 the family's finances began to crumble and Howard left Pittsburgh again, this time for the Dakota Badlands, where he knew he could find work. He was an accomplished hunter, and along with a partner named E. G. Paddock, he supported himself by supplying meat to the men building the Northern Pacific Railway.

He did well enough to buy property near Medora, North Dakota, and made his home in an abandoned cabin once used by a stage company. He had big plans, which he demonstrated with the name of his new enterprise: the Custer Trail Ranch, so called because the general, who had been killed a few years earlier at the Battle of the Little Bighorn (or the Greasy Grass, as the Lakota and Cheyenne called it), had allegedly once camped in the area.

In 1881 Alden Eaton joined his brother in Medora, and that same year the men invited an acquaintance from Pennsylvania, A. C. Huidekoper, to come out for a buffalo hunt. Huidekoper had seen the Dakotas two years earlier and didn't need much convincing. Both Eatons raved about the potential of the Badlands as cattle country, and in 1882 the brothers and Huidekoper started the Custer Trail Cattle Company, with the latter supplying the funding to buy the initial stock. Willis Eaton came West the same year and helped build new cabins as the three planned their prosperous future.

The busy Eatons wrote letters about life in Dakota to their friends back East, and men started showing up in Medora, both to see the wild country and to follow Howard on hunting trips. Though pleased that they had visitors to whom they could show off their ranch and their packing skills, the Eatons also realized how their hospitality ate into the cattle profits. Some men offered to cover their costs, but not all of them. With the entrepreneurial spirit that sent them West in the first place, the Eaton brothers decided to formally charge visitors to stay in one of their cabins. They bought a guest book, and in 1882 Bert Rumsey of Buffalo, New York, was the first to sign it. He was a wealthy hunter and polo player, and he returned to Wyoming a few more times to bring back some big game.

Visitors to the Custer Trail Ranch paid $10 per week (nearly $300 today), but this was not a daunting amount to independently wealthy men who could afford the long trip out West.[2] The Eatons' neighbors and the thriving business owners in nearby Medora soon had a name for them: dudes.

"Dude" is one of those words whose meaning changes over time but has proved to be so useful it's never gone out of style. Style is appropriate here, because the origin of "dude" began with clothing.

In the eighth century the word "duddes" was a northern English term for clothes, and seven hundred years later "dudes" meant coarse garments or peasant wear. A "dudesman" was a scarecrow in clothing so raggedy no commoner would be seen in it. By the seventeenth century the word had evolved to "duds" and meant clothes of any kind, no matter what they looked like. But the fortunes of the word changed when the British crossed the Atlantic to the New World.

In early America, "duds" still meant clothing, and though scholars aren't quite sure how it happened, "dude" reappeared in the mid- to late nineteenth century. By this time, the word referred to the person who wore fancy "duds," and it was often used to mean a "dandy": a snappy dresser who reveled in others seeing just how well turned out he was. And of course, these "dandies" were all men.

The 1880s, the decade that saw the creation of the first real dude ranch, also saw the word "dude" itself take off. In 1883 a poem titled "The Delighted Dude" made the rounds of American newspapers. Written in the first person, each stanza is a celebration of the writer's style, gait, clothing, and hair. "My clothes fit tight as a papered wall / You could pick me out of a thousand," it begins. The Dude despises "the rough, rude press / Who mock my dress" and knows that others secretly envy him. The poem ends: "But best of all, few can intrude / Upon our brood / For we exclude / Every fellow that's not a dude / And he is one in a thousand."[3]

Tight pants were the dude's most prominent feature, and these were either most offensive or most amusing. "How large an idea does it take to fill a dude's head as completely as his thin legs fill his tight trowsers?" asked a writer for the *Albany Express*.[4]

But not all dudes were men who thought too much of themselves. A young man named P. C. Collins, referred to as "the dashing and handsome 'Dude' of everybody's acquaintance," was featured in a Lima, Ohio, newspaper article in 1881. He was the new owner of a saddlery and harness shop where he no doubt wore appropriate, unfussy work clothing. However, his off-duty wardrobe must have been finer than most leatherworkers were accustomed to wearing—hence the nickname. But it's given with affection, not derision.[5]

That was rare. By early 1883 newspapers from New York to New Mexico were running multiple articles about dudes: what they looked like, where they lived, how attractive they were to women, and how annoying and stupid they were. Their attention to clothes made them unmanly, and there were also hints of homosexuality. "Well what is a dude? A dude is one who would / Be a woman if he could / As that he can't does all he can / To show the world that he's not a man."[6]

There seemed to be no racial barrier to being a dude either, at least in the 1880s. "Two colored dudes" wandered back and forth on the newly opened Brooklyn Bridge wearing high, stiff collars stenciled with the name of a popular laundry soap as an advertisement. "The practical use to which even a dude can be put was illustrated in their cases."[7]

And in 1889 Mark Twain used the word in his novel *A Connecticut Yankee in King Arthur's Court*, giving it an anti-American spin. He said that the only Americans who still venerated British rank and titles were "dudes and dudesses," and because the Knights of the Round Table did the same, he called them "iron dudes." Early illustrations for the book depict the knights in suits of armor that look dandyish rather than daunting.[8]

The men who stayed with the Eatons would often wander into Medora or its rival town, Little Missouri, just across the river of the same name, and they quickly earned their dude credentials. They would visit the two villages' many saloons, including Bill Williams's, where they were a constant source of amusement. They could also go to Little Tom's saloon, where Tom himself, the Festive Barkeep, served Dude Soda, which was probably weak beer.

Howard Eaton's name showed up frequently in the local newspaper, the *Bad Lands Cow Boy*. And the Eatons' ranch was proving to be a popular place, even if many of these early visitors were friends or business acquaintances. Dude ranches got their real start with networks just like these.

In the early 1880s dudes were a popular topic in newspaper stories, at social clubs, and in parlors. People—mostly men—sneered at the dudes' prissy clothing and affectations. The word had been around for a long time, so why did it explode into popular consciousness just now?

One reason was fear. In 1880 Dr. George M. Beard coined the word "neurasthenia," defining it as a type of nervousness that afflicted overcivilized men and endangered their virility. Dr. Beard's neurasthenics were white, middle-class husbands, fathers, and brothers, self-proclaimed slaves to the horrors of city life and victims of the tides of new immigrants whose culture threatened to swamp their own. Immigrants were not sober, upright, Protestant, churchgoing men, and neither were dudes who dressed in tight pants and didn't look as if they ever did a day's hard work. Simmering fears about the women who were venturing out of their domestic sphere to help the poor and fight for the vote linked a perceived toxic femininity to neurasthenia and tied them up together in the figure of the dude.

Then, in 1883, a new type of entertainment debuted in North Platte, Nebraska, and presented to a worried public a view of America perfectly suited to ease these anxieties: Buffalo Bill's Wild West. William F. Cody, a.k.a. Buffalo Bill, was a scout, Indian fighter, actor, and dime novel hero. He created a spectacle (which was never called a "show") designed to be an authentic representation of the frontier story and the importance of the West in forming the American character. Among the presenters were cowboys who demonstrated their skills with ropes and bucking horses. They were already considered paragons of masculinity and were on the cusp of moving from hired hand to cultural symbol. For now, their appearance in the Wild West meant they stood in as the absolute opposite of the dude. This contrast was made clear in many magazine and newspaper stories, even if a lot of them were also yarns.

"The dudes of Butte wear plug hats. One cowboy raid will effect a change in the fashion," ran a bit of filler in the *Bismarck Tribune* in 1883. Plug hats were fancy top hats, and these were obviously an affront to cowboy sensibilities in Montana. In 1886 the *Bad Lands Cow Boy* published a story titled "A Festive Cow Puncher," which described cowboys as running over with wit, merriment, and good humor. The writer then presented an allegedly true story of seeing a dude step out of a hotel in Cheyenne wearing a silk hat, lavender trousers, a cutaway coat, a red velvet scarf, and patent-leather shoes. Two cowboys roped the dude, dirtied up his hat and shoes, and then told him to put on some more appropriate clothes. While this sounds too made up to be true (why would anyone dress like that in Cheyenne?), the story serves a purpose. Dudes needed to be brought down a peg, and cowboys were the men to do it.

Some writers took a different view of cowboys and dudes:

> A traveler in the west says that it is the rule for men of the plains, and particularly for cowboys, to speak contemptuously of eastern "dudes." But, in fact, most of them are as much the slaves of fashion as any one. They have an expensive suit of a white felt hat, a pair of fancy leather chapareros or overalls, French heel boots and a red silk handkerchief. Fancy ornamented pistols take a large part of many of the cowboys' earnings.[9]

Exposure to cowboys and the West itself became an important cure for neurasthenia and for the ills and temptations of urban life. Eastern parents, worried that their sons were succumbing to riotous and alcoholic living, decided that a few weeks of hard work in the West would straighten them out. Some heard about Eatons' through friends and asked the brothers whether they would take in their boys and convince them to reform. Once assured that the young men would not have access to drink, these mothers and fathers put their sons on the train. Things didn't always work out the way they wanted, though. Locals noticed that the dudes regularly came back from town with armfuls of bottles, and some cowboys swore that the crotch of every tree within a hundred yards of Eatons' ranch had a bottle in it.

These cowboys worked at another ranch, the Maltese Cross. It was owned by the most famous dude ever to show up in Medora: Theodore Roosevelt.

In 1883 the vigorous young Roosevelt was an author, outdoorsman, and rising political star, serving in the New York State Assembly as Republican speaker. He was also a hunter, and in May 1883 he met Henry Honeychurch Gorringe, a former naval officer who had just returned from the Dakota Badlands, where he was planning to run cattle and open a private hunting lodge. Roosevelt had been reading about the West and about the great sport men were finding there. One intriguing item was a letter published in a New York paper, written by Howard Eaton to an eastern friend, praising Medora and the region of the Little Missouri. Roosevelt decided to go out there and shoot a buffalo before they were all gone. Gorringe, whose property was near the Eatons,' suggested he come out to Dakota.

Roosevelt stepped off the Northern Pacific train in Little Missouri on September 8. He hired a local guide and after a couple of attempts, he bagged his buffalo. He also visited with local ranchers for a few weeks, though it's unclear whether he met the Eatons. Roosevelt was intrigued with the cattle business and started looking around for a ranch of his own. Before he went back to New York at the end of the month he bought the Chimney Butte Ranch, seven miles south of Medora, known locally as the Maltese Cross for the design of its brand. He was an enthusiastic, if absentee, owner. But his life changed the following year, and he would discover that the West had more to offer than livestock.

On February 14, 1884, Roosevelt's mother, Martha, and his wife, Alice (who had given birth to their first child two days earlier), both died. Despite his grief he pulled himself together and in June went to Chicago to attend the Republican National Convention as a delegate. He parted with many of his fellow delegates by backing George Edmunds as the candidate, rather than James G. Blaine, earning for himself and other Edmunds supporters the epithet "dudes." The insult was aimed at the majority of the delegates against Blaine, who were from New York or other eastern states. Perhaps this was a slur on their lack of manliness for not sticking with the party line. In any case, the dudes were not successful, and Blaine clinched the nomination, though he lost to Grover Cleveland in the presidential election later that year.

Roosevelt did not stick around after the convention was over. He got onto a westbound train and arrived at his ranch on June 9. Sometime that summer he signed the book at Eatons,' though he was probably just a visitor and not a guest. On the previous year's trip as well as this one, his appearance had marked him as a dude because he wore glasses and had a fondness for buckskins. Locals like Howard Eaton knew how wildly impractical the latter were, and he may have mentioned this to Roosevelt. "Buckskin shirts were all right as long as they didn't get wet, but when they got wet they'd shrunk [sic] up. I never did like that buckskin hunting shirt he had but he wouldn't have anything else."[10] Roosevelt proved his mettle, though, and won the respect of everyone from ranch owners to ranch hands.

The Eatons were cattlemen first and hosts second. Their concerns were with the stock and the relationships they had with other ranchers in the area. In June 1884, for example, the Eatons and other local ranch owners put an ad in the *Bad Lands Cow Boy* offering a $250 reward for anyone who could help them find the men who set fire to nearby grasslands. But the Big Die-Up decimated the Eatons' cattle, and by some accounts their herd of 1,500 was whittled down to 150.[11]

The Eaton brothers had other skills, however, especially Howard. He continued to lead pack trips for sightseers and hunters, and in 1898 he took a group of forty men on a trip into Yellowstone. Paying guests continued to arrive, and visitors were a regular source of income by the early 1890s. And although Howard Eaton went to Yellowstone every year, he didn't know all its hunting spots. One day while riding in the park, he met a man named Dick Randall, and the two got to talking. Randall told Eaton about the best places to take his hunters, and it's likely Eaton recognized that here was someone with skills equal to his. Within a few years Randall would also mirror Eaton in another way.

James "Dick" Randall was a midwesterner, born in Iowa in 1866. Like Howard Eaton, he left home early and ended up in the West. Randall's brother was living in Junction City, Montana, in 1884, and Dick joined him there, going to work for a man who managed the nearby 7 Bar 7. The ranch did not escape the decimation of the winter of 1886–87, and Randall knew he needed to find another line of work. He and a friend, June Buzzell, had a cabin in Gardiner, near the north end of Yellowstone, where they had done some big game hunting. In the spring of 1887, with Gardiner as their base, they bought eighty horses from a local Indian tribe and drove them into the park to sell or rent to other men to use on pack trips. That summer they managed the string of horses for Yellowstone's stage company, run by a seasoned outdoorsman named George Proctor. He taught Randall and Buzzell everything he knew, and the two men started leading trips of their own.

Randall married local girl Dora Roseborough in 1892, and their son Lesley, later known as Gay, was born the following year in Gardiner. One of their neighbors was Calamity Jane, and young Gay loved to wander over to her cabin, where she would fuss over him and give him cookies. Dora did not think the rough-edged woman was a good influence on her son and washed his mouth out with soap when she heard that Calamity had kissed him.[12]

Dick Randall was now one of the best guides in the region, and in 1898 he realized he needed a larger headquarters for his business. He soon found another cabin with good land at Cedar Creek, about twelve miles from Gardiner. The two men who owned the property were looking to sell because they had been robbing the Yellowstone stages and decided that things were getting too hot for them to stick around. Randall bought their horses and equipment, in addition to the house, and he and Dora moved in.

He added a kitchen and a couple of bedrooms to the cabin and built corrals, a barn, a root cellar, and a blacksmith's workshop. A garden was the final touch, and Randall soon welcomed his hunting and packing clients. Some of them were well known or on their way to being famous: writer Owen Wister, Northern Pacific Railroad president Henry Villard, even Theodore Roosevelt.

Many enthusiastic hunters showed up at Cedar Creek early for their trips so they could get accustomed to riding and the rigors of outdoor life. They helped out with ranch work and ate their meals with the Randalls and their hands. These men also needed a place to sleep, and because the house was too small for everyone, Randall put up tents on his property with wooden floors and sides. These were fine for single men, but some who came to visit year after year started to bring their families. Dick and Dora had to grow more food, raise more poultry, and build actual cabins to meet their needs.

Men like Randall and the Eaton brothers, who were famed for their skills on the trail, were now providing a new kind of lodging. Locals, guests, and the popular press dubbed their places "dude ranches."

The first person to call the Eatons' Custer Trail Ranch a dude ranch was a reporter for the *Mandan Pioneer* newspaper, and his description was reprinted in a Bismarck paper in 1899. "The *Mandan Pioneer* tells of the Eaton Brothers' 'dude' ranch at Medora where debilitated youths from the east spend the summer and rusticate among the Bad Lands, become strong and lusty in the invigorating air."[13]

This article generated another one in April of the following year. Eatons' popularity was growing, and nerve-racked eastern men continued to come out for some toughening up. Hunters who wanted to go on one of Howard's pack trips were still in the majority, though.

The Eaton brothers were now in their midforties to early fifties and could easily have rested on their dude ranch laurels and made a good living, even with the vagaries of the cattle business. Howard and Willis were still single; Alden was the only brother from the Custer Trail Ranch to marry and have a family (another brother, Charles, had a ranch nearby, though he and his wife returned to Pittsburgh in 1887). At least one sister and her family also lived in Dakota, while others came for regular visits. But in 1903 the brothers decided to sell Custer Trail and move west to Wyoming.

The reasons are a little fuzzy. Relocating to Wyoming meant they were closer to Yellowstone for hunting and sightseeing trips. The region also had better riding trails for dudes. But one family member said the brothers sold out simply because someone made them a good offer for the ranch.[14] Whatever their motivation, the decision made national news. With headlines like "Famous Dude Ranch in Billings County Has Passed into Other Hands" and "Dude Ranch Sold: Once Noted as a Plant for the Reformation of Eastern Young Men," the Eatons' move was reported from Delaware to California.[15]

Their new home was in Wolf, at the base of the Bighorn Mountains about eighteen miles west of Sheridan. The property already had a fine ranch house, and Sheridan was a more modern place than Medora, with better amenities. On April 18, 1904, Howard and Willis Eaton signed their new guest book, and other family members arrived a short time later. While Custer Trail was mainly a cattle ranch, Eatons' in Wolf was, from its first day, a dude ranch.

Chapter 2

The Eatons' success inspired others to try dude ranching in the early years of the twentieth century. Buffalo Bill himself built a string of lodges between Cody and Yellowstone that were filled with visitors eager to get close to anything associated with the famous showman. The Jackson Hole area was also a haven for big game hunters, though not so great for the cattle business. The first place near Jackson that opened exclusively as a dude ranch was the JY.

Its cofounder had one of the most colorful names in the business: Struthers Burt. Born in Baltimore in 1881, he went to Princeton and after graduation studied at Oxford and at the University of Munich. He was a writer, poet, and frequent traveler to the West, having heard stories all his life from an uncle who had a ranch in California. During one summer in Wyoming, he hunted game, drank in the scenery, and "was completely ignorant of the fact that I had found my future home—the place where so much was to happen to me. I only knew that I was happy and that the country filled every nook and cranny of my desire."[1]

He then met another former easterner, Louis Joy, who had some land in the area. They decided to open a dude ranch, which they called the JY, and welcomed their first five visitors in 1908. The Burt-Joy partnership lasted only until 1911, when they parted company and then ran dude ranches of their own. Joy kept the JY and Burt opened the Bar B C with a local man, Dr. Horace Carncross.

Meanwhile, back in Montana, Dick Randall's packing and hosting business was booming. In 1910–11 the Randalls bought more horses and built more cabins to meet the increasing flurry of hunters and nature lovers. They also built a lodge on a piece of property about thirty-five miles away on Hell Roaring Creek, where they officially started their dude business. Randall's brand for his livestock was "OTO," which he said was simply a design and had no special meaning. It was easy to make and easy to read on the side of a horse, steer, or saddle. Within a few years "OTO" was the official name of Randall's dude ranch.

He also had some competition. In 1907 a stage line owner named Pete Karst opened a small dude ranch with a few cabins in Gallatin Canyon, but Randall wasn't worried about him. There were dudes enough for everyone.

In August 1912 the *Denver Republican* ran a poem in its pages titled "The Dude Ranch," which was picked up by papers all over the country. The concept continued to fascinate, and the poem met readers' notions of what a dude ranch was.

> We used to run a cow ranch,
> In all that old term meant.
> But all our ancient glories
> In recent years have went.
> We're takin' summer boarders.
> And, puttin' it quite rude,
> It's now the cowboy's province
> To herd the festive dude.[2]

No one knows who coined the term "dude ranch," but the name is perfect. A ranch, of course, is a place where livestock are fed, watered, kept more or less confined, and then sent away to meet a new fate. Cattle were a commodity, and so were dudes. They also had to be fed and watered, with daily activities to keep them occupied within the confines of the ranch. And when they went home, the owners hoped they were changed by their experience.

Although society still sneered at dudes, early ranch owners began to look at them differently and ended up changing the definition of the word. In August 1913 *Collier's* magazine published "Joy-Ranching and Dude Wrangling," a long article about ranch life in the West. The author, Jesse Lynch Williams, was a journalist, novelist, and Pulitzer Prize–winning playwright who lived in New York and Princeton. He visited some western cattle ranches and dude ranches and was surprised to hear that "dude" was no longer an epithet, but simply a term to classify the tourists who came to ranches, whether they were expert riders or tenderfeet. Men like Howard Eaton, Dick Randall, and Struthers Burt felt the same way about their dudes.

For the most part, the people who came West for a good time were wealthy men (and a few women), accustomed to fine china and soft sheets in quiet hotels. As hunters, they could rough it in a camp, because that's what they expected. But when they signed the guest book at a dude ranch, they experienced something unique.

Their lodging was the ranch owner's home, where they would also see his wife and children, if he had them. Hotel owners were mostly invisible to their guests, unless the latter had a problem that needed to be bumped up to management. Hotels sold rooms and meals. Dude ranch owners shared rooms and meals. They personified the word "host" in its earliest definition as a person who provides lodging and entertainment to paying customers. And in the years just prior to America's entry into World War I, these customers were no longer dandies or figures of fun. They were tourists.

Historian Daniel Boorstin once wrote about the difference between the words "traveler" and "tourist." A traveler experienced "travail" to get somewhere: hardship, inconvenience, even possible injury. It was dangerous work to get to your destination, and Isabella Bird's struggle to navigate the wilds of Colorado in 1873 fits the definition of "traveler." By contrast, a tourist doesn't reach a goal after miles of bad roads or weeks of hard riding. He or she simply arrives after a fairly comfortable trip. This term describes the dudes who stashed bottles of whiskey in the trees near the Eatons' ranch. Tourism was also limited to people of means who had the ability to spend weeks away from home. Another essential was conveniently located railroad depots.

These conditions improved as the 1890s waned and tourism became less of an elite activity, now reachable to people further down the social scale. Sightseers poured into the West in successive waves from the late nineteenth century through the 1910s, intrigued by the stories that hunters and dude ranch visitors came home with. But spending a few weeks in a cabin on a cattle ranch wasn't enough to pique the interest of easterners used to spending their summers in Newport or European watering holes. Something more intangible inspired these visitors to venture out West, as it did the increasing numbers of men and women from the emerging middle class who were able to take vacations.

Buffalo Bill knew what he was doing back in 1883 when he named his spectacle "Wild West." He saw that the region was fast being "tamed," and giving people a taste of its former raucous past was a good way to pack the stands. Bill Cody helped create a view of the West that was perfect for a country already nervous about its identity. Big eastern factories were now shipping their products by railroads that snaked through former agricultural land. Barbed wire had closed the open range, and farmers and bankers were moving farther westward, creating new towns along the way. The frontier had always been in the East's backyard, serving as a sort of escape hatch, but now it was disappearing. Rough-and-tumble America was becoming too civilized.

The cure for this malady of urbanization was the same as it had been for boys on the verge of falling into louche lifestyles: a dose of the West. But seekers didn't need just scenery or a few days on horseback. There had to be a frisson of danger involved, a reminder of the manliness that once was, even if the actual danger of life in the Old West was fading fast. A manufactured experience of the cattle frontier was soothing without being lethal.

The West symbolized something else to these men, too. They were like adolescents who desperately want to grow up but once they get to adulthood, once they have jobs and responsibilities, they want to return to the freedom and occasional recklessness of their youth. The West was the teenager they once were.

Dude ranches helped fill this need. Taking horseback rides on steep trails in Wyoming and Montana could be treacherous, and so could helping a dude ranch owner round up his cattle or bring in the horses from the corrals, if the guest was so inclined. But this experience could not tip into real danger, and the Wild West—either as the name of Buffalo Bill's extravaganza or as a phrase in a tourist guidebook—was not a literal definition.

Dude ranching also got a boost from a program created by Fisher Sanford Harris, manager of the Knutsford Hotel in Salt Lake City, as well as Heber M. Wells, president of the Salt Lake City Commercial Club. These men had been watching vacation trends, monitoring where tourist dollars were going, and were appalled: Americans were spending $150 million a year on visits to Europe. Harris and Wells thought some of that money should be kept at home, and in 1905 they conceived a promotional campaign that was soon adopted around the country. They called it See America First.

Their program piggybacked on books and travel guides that had been published since the 1870s, urging tourists to explore the wondrous West. These also tapped into a strand of transcendentalism that turned time among great landscapes into a religious experience. Boosters said that America's natural wonders surpassed Europe's tired old ruins, and by the time Harris and Wells conceived See America First, which they described as "a propaganda of patriotism," tourists were ready to believe them.[3]

When Mary Roberts Rinehart showed up at Eatons' dude ranch in the summer of 1915 to join the Glacier Park pack trip, she was interested to see that at least half the folks on horseback were women, and that few of them were novices at outdoor activities. Women had been going out West for decades, with goals unique to their gender. The main one was liberation: from household chores, from confining clothing, from suffocating social rules. Like their husbands, fathers, and brothers, these women came from the monied or at least upper middle class, but instead of returning East with venison or a set of elk antlers, they went back with photographs, diaries, and experiences that they took into the rest of their lives. They shared their travels with friends, family members (the ones who didn't disapprove), and members of the many clubs to which they belonged.

They often went to dude ranches, though not always for vacation. In June 1907 a Philadelphia woman named Evelyn Raue left her physician husband and traveled to Aldrich Lodge, a cattle ranch on the south fork of the Shoshone River near Cody that also took in a few guests. Her lover, G. Gordon Massey, the son of a railroad magnate, had a big drinking problem and went out to Wyoming to dry out, leaving behind his wife and three children. When he got to the ranch, he made little effort to get sober, finding like-minded men to share bottles of champagne with. Evelyn's arrival at the ranch did nothing to stop him, and when Aldrich took away his liquor, Massey ran off to town with a shady local named Sam Berry. Evelyn then took charge. She hopped onto a horse and rode to Cody, grabbed her errant boyfriend, hired a carriage, and brought him back to the ranch, swearing that she would see him sobered up if it cost her life. Evelyn later reported that Massey improved after ten days at the dude ranch. (His wife filed for divorce.)

Even allowing for the sensational way this story was written up for the newspapers, this early twentieth-century female dude ranch visitor was obviously equal to anything the wilds of Wyoming had to offer. Women, whether with their husbands, in the company of their girlfriends, or even by themselves, saw the dude ranch as a place where they could have an authentic western experience, but one whose edges were softened by the good care of the ranch owner and his wife.

One young woman from Kansas took a solo trip to a Colorado dude ranch, and her exploits made local news. Gladys Parker was in her early thirties and unmarried, worked occasionally as a clerk, and was beloved in Hutchinson, Kansas, for her charity work, especially with the Campfire Girls. In her teens she had become ill and spent a few weeks on a local farm doing chores, caring for chickens, and generally spending her days in nature. She went home healthy and was later described as someone who was very fond of outdoor activities. Then, in the summer of 1916, she took the train to Colorado to spend a few weeks at some well-known dude ranches. By herself.

She went first to Arapahoe, situated between Lake Granby and Monarch Lake, where she fished and rode horseback. After two weeks she traveled to the larger McDonald spread. There she stayed in her own cabin, danced nightly in the outdoor pavilion, and continued to fish and ride. Vacationing alone didn't seem to raise any eyebrows back home, and when she returned to Hutchinson, she went right back to her family and her community activities. Perhaps as a confirmed spinster she was already an eccentric, and going on a solo western adventure was just part of the package. What the dude ranch owners and the other guests thought about her single status is unknown, but it's doubtful anyone in Colorado raised their eyebrows, either.

Eatons,' still the most famous dude ranch, had been welcoming women since its first day at the new location in Wolf. By 1905, it had a ranch house just for female guests called the "Hen House" or sometimes "The Hennery," which was rarely empty.

Of course, women were already at dude ranches: they ran them alongside their husbands. Dora Randall managed the dudes at the OTO while Dick concentrated on guiding hunters around Montana. Lists of other dude ranch founders at the turn of the twentieth century are not complete without the names of their wives: Sophia Holzwarth at Neversummer Ranch in Colorado; Helen Van Cleve at Lazy K Bar in Montana; Katherine Newlin Burt at the Bar B C in Wyoming; and Peg Murphy at Montana's Ox Yoke Ranch, among them. Many more women would become famous for their dude ranches in the coming decades. And some of them wouldn't have husbands.

In 1915 a new place opened near Cody, founded by a charismatic man who, in the following decade, would help create the modern dude ranch industry.

Irving H. Larom, later known as Larry, was born into a wealthy New York family in 1889. His father was a partner in the Mark Cross company, the famed leather goods firm, and young Irving attended Princeton. During his time there he met a student from Yale, another scion of American business, Winthrop Brooks, whose grandfather had founded Brooks Brothers.

Larom was brought up to be an outdoorsman and spent many happy hours hiking in the Adirondacks and Catskills. As a young man, he saw Buffalo Bill's Wild West at Madison Square Garden during one of its New York tours. On one visit he actually met the great man, who invited him to ride in the Deadwood Stagecoach portion of the spectacle. This sparked Larom's growing fascination with the West.

He spent the summer of 1910 in a cabin on the south fork of Wyoming's Shoshone River, owned by famed guide and hunter Jim McLaughlin. Larom ran into Buffalo Bill again on this trip and then returned for three more summers. Winthrop Brooks came with him on a 1914 visit, and Larom realized that his future was in the West. He and Brooks bought McLaughlin's homestead in June 1915 and started their Valley Ranch with a couple of rickety buildings and the enthusiasm of youth.

Larom knew exactly what he wanted his place to be. "The purpose of [the ranch] in general was to give my friends in the East with homes on Long Island and Newport and all over the chance to get away from the social cocktail party group and come out here and enjoy the 'simplicity of living.' That was my slogan, 'simplicity of life.' . . . And there were none of the contaminations of the usual social life in the East."[4] How many of his friends actually wanted to live simply is debatable, but this attitude perfectly defined Larom himself.

He and Brooks threw themselves into improving and advertising their new venture right away. They printed a brochure highlighting its log buildings, its great fishing and hunting, riding, and multiday pack trips. The pamphlet also included detailed information about train schedules to Cody from major cities. The two men, like Struthers Burt in Jackson, were well-off and educated, and they had deep connections to people of their own class in these eastern cities, all of whom were potential guests.

Larom and Brooks worked hard to show how authentically western the Valley Ranch was. During the first two summers, they staged a Wild West show for their guests, undoubtedly in homage to neighbor Buffalo Bill. There were horse races and demonstrations of cowboy skills in bronc riding and bulldogging, followed by a dance in the evening. Cody's business owners donated prizes for the contest winners, and guests also got the extra thrill of seeing Crow Indians from a Montana reservation mingling in the crowds.

Larom had a knack for both hospitality and marketing. Though neither he nor Brooks had any training or experience in such a people-driven occupation, they came from families for whom business was like breathing. Being a host to people like himself at his own western spread was deeply satisfying to Larom and was nothing at all like the life he would have had in New York. Which was probably the point.

In April 1917 the United States entered World War I, and Larom was drafted for service. He got a deferment until June 1918 and then boarded the eastbound train for induction. Winthrop Brooks, now married, stayed at Valley Ranch to manage the business, and in August everyone in Cody was aflutter with the news that a movie crew had arrived in town.

Geraldine Farrar was a singer with New York's Metropolitan Opera, and she also acted in silent films after the opera season closed. She was set to star in the western melodrama *The Hell Cat*, and the entire production was filmed in and around Cody. For the first few weeks everyone stayed at the Irma Hotel in town, managed by Irma Garlow, Buffalo Bill's daughter. She and her husband, Fred, entertained the company, and local cowboys were hired as extras.

In the film, Farrar plays Pancha O'Brien, the half-Irish, half-Spanish daughter of a sheep rancher who is kidnapped by the cattle rancher who wants to marry her. She eventually stabs her unwanted suitor to death and is then free to marry the sheriff, played by popular leading man Milton Sills. The film gives a nod to the always contentious relationship between sheep and cattle men and is a classic example of an early western melodrama.

The West had provided source material for silent film plot lines for years. *The Great Train Robbery*, a twelve-minute, rip-snortin' adventure that debuted in 1903, is considered the first real western because it is a narrative story, rather than the scenic travelogues and footage of Buffalo Bill's Wild West that moviegoers were familiar with. Actors such as Bronco Billy Anderson and William S. Hart soon made careers out of playing tough cowboy characters. In 1915 D. W. Griffith made the first feature-length film, *The Birth of a Nation*, and moviemakers vied with each other to do the same with westerns.

The Hell Cat was one of these. It was produced and distributed in Fort Lee, New Jersey, by Goldwyn Pictures (which was just about to move to Hollywood), and the company wanted a real ranch background for the story, which it got. Early scenes were filmed at the Hargreaves Ranch, on Cottonwood Creek north of Cody. The company rented sheep, cattle, and horses to fill any empty spaces, and a special chuck wagon was rolled in to provide food for the actors, crew, and extras. The chief cameraman shipped each day's footage to New York by driving to Billings and putting the reels on the eastbound train.

During the last few weeks of filming, the actors and crew stayed at the Valley Ranch. Farrar wasn't impressed with dude ranch life, and in her memoir, *Such Sweet Compulsion*, she described the experience as "discomfort and irritation." She was very happy to get back to New York when filming was finished. *The Hell Cat* was released in December 1918 to generally good reviews, especially for Farrar.[5]

The Valley Ranch was simply local color for this movie, whose plot had nothing to do with dude ranching. But the following year, dudes would show up on the screen.

Clarence L. Chester was a New York movie director and producer, and in 1918 the popular sports magazine *Outing* approached him about making a series of outdoorsy one-reel short subject films. The topics were far-ranging but always included some element of adventure and travel to places like Fiji or Quebec, and many were filmed as stories rather than straight travelogues. They were called "Outing-Chester Scenics" and were made well into the early 1920s. Film number fifteen, which arrived in theaters in June 1919, was called *Wrangling Dudes*.

Advertising for the movie appeared in *Outing*'s pages, and the magazine also sent copy to newspapers ahead of the movie's release. One ad said that *Wrangling Dudes* would "reveal the activities on one of the ranches in the West said to be maintained for the purpose of providing thrills for credulous tourists who have gotten their ideas of the West from novels and the movies."

Another ad went this way: "When an eastern tenderfoot goes west he expects to find it wild and wooly. Up in Montana they stage a wilder west than ever existed; and as for wool—they pull that over the tenderfoot's eyes." But then there's a review from the *Brooklyn Daily Eagle*, which describes the film as a "new Outing-Chester travel scenic entitled 'Wrangling Dudes,' showing cowboy life in Wyoming." The movie was probably made in Montana, as that information came directly from *Outing* magazine. But apparently some papers in New York, as well as a few in Canada, didn't know the difference between Montana and Wyoming.[6]

The western themes in films like *The Hell Cat* and *Wrangling Dudes* served the same purpose as the ever-growing collection of dude ranches. They presented the Wild West to audiences sitting comfortably in plush theater seats, just as ranches did to dudes sitting uncomfortably on western saddles.

The idea that dudes needed to be "wrangled" had been floating around since the establishment of the earliest dude ranches. By the 1910s Jackson Hole was known as a place where dude wrangling was one of the chief occupations, along with cattle raising and farming. The term was introduced to a national audience in 1912 in a long newspaper article titled "Dude Ranching in the West" and was described this way: "'Dude wrangling' is the refinement of the ranchman's art, and comes as the senior course in the visitor's education. He who wrangles dudes looks after their well-being on extensive overland trips."[7] At this point, packing and hunting were still the main activities at places like the newish OTO ranch and at Eatons,' but the dudes still needed to be managed.

It makes sense that a cowboying term like "wrangle" was applied to dude ranching. "Wrangling" is another word for "arguing," which is an appropriate description of trying to get cattle to go where they're supposed to. If a ranch was a place where dudes were herded, cowboys were the ones to do the wrangling.

By the time *Wrangling Dudes* was released in 1919, cowboys were firmly enshrined as the symbol of a West that was receding into the sunset. They represented freedom from the constraints that defined life in the East. They were heroic in the face of danger. They had skills never seen on Wall Street. People made movies about them. Women found them irresistible. And some were famous for the time they spent performing in Wild West shows or leading European royalty on hunting trips.

The transition from cattle drive hired hand to mythological figure had happened quickly. Buffalo Bill's Wild West first put cowboys on a national, and then international stage, even though they had a reputation for being uncouth, dusty drifters, perching on the edge of lawlessness. The "cow-boys" who fought the Earp brothers and Doc Holliday at the O.K. Corral in Tombstone in 1881 fit this description. But popular literature would both repair and regenerate the cowboy's reputation.

In the 1860s the "dime novel," so called for its cheap paper and price, appeared on newsstands in big cities as well as small towns, aimed at young boys from the working classes. Seventy-five percent of the one thousand books published each year included stories about frontier adventures and Indian scouts.

Inspired by James Fenimore Cooper's *Leatherstocking Tales*, the little novels emphasized the allure of the outsider. Cowboys started showing up on their pages in the 1870s, with Buck Taylor becoming the first celebrity cowhand in a series of books introduced in 1887. He had been part of Cody's Wild West, though in his stories, he fights Indians rather than herding cattle. The big boost for the reformed image of the cowboy came with Owen Wister's 1902 novel, *The Virginian*. His hero was the laconic, gentlemanly, horse-thief-hanging character we still see on the page and the movie screen.

But before Wister there was Emerson Hough, whose 1897 nonfiction book, *The Story of the Cowboy*, set him up for immortality, along with an acknowledgment that the West was changing, and that the "Long Trail" was the connection to a misty, historical past. Hough also wrote fiction and placed cowboys and other western characters firmly into historically accurate settings, like railroad towns and cattle drives. The success of his works, as well as Wister's *Virginian*, inspired authors like Zane Grey to contribute to the genre, as he did in 1912 with *Riders of the Purple Sage*.

Male writers did not have the monopoly on forging the literary cowboy, or even the authenticity to do so. B. M. Bower was the pen name of Bertha Muzzy Bower, a Minnesota native whose family moved to Montana in 1889 when she was a teen. After working as a teacher, she married Clayton Bower, who worked off and on as a cowboy and laborer. The couple had three children and in 1900 Bertha bought a typewriter and began to submit stories to magazines, partly as a way to deal with her crumbling marriage. She and her husband now lived at the TL ranch, where Clayton was a hand. Surrounded by cowboys who lived in bunkhouses and who spent their spare time doing rope and riding tricks when they weren't managing roundups, Bower found a new story to tell. In 1904 she published her first novel, *Chip of the Flying U*, which was filled with the western and cowboy details that readers wanted.

It also had a female doctor as a surprising lead character. The male-sounding pseudonym B. M. Bower helped sales, and her audiences probably never knew how closely Bertha's life mirrored her art. One rave review praised the book and its assumed male author because the heroes were a lady doctor and a cowboy, moving the story beyond the usual hackneyed characters and western situations.

Magazines, Wild West shows, novels, and dime novels fueled the craze for the cowboy, but dude ranch owners like Howard Eaton, Dick Randall, and Larry Larom weren't prepared for how popular their cowboys would be. They were just the hired hands responsible for keeping the dudes in line.

The work wasn't onerous, perhaps just rounding up horses in the morning for the day's ride and leading the dudes down a trail or two. Sometimes the dudes just wanted to sit on the corral and watch the cowboys at work or ask them about their life on the range. More adventurous guests could help with the daily chores. In these early years, cowboys moved easily between their four-footed and two-footed charges, but within a decade the dude ranch would bring big changes to the cowboy way.

Chapter 3

By the time *Wrangling Dudes* was released in 1919, more people knew what a dude ranch was, and more people had spent time on one. This was due, in great part, to the upheavals of World War I.

The war over there, which the United States entered in 1917, had a huge impact on the tourist business over here. Taking long vacations in Europe was no longer an option, even for the wealthy, so families began to look around for other leisure ideas. The See America First campaign was still preaching the gospel of western travel, and so was the US Department of the Interior, which spent money advertising the national parks. Some ranchers had to give up their horses to the war effort, but thanks to the increasing use of gasoline-powered trucks and other equipment, horses that did not go overseas were available for trail rides and pack trips.

At the same time, a drop in cattle prices after 1919 and a drought that increased the price of hay meant that the livestock business was even more precarious than usual. Many ranchers in Montana, Wyoming, and Colorado looked around at their dude ranching neighbors and decided to try herding dudes instead.

When Mary Roberts Rinehart's physician husband urged her to go on Howard Eaton's pack trip in 1915, he knew that the emotional wounds of war—for journalists like his wife, as well as for soldiers—were often healed by spending time in nature. Doctors and philosophers had observed the restorative benefits of the outdoors for decades, and those who studied shell shock (as posttraumatic stress disorder was then called) saw how wild places could ease the disordered mind.

Elizabeth Frazer, a war correspondent and writer for the *Saturday Evening Post*, saw this firsthand. When she came back from Europe, ignorant people asked her whether she was sad to be back in America after seeing the glories of the Continent, a query she thought was sheer foolishness. She didn't know how to respond to people who talked this way, but then she met a man at a Jackson Hole dude ranch who expressed her feelings perfectly.

He was a recently demobilized soldier who had seen famine and death from France to Poland. One day a "romantic, sentimental lady tourist" from back East asked him whether he didn't think Europe was so much more picturesque than America. The man, "seventy-four inches of western sunburned brawn, laconic, humorous, stood looking down on her much as a big benevolent Saint Bernard looks down on a lady's tiny, yapping wrist watch pet." After staring at the lady dude for a few moments, his gaze shifted. "Then he looked off at the encircling mountains, stark granite shafts and peaks and pinnacles, painted with the first snow of the season; then he looked at me, got no help, and suddenly he gave the whole proposition up, jerked out a brief 'Oh—hell!' and walked away."[1]

There was a term for these western lady tourists, which appeared in the lexicon at about the same time as "dude": "dudine." From the 1880s to the early part of the twentieth century, being called a dudine in public or in print was as insulting as being called a dude (though the recipients of the insults usually didn't care what they were called). One bit of newspaper filler from 1889 had a dude asking a famous dudine why she dyed her hair. She replied that her husband wanted her hair to match the color of his horses.

Then there was this pithy item: "Dudes and dudines are all one; both sissies."[2]

By the end of World War I, ranch owners had embraced "dudine," which replaced "lady tourist" and other similar terms. Some writers and ranchers thought "dudette" was more appropriate, but it didn't catch on, except as a term for children on dude ranches and, in 1919, as the name of a famous racehorse. "Dudine" did not have the infantilizing "-ette" appended at the end of the male form of the word, making it a term of gender equality almost unmatched in the English language. In the lodge and on the trail, dudes and dudines were all one.

Dude ranching as a business and a vacation destination spread like sagebrush as the 1920s opened, helped along by journalists and writers. Hal G. Evarts was the outdoors editor for the *Saturday Evening Post* and a writer of sprawling western adventure novels, some of which were made into early films. In 1920 he wrote an article for the *Post* titled "Dude Wranglers." Evarts describes his visit to a Wyoming dude ranch, which he shares with another guest, a dyspeptic and insomniac eastern businessman. In Evarts's long profile the reader learns about a typical dude ranch vacation through the eyes of this man, named T. Warrington Smith.

Smith's decision to come to Wyoming was made on impulse and regretted as soon as he stepped off the train. The people he encountered were unlike anyone he knew back home, and so were the sleeping arrangements, the food, and the daily activities. He kept to himself at first and spent little time with the other dudes, but soon the wranglers, with their colorful language and even more colorful backstories, drew him out. So did the cook, who made food that Smith had never eaten before but found surprisingly delicious. Evarts noticed that he took to dude ranch life more quickly than some of the other visitors, and Smith soon decided to take a two-week pack trip with a Detroit banker who was also staying at the ranch.

When it was time to go home, Smith was a different man and had already made plans to return the following spring. Evarts ran into Smith in town on the day he was catching his train home. They had lunch together at a local hotel and shared their table with a visiting salesman. He looked at Smith's tanned face and well-worn outdoor clothing and asked whether he was a rancher or a tourist. "Neither," said Mr. Smith. "I'm a chronic dude."[3] Whether Smith was a real guest or a composite created to make a point, Evarts perfectly illustrated how the dude ranch was supposed to work on jangled eastern nerves.

Journalists profiled dude wranglers and guests as the 1920s progressed, but one novelist saw their story potential much earlier and put dude ranching on the literary map.

Caroline Lockhart was an Illinois native, born in 1871 and educated in Pennsylvania. In 1889, at the age of eighteen, she got a job as a reporter for the *Boston Post*. In 1899 Buffalo Bill's Wild West came to town, and Lockhart's editor sent her to do a story on the famous showman. She was bowled over by the man and his western pageant, and they stayed on her mind even after she moved on to the *Philadelphia Bulletin* in 1902. She then took a western excursion and later published "A Girl in the Rockies" for *Lippincott's Monthly*. In 1904 the *Bulletin* sent her to Montana to do a story on the Blackfoot Indians. She took a side trip to Cody and was so taken with the town she decided to move there, and she soon became a one-woman chamber of commerce for the western way of life.

Lockhart was thrilled to be among cowboys, Indians, and especially horses, which she loved. She was unconventional and independent. She earned her own living, had big ambitions, carried on (unmarried) sexual relationships with cowboys, was for suffrage, and was against Prohibition. She was determined to write the West into existence—as she saw it—for the hopelessly mediocre folks in the Midwest and East. But unlike writers such as Owen Wister, Zane Grey, and B. M. Bower, she wrote about the West she was living in, not the faded, romanticized days of cattle drives and horse thieves. Her adopted region had a future that was built solidly on its past but wasn't mired in it. To make this clear, she wrote the first nationally published short story about dude ranching.

Lockhart knew people who ran informal dude ranches around Cody, so she had firsthand inspiration for her characters. She titled her piece "The Dude Wrangler," and it ran in the women's magazine *The Red Book* in November 1907. It's a gently mocking story of a local wrangler trying to herd a group of easterners through Yellowstone, with harrowing adventures along the way.

Two years later, she set a short story on a dude ranch. "Jim's Dude," published in the February 1909 issue of *McClure's Magazine*, is a sweet tale about a rough cowboy who works on a dude ranch and falls in love with a glasses-wearing, sickly teacher who is visiting the ranch from back East. Lockhart knew both cowboys and dudines and instinctively understood the meaning of the dude ranch for the western image. The following year, Lockhart published her sixth novel and took the title from her first dude ranch story: *The Dude Wrangler*. Like her earlier, shorter works, hers was the first novel to tackle the phenomenon of dude ranching, and it set up the themes that other authors would follow for years.

The main character is a foppish young man named Wallie Macpherson. He paints, did not fight in World War I, and spends summers with his aunts. During one season he meets a Wyoming cowboy named Pinkey Fripp. Pinkey comes by the resort where Wallie is staying to visit another guest, a cowgirl named Helene, who is also from Wyoming. Pinkey's disdain for dudes shames Wallie, who decides to throw away his soft life, buy some property out West, and see whether he can make a man of himself. Every chapter of the book sends up Wallie's deficiencies, and after failing in the farming business he decides to open a dude ranch with Pinkey, who is now his bosom friend. Pinkey thinks this is a fine idea, and they discuss just how perfect their place is: it's got scenery, climate, great fishing and hunting, and Yellowstone Park in their front yard. Unfortunately for the boys, dude ranching doesn't go well either, but in the end Wallie manages to cowboy up and wins Helene.

Most reviewers liked the book and understood the theme of the effete easterner turning into a strong western man. *The Dude Wrangler* would remain the sole novel about dude ranching for nearly a decade.

Lockhart believed dude ranches were here to stay, but though they were perfect fodder for her fiction, she was conflicted about their meaning. They provided an authentic western experience in an inauthentic way, and that offended her view of the West as a place for real men and women. But she knew dude ranches also supported the local economy, and for that she could look the other way, in person and on the page.

When writers, filmmakers, and journalists turned their talents to dude ranching in the early part of the century, they set their stories in the Rocky Mountain West, which makes sense. The first dude ranches got their start there, and hunting and fishing were still the biggest draws for customers, as well as proximity to places like Yellowstone. Craggy mountains and roaring rivers made good copy and impressive photographs. But in the years before America's entry into World War I, tourists began to realize that when it came to scenery and outdoor experiences, there was more than one West to choose from.

The deserts of Arizona, New Mexico, Utah, and Southern California had long been viewed as terrifying wastelands devoid of water and greenery, something to endure on your way to somewhere else. Farmers certainly avoided the desert, except those who were tricked into believing that "rain follows the plow." The generations of immigrants from Mexico who ran ranches or businesses in the small towns of the desert West found it similar to home and thrived because they knew how. But in the 1890s, artists, writers, and others who didn't need to rely on the land for sustenance discovered the desert and called its stark landscapes beautiful.

New Englander Charles Fletcher Lummis walked across the country in 1884 to take a job at the *Los Angeles Times* and spent the rest of his life touting the Southwest as a magical place, also taking the helm at a tourism magazine called *Land of Sunshine* in 1894. The Santa Fe Railroad made travel to the Grand Canyon easier in 1901 when it created the Grand Canyon Railway Company, which took tourists from Williams, Arizona, to the South Rim. Mary Austin found refuge in the Mojave Desert from a stifling marriage and social conventions in general, and she wrote about the power of place in books like *Land of Little Rain* in 1903.

Without these early boosters, dude ranching in the Southwest probably would have started much later, and its beginnings mirrored early efforts in the Rockies. Wealthy men came out to the desert, many for health reasons, because the dry air was good for lung ailments. Entranced with what they saw, they built vacation lodges and invited their friends to visit. The Southwest wasn't all desert, so guests could fish lakes and streams, and there was also huntable game.

Chicago grain magnate W. H. Bartlett moved to New Mexico for his health, went full cowboy, and added cattle ranching to his desert footprint. Bartlett built the Vermejo Park Ranch in northern New Mexico in 1901 so he could share it with his fellow midwesterners and continue to thrive in the western climate. The ranch later passed into the hands of Harry Chandler, publisher of the *Los Angeles Times*, who turned it into a private club in the 1920s.

But for the most part, early dude ranches in the Southwest were aimed at tourists who wanted to spend a few weeks in the desert and live to tell their stories back home. One of the first, and probably the first in Arizona, was the Garden of Allah just outside Wickenburg. The property had been a thriving nineteenth-century farm owned by Fritz Brill, and in 1912 Dr. John Sanger and a partner named Chapman (possibly Phoenix businessman Lebbeus Chapman) bought the buildings and grounds. Sanger was from New York and a retired physician.

Guests stayed in cabins by the Hassayampa River, and though the Garden of Allah was more like a resort than a rugged western retreat, it was a popular place for visitors from Phoenix who wanted to escape the summer heat. Sanger and Chapman couldn't keep the place up, and Sanger disappeared in 1915, so the property was sold off. Ten years later, a couple named Weaver started it up again as the Circle Flying W, and Wickenburg's future as the Dude Ranch Capital of the World began.

One of the earliest New Mexico dude ranches also started life as a private club. The Ramon Vigil Ranch, on the Pajarito Plateau east of Santa Fe, was the home of the Pajarito Club, founded in 1913 by four Michigan executives in the auto and banking business. Like the Vermejo Park Ranch, Pajarito existed solely for the pleasure of its owners' wealthy eastern friends. But by 1916 the absent partners were squabbling about the club's financial future. They discussed turning it into a dude ranch and making their friends pay for their desert luxuries.

In that year, a newly married couple, Carol Stanley and Roy Pfäffle, came to the ranch for a short visit. Stanley was a gifted musician from Maine, and in 1915 her friends suggested she go to the Southwest to get over a scandalous love affair. She stayed on and in 1916 was spending time in Santa Fe, where she met Pfäffle, an Iowa-born forest ranger who took tourists on desert horseback excursions. The two married in October 1916, and the following January they opened a larger-scale outfitting business in Española.

After their stay at the Ramon Vigil Ranch, the owners asked Pfäffle and Stanley to manage the place as a dude ranch, as well as another called Bishop's Lodge. In 1920 the couple bought a property they named San Gabriel and turned it into a dude ranch. They had many local friends who had friends in the East and Midwest, and by the mid-1920s San Gabriel was a popular stopping place for out-of-towners, including author Willa Cather and her partner Edith Lewis.

Pfäffle was a gambler and in 1928 he won a 157-acre piece of property in a poker game near Abiquiu, but he and Stanley eventually lost the San Gabriel Ranch. The couple divorced and Stanley moved to the Abiquiu homestead, which she developed into a dude ranch and renamed Ghost Ranch. It is famed today for its association with painter Georgia O'Keeffe, who had a home nearby, and it inspired much of her work.

Despite its long history with the cattle business, Texas did not boom as a center of dude ranching except in the hill country around Bandera, about fifty miles from San Antonio. In 1921 local rancher Ebenezer Buck invited his Houston friends out to his place to stay, where he fed them well and showed them the ranching life for ten dollars a week. Buck's enterprise was the earliest, though a few other ranches opened up around Bandera later in the century.[4]

Southwestern dude ranches offered tourists the basics: a rustic place to stay, the use of a horse, good food, and glorious views. But the experiences there were unique, especially in landscape and climate, not to mention the species of fish and game available to sportsmen and women. Vast desert vistas, cacti, unfamiliar trees, and only scattered bodies of water meant that visitors went home knowing that their dude ranch vacation was very different from the one their neighbor had taken in Montana or Wyoming. They also went on their excursions at different times of the year. People who needed to escape the winters of Chicago or Boston could vacation at an Arizona dude ranch in December and January and breathe deeply without freezing their lungs. Wyoming and Montana ranch owners usually closed their places down during the winter, except for the hardiest of proprietors and the few guests willing to risk being snowbound.

Dude ranching was proving to be adaptable to any region, which meant that it was slowly becoming a real industry, not just a wealthy man's hobby. This likely pleased Howard Eaton. He lived long enough to see that the new kind of vacation he popularized in 1882 was thriving and giving Americans a taste of the West that he loved. He died in Sheridan, Wyoming, in April 1922 of peritonitis, contracted after an operation for appendicitis. Celebrated artists and writers like Charles Russell and Mary Roberts Rinehart spoke publicly about the loss, and newspapers across the country carried his obituary. The best headline came out of the *Pittsburgh Daily Post*, Eaton's hometown paper: "Howard Eaton Missed 'Dying with Boots On.'" After funeral services in Sheridan, his body was returned to Pittsburgh and cremated.

By the 1920s dude ranches were no longer the places mothers and wives sent their sons and husbands to dry out or man up. Most men came out just for the shooting, fishing, and other outdoor activities, a necessary break from the stresses of business life. For women, though, the dude ranch was still a place of freedom and a respite from constraints. Stories of ladies on vacation in the West, especially without their men along, continued to fill the columns of national newspapers. Especially if they were spunky.

Peggy Thayer, for example.

She was born in 1898 in Philadelphia, and her father was John B. Thayer, second vice president of the Pennsylvania Railroad. Thayer and his wife, Marion Longstreth, had two daughters and two sons, and in 1912 Mr. and Mrs. Thayer and their son Jack went to Europe and spent time as guests of the American consul in Berlin. On April 10 they boarded their ship for home: the RMS *Titanic*.

Marion Thayer, Jack, and a maid survived the sinking, but John B. did not.

The family put itself back together, and since they were wealthy, they had all the material comforts necessary for healing. But disasters leave long cracks in survivors. Peggy Thayer was a preteen when she lost her father in a manner that was both terrible and terribly public, and as she moved forward in her life, she dealt with her loss in ways that shocked mainline Philadelphia society.

In the fall of 1917, as America sent more troops to France and Belgium, few girls came out as debutantes. It didn't seem proper during wartime. Thayer was one of the girls who didn't get a formal entry to society, but she didn't care, because she had other things to do. By the following spring she was in rural Pennsylvania working on a farm. She then took a nursing course, and when the influenza epidemic roared through Philadelphia in 1918, she helped nurse the sick.

After the war, Thayer traveled with friends and visited Yellowstone on one western trip in 1919. By this time her family noticed something alarming. She expressed disdain for the social duties that were expected of her and gravitated toward anything that was remotely exciting, shocking, or dangerous. She was especially fond of riding but did not post sedately in her saddle on rides in nearby parkland. One friend remarked, "She rode as if she had some place to go and wanted to get there."[5]

It was therefore inevitable that she should take a dude ranch vacation. In the summer of 1920 Thayer and one of her aunts took the train to Jackson Hole and checked in to the JY Ranch. One western trip was eccentricity; a second one the following summer was just flabbergasting. Not only that, she entered the dude events during a local rodeo and won a horse race on a recently broken bronco that tried to buck her off before the race started. She enjoyed showing off her silver cup to family and friends, shocking them with the story of her daring, a tale that also made the rounds of the society pages.

Thayer spent only two seasons at the JY, but the impulse that sent her there molded the rest of her life. After she came home, she opened a perfume shop, went on the stage, played semiprofessional tennis, and shot big game in Canada and Africa. What explains her longing for adventure, unconventionality, and even danger? Her father's horrible death at sea could have pushed her toward a life of safety and calm, but she went the other way. Dude ranching and the wild cowboy life gave her the excitement she craved. The tamer guests she met at the JY Ranch, as well as those from her own class, probably thought she was one of the most exciting young women they'd ever met. What fun she must have been.

Hollywood came back to dude ranch country in 1922 with *The Cowboy and the Lady*, starring former child star Mary Miles Minter. The film was based on a Clyde Fitch play that ran on the New York stage in 1899, and the producers wanted ranch-like authenticity again, so they filmed much of the action at Struthers Burt's Bar B C dude ranch in Jackson Hole.

In 1925 western star Franklyn Farnum starred in the first silent feature film to take dude ranching as part of its story line, called *The Galloping Dude*.

Farnum's character, vaguely from back East, inherits an Arizona ranch that has been turned into a dude ranch, and hilarity ensues when he comes out to investigate the place. Farnum was known for horsemanship and comedy, and though he appeared in films for the rest of his life, his career did not reach the heights of his costar Jean Arthur. *The Galloping Dude* was filmed at the Gillibrand family cattle ranch near Santa Susana, California, about thirty miles northwest of Hollywood in Simi Valley. This area was also home to Corriganville, a studio and movie ranch where dozens of films and television westerns were filmed from the 1940s to the 1960s.

The following year, western superstar Tom Mix starred in a silent called *Hard-Boiled*. He plays yet another dude (this time from Chicago), whose rich uncle asks him to go out West to inspect a dude ranch called Boiling Springs. The ranch needs looking into because it's run by a woman named Abigail and her niece Marjorie who aren't hard enough on the staff, so not much is getting done. Mix decides to pose as a doctor so no one knows what he's up to, and he eventually falls in love with Marjorie. With the help of Tony the Wonder Horse, he thwarts a robbery and a kidnapping and wins the heart of his cowgirl.

Hoot Gibson, another big cowboy star known for his daredevil riding, enjoyed success with his 1928 silent, *The Flyin' Cowboy.* He plays a real cowboy whose job is entertaining dudes at the Bar-X, and he thwarts gangsters who try to carry off his lady love and her pearls, demonstrating his equally well-known skill with a lariat. Like *Hard-Boiled*, the film fits solidly into the western genre: good guys (West) vs. bad guys (East), tough but still vulnerable females who needed rescuing, a horseback chase sequence, and the western architecture, design, and scenery that audiences loved.

Actors and directors caught the dude ranch bug in the mid-1920s, if you can believe the newspaper stories. In August 1926 the *Los Angeles Times* reported that director Hal Roach—who made comedic genius Harold Lloyd famous, brought Laurel and Hardy together, and created the *Our Gang* films—was planning to build a dude ranch outside Las Vegas. He did build a ranch, but it was his movie studio, and it was in Culver City.

Films set on dude ranches with huge stars like Tom Mix, Franklyn Farnum, and Hoot Gibson were free advertising for ranches all over the West. Their owners saw the results in increased visitors and income. Larry Larom of Cody's Valley Ranch, who kept track of these things, said that dude ranching revenues in Montana and Wyoming doubled between 1916 and 1926, and tripled between 1921 and 1926. He believed that the business was no longer an experiment, but a viable tourism asset to the Rocky Mountain region. Larom was always looking for ways to make dude ranching popular and profitable, and he started talking to other ranchers about how to make this happen.[6]

On September 28, 1926, twenty-six dude ranch owners met at the Bozeman Hotel in Montana and elected officers for a new organization. Larry Larom was named president, and the vice president, secretary, treasurer, and board of directors came from dude ranches in Montana (Bozeman, Red Lodge, Missoula, Corwin Springs, Cooke City, Big Timber) and Wyoming (Shell, Cody). Among them were Dick Randall of the OTO and Paul Van Cleve of the Lazy K Bar. The stated purpose of the group was to discuss their problems and standardize the business.

They also had an important decision to make. What about the word "dude"? Was it undignified as a name for their growing industry, and insulting to their guests? After a brief discussion, the men decided that there was nothing wrong with "dude" or "dude ranch," and that these terms were already in common usage anyway. With a unanimous vote, they named their new venture the Dude Ranchers' Association.

Chapter 4

The members of the Dude Ranchers' Association had lofty goals in mind for their new venture. Ranchers wanted to figure out the best way to care for their guests, which meant they had to communicate more with each other. They wanted their practices to become standardized so guests would have a better experience, leading to repeat visits. And they wanted to improve their sales and marketing.

By the time the DRA was organized, dude ranch revenues for Montana and Wyoming were already at about $1 million. Merchants in Gunnison, Colorado, counted dude ranching as one of the most important contributors to tourism dollars in their town, which they estimated at $60,000. This spurred the local commercial club to lobby for building more dude ranches in the county.

The DRA's officers knew they had to take advantage of this momentum, and they had a powerfully ally. Railroads such as the Northern Pacific, Union Pacific, Burlington, and Great Northern had made remote dude ranches more accessible to eastern visitors in the late nineteenth and early twentieth centuries. The Santa Fe and Southern Pacific would later bring visitors to ranches in the Southwest. Railroads were also essential for bringing in supplies and seasonal workers.

Railway companies spent a lot of advertising dollars on brochures luring tourists to the national parks before and during World War I, as these were also served by the various rail lines. But executives did not think dude ranches were that important to their bottom line until the early 1920s and the first meeting of the Dude Ranchers' Association. Ernest Miller, of the Elkhorn Ranch near Bozeman, knew Max Goodsill, who was the general passenger agent of the Northern Pacific. Miller was another dude ranch owner who thought the industry needed its own trade group, and he told Goodsill that railroads should support this idea. Goodsill was intrigued, so he then talked to A. B. Smith, the line's passenger traffic manager. He also understood how much dude ranches were adding to tourism's coffers, so Smith helped organize the first Dude Ranchers' Association meeting at the Bozeman Hotel.

Afterward, railroad companies were all in. The Northern Pacific line included dude ranch advertising in its 1928 budget, and by 1930 the railroads that served ranching locations featured individual ranches in their glossy brochures. They also placed ads in newspapers wherever potential vacationers might be. These featured fine drawings of mountains and lakes, images of men and women in cowboy hats and bandannas, and language like this from the Northern Pacific Railway's ad for Montana and Wyoming: "Everybody likes a 'Dude Ranch.' Rest and relax, or ride, fish, hike, hunt and explore. Eat and sleep as never before in this glorious mountain air."[1] These brochures filled the windows of travel agencies in New York, Boston, Philadelphia, and other cities where tired easterners looked for vacation ideas (not to mention places like San Francisco and Los Angeles).

Walter H. James, a professor of mechanical engineering at the Massachusetts Institute of Technology, wrote to a number of railroad and steamboat offices in the spring of 1929 for information about summer travel in the West. He and his wife, Ida, were about to celebrate their thirtieth wedding anniversary, and they wanted to do something unique.

A booklet from the Northern Pacific Railway showed up in their mailbox one day and the Jameses were intrigued by the photos and descriptions of Wyoming and Montana dude ranches. They wrote to a few of them and among the replies was a cordial and businesslike letter from W. E. Binko, who ran the Binko Dude Ranch at Clearwater, Montana, about fifty miles from Missoula. He followed up his letter with two small albums of photos of the ranch buildings and surrounding landscape. Walter and Ida decided to give dude ranches a try and had definite ideas about what they did and did *not* want for their vacation. No stylish hotel-type accommodations or crush of guests for them. They wanted a small ranch with mountain views, a place that was a genuine reflection of the glorious West. After weighing all the other ranches in the balance, the Jameses made a reservation at Binko's for two weeks in July 1929.

Walter James kept a diary of their adventures that summer. Being a meticulous scientist, he also recorded the costs of the trip and a detailed description of the trains he and his wife took to get to Montana. Once they arrived, they rode, took a pack trip, and loved every minute of every day because they got their real western experience. They thought they might go back to a dude ranch in two or three years but, as James put it, "We should have known better.

There is something about the West which gets into the blood and calls one back from the city to the freer life of the hills and plains." The couple returned to Montana twice more, staying at the Broken Arrow and Three Circle dude ranches, where they happily relived their western dream.²

Ranch owners were pleased that the railroads put money into advertising. But some of them also felt that dude ranching would benefit from a more personal touch. Larry Larom regularly went back to New York in the winter months to speak to friends and give talks about the Valley Ranch, praising the benefits of spending weeks at a dude ranch and spreading his gospel of simplicity. Winthrop Brooks, now employed full time in the family business, Brooks Brothers, gave Larom space in the company's offices for advertising material.

The OTO's Dick Randall took his marketing visits to other cities. In 1924 an educational filmmaker named Charles Herbert spent time on the OTO while filming a local fair and put together a reel titled "What the Dudes Do on a Dude Ranch." Randall took copies of this film to Marshall Field's in Chicago and Gimbels in Philadelphia and talked to the people responsible for creating window displays. He told them that advertising dude ranches would help their sportswear sales and showed them how to use the film with their customers. In 1928 he found out that a movie actor in Los Angeles had commissioned a silver-mounted saddle for himself but then changed his mind and didn't buy it. Randall was spending the winter in LA, so when it was time to go East to talk to potential dude ranch customers, he bought the saddle and shipped it by rail to Chicago to exhibit at local stores.

In the mid-1920s Larom and the Eatons started sending out sprightly newsletters to their former guests, hoping to entice them to come back another year. The Eatons' effort was called *Wranglin' Notes* and featured illustrations from an up-and-coming artist named Joe DeYong, a protégé of Montana artist Charles Russell. DeYong would later end up in Hollywood, consulting on western authenticity in the movies. Larom's newsletter was called *Corral Dust*, and he or his secretary mailed a sprig of sagebrush with every issue. Over the next few decades other dude ranchers took up the pen to create newsletters of their own.

Larom and Randall gave their talks, schmoozed marketing executives at stores, clubs, and commercial organizations, and did a good job drumming up both interest and business. Other ranch owners sent out letters and brochures or paid for advertising in New York and elsewhere. These efforts were aimed at very specific audiences. Because not everyone was welcome at their ranches.

In order to book a stay at many of the larger dude ranches, a potential guest had to first provide personal and financial references. Ranch owners wanted to make sure guests coming all the way from New York or Chicago would be able to pay for their stay once they showed up. But these references, which could include membership in social clubs, or the name of someone who had already stayed at the ranch, were designed to weed out one particular group of people, regardless of the education, money, or social connections they had: Jews.

This attitude did not take history into account, because the West had been home to Jewish immigrants, entrepreneurs, and families since the middle of the nineteenth century. The European revolutions of 1848 and the anti-Jewish violence of the 1880s saw thousands of Jews arrive in American ports, mostly in New York. The handful of Jewish residents in the United States in 1850 grew to about 300,000 by 1920.[3]

Thousands of established Jewish merchants moved to San Francisco and the gold country during the California Gold Rush, and mineral strikes in Nevada and Colorado in the 1850s tempted others to try their luck selling supplies to miners. In the nineteenth century, names like Zeckendorf, Steinfeld, and Goldwater in Arizona, Strauss in California, Goodstein in Wyoming, and Basinski in Montana, among many others, illustrate how early and how deeply Jewish life penetrated eastward from New York and westward from California.

Except in major cities like San Francisco, Jews in the West were generally a minority in their communities. And until a rise of anti-Semitism in the United States in the 1920s, most Jews did not face the kind of active or violent discrimination they saw in New York, not to mention their home countries. If it existed, anti-Semitism generally reared its head through laws against doing business on Sundays, bad ratings in eastern-run credit bureaus, and restrictions against Jews at hotels and clubs.

Jewish immigrants wanted to be Americans, and their skills in the mercantile and banking business meant that they were valuable contributors to the financial success of the towns in which they lived. They also formed charitable organizations to help not only their fellow Jews but also their Christian neighbors. By World War I many Jews in the West were the second or even third generation of their families, no longer immigrants but natives, and deeply embedded in the cultural, financial, and religious life of their communities.

Even if institutional discrimination was limited, individual attitudes toward Jews could make life uncomfortable. Western towns were often founded by people who had come there from somewhere else, and they brought their prejudices with them. Such was the case for New York native Larry Larom, and the Pittsburgh-born Eatons.

Ranchers and the writers of railroad advertising included coded language in their correspondence and brochures that assured their Christian guests that they would not be sharing their vacations with Jews. This example, from a 1913 Eatons' Ranch brochure, is typical:

> To the end that pleasant associations may be found at the ranch, special effort is put forth to avoid misunderstanding of the ranch standards. Throughout this booklet the class of patronage sought is clearly indicated and certain conditions are enumerated whereby anyone may safely judge. In the record of many years' work the ranch has won a host of friends through its standard of solicitude for the real welfare of each visitor, and its future will be more strongly devoted to this principle.[4]

Larry Larom used similar language in his advertising, but he was more explicit with his staff and others who shared his views. Secretary Elizabeth Phillips was responsible for reading the letters from people who wanted to come out to the ranch, and she wrote to Larom about potentially unwelcome applicants when he was out of town. In March 1923 Phillips and Larom traded notes about the request from a Miss Gloria Frink, who wanted to make a reservation. "Sounded like a good letter but I was a little doubtful of the name. Might it be Jewish?" Phillips wrote.

Larom replied, "If you receive word from Miss Frink send the letter to me or stall her off until we find out more about her." Miss Frink never followed up with a second request. Later that summer Larom wrote to Phillips about another dude rancher named Joe, who had "only two Jew dudes."[5]

Joe might have been Joe Jones, who ran the nearby Majo Ranch. He died in September 1929, and Larom was worried that a Jew might buy the place. The post office for the region of the Shoshone River's south fork was at the Valley Ranch (another one of Larom's marketing coups), and he was also concerned that if Jews took over at Majo, then his own guests would have to mingle with them.

How dude ranchers like Larom and the Eatons really felt about Jews is hard to judge. Their restrictive policies were common at hotels, colleges, and clubs all over the United States, and ranchers knew that they had to please the majority of their guests, even if this meant barring the minority.

Outside observers of dude ranching also understood this attitude, though they didn't necessarily agree with it. In 1929 Glen A. Smith, assistant district forester for Missoula, told the *Great Falls Tribune* that dude ranches in western Montana needed to up their game in order to compete for the lucrative dude tourist business. In addition to well-equipped cabins, good horses, and good food, the "big money" dudes of the East also expected something else. "There are other problems, too, of religion, race and caste that westerners rarely think of but which are essentially important to these visitors."[6] Forester Smith might not have had anything against Jews, but he knew people who did.

By the time the Dude Ranchers' Association was organized, the daily routine at most ranches was about the same: three hearty meals a day served in the main lodge or cabin, and trail rides at least once a day, with each guest assigned a horse best suited to his or her riding experience. Guests could go fishing if there were good streams nearby, and card games or informal musical interludes filled the evenings. Some ranches also offered pack trips, especially if they were near the national parks.

Mary Roberts Rinehart, in her many visits to Eatons,' enjoyed weeks on horseback and all the other activities that dude ranch guests enjoyed. But as a friend of the Eaton family, she also understood the dude ranch from the owner's perspective and wrote up her impressions of what these men and women accomplished over the course of a season:

> Yet good weather or bad, it must feed its two hundred guests and also its office force, cowboys, wranglers, guides, waitresses, gardeners, cooks, dishwashers, blacksmiths, and laundry maids. It must wash all the household linen, and sometimes that of its guests. It must provide light and heat not only for its main establishment, but its outlying cabins and tent houses . . . it must feed and care for hundreds of saddle horses and provide saddles for

them and men to wrangle them, feed them, shoe them, saddle them, and vaccinate them.[7]

Not every dude ranch was the size of Eatons,' and the scale of the enterprise was unique for each ranch, but the tasks and the staff were the same. Rinehart neglected to mention one of the most important people on the dude ranch: the co-owner, generally called the dude ranch wife.

Larry Larom knew he would not be able to run the Valley Ranch without his wife, Irma. The two had met in Cody, where Irma was working as a librarian, and they were married in 1920. She had also been a teacher, and her parents were Wyoming working class, not exactly the kind of guest Larom wanted at his dude ranch. But his business sense told him that a woman from his own class would not be able to manage the workload and struggles of ranch life. He said as much to Winthrop Brooks in a 1923 letter:

> As for Irma, she cleans and cares for our house, makes a decent home for me . . . and puts up with a lot of noise, trouble and worries which the average wife would not stand, for a woman to live continually with all manner of strangers around her, such as this business is, and cut off from regular friends and associations, pleasures, theaters and the usual entertainments in life, is a most difficult thing. The wives of you men who live in the East wouldn't and couldn't stand it, year after year.[8]

Except for serving as a hostess at meals, the dude ranch wife generally wielded her power from behind the scenes. But she knew everything her staff members did, even if some of them, on paper, were under her husband's authority. The most important of these were the cowboys.

Employers, guests, and the local press had many different names for these men. They were cowboys, cowpunchers, wranglers, or dude wranglers. As they had done earlier in the 1910s, cowboys just added dude wrangling to their daily duties on ranches that had previously only run cattle. When cattle ranches went under, cowboys needed to find work, and jobs on dude ranches were pretty easy to find. Some men enjoyed this change. Wrangling people was easier than herding steers, and the more gregarious cowboys enjoyed spending time with the guests. Others found humans difficult to deal with but persevered until they found a job where they had only livestock to manage.

Cowboys were still icons of masculinity, especially since they were showing up more frequently on movie screens as horseback-riding heroes. Dude wranglers, on the other hand, even if they had years of cowboying under their belts, were becoming figures of fun. Consider this filler from a variety of newspapers in January 1928: "Dude ranch owners are organizing an association, with the result that the cowboy will be asked to throw away his six shooter and buy a saxophone."[9]

It took a strong, self-reliant personality to ignore this cultural onslaught. If you think about it, that's the definition of a cowboy. Dude wranglers did not think the work was beneath them. They had a measure of autonomy because the dudes had to follow their instructions on trail rides or any other activity that involved horses. Their skills were valued, and the dudes were thrilled to be in the presence of the kind of men they had only read about.

But not all dude ranch owners valued their cowboys equally, and sometimes the men who were new to the West treated their wranglers as lowly hired hands. Reporters for western newspapers made a distinction between cowboys and wranglers, as well as the class difference between owners and workers, and the easterners did not always fare well.

In 1922, a World War I veteran from New York named E. M. Joyce—always called Captain—opened the Seven Dash dude ranch near Willcox, Arizona, about eighty miles east of Tucson. Joyce had moved to Arizona after he was discharged from the Signal Corps, and by 1920 he was married and managing a ranch at Willcox. The father of his wife, Lillian, owned the Seven Dash property, and Joyce and his wife ran dudes there for about a year after they took it over. They then sold it, bought property near Redington, north of Tucson, and in 1923 opened the Carlink Dude Ranch.

One of their wranglers was a young man from Texas named Jess Whitley. He was also a veteran and had been a wagoner in France, driving horse-drawn vehicles of supplies for Ambulance Company 360. He had worked on ranches in his home state, and sometime after returning from Europe, he moved to Arizona to find a job.

He was just an anonymous hand, like so many others, until November 23, 1924, when Captain Joyce shot him dead in the yard of the Carlink ranch.

From the moment Joyce was arrested, local newspapers filled their pages with the lurid story. The victim was described simply as "a dude wrangler named Whitley," and the headlines mentioned Whitley by name in only the first story published after the murder. He was just a cowpuncher, or a cowboy, or a dead vaquero. All the attention went to Joyce and the reason he killed the wrangler, which didn't come out until a few days later: Whitley had been having an affair with Joyce's wife.

More details emerged before the trial began in Tucson in January 1925, and reporters described Whitley's work as a dude wrangler. Whitley had also worked for another local rancher and had many friends, most of whom showed up at the trial every day wearing their big hats, boots, and spurs. The *Tucson Citizen* made its view of the defendant clear in its pages: "Joyce's only resemblance to the ranch life was the large cowboy hat which he wore to the court room."

The trial lasted just over two weeks. Lillian Joyce had to admit to the affair on the stand and read from the letters she had sent to Whitley. Captain Joyce said he shot the young man because he wanted to protect the integrity of his home, and he was driven to his actions by shell shock. The jury didn't buy it, and he was convicted of manslaughter. Lillian divorced him and later remarried, and Joyce was released from prison in 1928. Reporters followed him until the end of his life, recording his arrest for writing a bad check in 1930, and his remarriage the same year. He ran another dude ranch for a while in the 1940s and died in 1956.

Cochise County officials sent Jess Whitley's body to an aunt in Texas after the inquest was over at the end of November 1924. He disappeared from the historical record, even in his home state. Murderers make better copy.

Newspapers wrote about Whitley's work as a dude wrangler with detachment in the aftermath of his death and during Joyce's trial. But that was just respect for the dead. Wranglers still came in for their share of jokes in person and in print. C. Wiles Hallock, a Colorado-born journalist of the *Denver Post* and poet laureate, published a satirical poem about wranglers in 1928 titled "Pride of a Puncher." A Texas cowboy, who earns his pay by the sweat of his horse and his brow, laments how many of his buddies, including famous cowboys like Will Rogers and Tom Mix, have been tempted to work on dude ranches. "An' it surely galls when yore sidekick falls / Fer th' dude-ranch wranglin' game!"[10]

This kind of press did not keep eastern men from flocking to dude ranches for vacations with their families or friends. They still expected to see real cowboys, even if they were called dude wranglers, and still expected to have a cowboy experience of their own. Among them was one of the quintessential "he-men" of the twentieth century, Ernest Hemingway.

Hemingway's big, outdoorsy personality, and the many photos of him with a fishing rod in his hand, make him look like a typical westerner, but the Illinois-born writer did not see the West until he was nearly thirty years old. In July 1918 Hemingway was nineteen, an ambulance driver serving in World War I Italy. Just a few weeks after he started his duties, a mortar shell struck his leg and he spent months of recovery in a Milan hospital. Another American was in the next room suffering from a bout of jaundice. The men got to talking and soon realized they shared a love of fishing and camping.

This other man was Henry Villard, who would later become a US ambassador and writer. He was also the namesake grandson of the Henry Villard who had visited Dick Randall's OTO dude ranch in Montana twenty years earlier. The younger man had inherited his grandfather's love for the western mountains, and he told Hemingway about the ranches around the south fork of the Shoshone River in Wyoming.

By the late 1920s Hemingway had published *In Our Time* and *The Sun Also Rises*. Villard's description of Wyoming stuck with him, though, and in 1928 he went West with Bill Horne, a friend and fellow ambulance driver.

Their destination was the Bighorn Mountains. They first stayed at a place called the Folly Ranch and then went to Sheridan, where Hemingway worked on the draft of *A Farewell to Arms* at the Sheridan Inn. His wife, Pauline, who had just given birth to their son Patrick, later joined him and they went to the Spear-O-Wigwam dude ranch, owned by former Wyoming senator Willis Spear and his daughter Elsa. The Hemingways spent weeks that summer in a little log cabin next to a burbling stream, went fishing, and one day drove to the town of Shell to meet veteran western writer Owen Wister. Hemingway finished writing *A Farewell to Arms* during his Spear-O-Wigwam sojourn.

He turned to the mountains again in 1930 with Pauline and the son from his first marriage. They started off at the Sunlight dude ranch in Wyoming's Sunlight Basin and also rode out at the Majo Ranch near Larry Larom's Valley Ranch, where Hemingway made news, though not the kind he wanted.

"Dude Injured at the Majo on Southfork" was the headline in the August 20, 1930, issue of the *Cody Enterprise*. The article read in part: "Ernest Hemingway was brought to Cody on Tuesday evening to receive surgical attention caused by an accident that afternoon when a horse (a bay named Goofy) bolted with him, carrying him through some heavy brush and tearing his face in such a manner as to require several stitches to patch up the wounds."[11]

Hemingway left the Sunlight ranch because so many guests knew who he was and he couldn't get any work done. He and his family then settled in at the L Bar T dude ranch near Cooke City, Montana. The owners of the ranch, Lawrence and Olive Norquist, had never heard of him, but they liked what they saw and gave Hemingway a cabin near a stand of lodgepole pines. There, no one bothered him, and he could do what he loved best: write and fish. One of the hunting guides, Ivan Wallace, remembered regularly talking to Hemingway about how good the fishing was, and the writer would reply sadly that he couldn't break away because he had work to do.[12]

This was the second time Hemingway had headed West when he needed to work on his writing. During the 1930 visit to the L Bar T, he revised his Nick Adams stories for a reissue of *In Our Time* and put in many hours on *Death in the Afternoon*. In 1932 he went back to the ranch, where he did the book's final edits, but didn't return again until 1938.

That summer was the most productive. In between sneaking off to fish (always on a Friday, according to Olive Norquist), he wrote the preface for *The First Forty-Nine Stories*, started on his Spanish Civil War tales, and wrote the first two chapters of *For Whom the Bell Tolls*. The Norquists were humble, unfussy people and did not advertise the fact that a famous writer was staying at their dude ranch, which Hemingway no doubt appreciated. His dude ranch stays freed him to do some of his best writing, and in the February 1939 issue of *Vogue*, he published a tribute to the L Bar T called "The Clark's Fork Valley, Wyoming."

The Hemingway we know was forged partly on the page and in the streams of the mountain West. And though it's hard to believe today, he was once called a dude.

Chapter 5

Dudines didn't have any trouble seeing dude wranglers as manly men, and their interest in cowboys set tongues wagging around the country. Especially when they married them.

In the winter of 1931 sisters Annie and Helen Crocker of Fitchburg, Massachusetts, spent a few months at the Two Shoe dude ranch near Castle Hot Springs, Arizona. The ranch was operated by Lawton Champie, an eastern-born champion rodeo performer who had lived in Arizona for years. Annie and Lawton surprised everyone when they married in April. Their union spawned headlines like "Fitchburg Girl to Wed Bronco-Buster" in the *Boston Globe*, and "Noted Cowboy Champ Marries" in the *Arizona Daily Star*. It's interesting that the Arizona paper didn't come up with a snappy description of Champie's bride, unlike the *Globe*'s comment about a bronco buster.[1]

In 1934 Anne Gould, great-granddaughter of financier Jay Gould, married a young Texas rancher named Frank Meador, who had come to New York to become an actor. They divorced in 1936 and Anne then married her second husband, Wyoming dude wrangler Herman Elsbury. She had met him during a summer at the Sunlight dude ranch a year before marrying Meador. "Gould Heiress Weds Dude Ranch Cowboy" was the typical headline when the news got out, and the couple tied the knot in Cheyenne. Elsbury wore a "super-gallon" sombrero, whipcord riding breeches, and cowboy boots, while his bride wore a sober gray traveling suit.[2]

Marriages between eastern girls and cowboys did not go unnoticed by dude ranch owners. By the 1930s a number of states had formed their own trade groups, and the secretary of the Colorado Dude Ranchers' Association, Lee Hermann, gave its members some advice about using romance in their advertising. "You must tell them, off-hand like, that you have handsome cowboys, moonlight on babbling brooks and all the other stage props that go to incubate the germ of tender romance." He reminded his colleagues that several heiresses had married dude ranch cowboys—citing Anne Gould in particular—and then said that ranchers wouldn't need an old age pension plan if they levied a 1 percent marriage bureau fee on the wealth of the women who came for vacation and went home with a husband.[3]

These marriages, however titillating, weren't always happy and didn't always last. Annie Crocker and Lawton Champie divorced after just a few years. Anne Gould left her wrangler for a guitar-playing cowboy, Ezra Wogoman, whom she married in 1941. In 1945 she married cowboy number four, Dominic Valentine (he played the fiddle), who had been best man at her previous wedding. They stayed together and lived in Prescott, Arizona, until her death in 1962. What's striking is that all of Anne's husbands were cowboys of a sort, and westerners above all.

Dude ranching started showing up in more books as the 1930s opened, and two of them took the story line about heiresses marrying cowhands and flipped it around. In Milton Krims's *Dude Ranch* and Zane Grey's *The Dude Ranger*, the women are the westerners. They live on their dude ranches, and the men come to the ranches from back East to find their futures.

Milton Krims was a journalist who also turned his hand to novels and screenplays. The main character in his 1930 book *Dude Ranch* is named Jerry Francis. He is a farm boy from some unspecified place who leaves home to try his luck as an actor and has been traveling around small-town America with a troupe of fellow thespians. He can ride a horse and has spent time around cows, but he is still a dude. Jerry and his friends find themselves stranded in a Texas cattle town, and they meet the owner of a dude ranch called the Bar O, Jim Townsend, who sees them as the solution to a problem. He explains to Jerry that his dudes want to do more than just ride horses in the surrounding countryside. "They expect to hear about cattle rustling and bad men and some even expect to find wild Indians roaming the plains."[4]

He wants to give his guests this authentic western experience, but his cowboys don't fit the stereotype. They are too quiet and industrious. So, he hires Jerry to play an outlaw named the Lone Rider of the Mojave, who terrorizes the new guests as they arrive on a stagecoach. His fellow actors join in as guests at the dude ranch, though they also have parts to play.

Townsend has a serene daughter named Grace who, even though she has a degree from Vassar, has come home to devote herself to the ranch. She and Jerry are instantly attracted to each other, and before the book ends Jerry thwarts real cattle rustlers, impresses the cowboys at the ranch, and wins

Grace's hand in marriage. He says goodbye to his friends as they take the train to other cow towns while he stays to run the Bar O.

Zane Grey is one of the biggest names in western fiction, even decades after his death in 1939. *Riders of the Purple Sage* is always in print and frequently filmed, and his novel *The Dude Ranger* was published in 1931. The story focuses on a dude, not a dude ranch: the main character is Iowa-born Ernest Selby, who inherits the Red Rock cattle ranch from an uncle. He gets a look at the ranch's financial records and realizes that livestock have been disappearing, so he decides to go out to Arizona incognito to find out what's going on. He takes on all the trappings of a dude and gets a job as a lowly cowboy on his own ranch. The love interest in this book is Anne, daughter of the crooked foreman who is responsible for the missing cattle, who's a bit haughty and doesn't want to marry a cowboy. Selby proves himself to Anne and surprises her by revealing who he really is. They marry and stay in Arizona to manage the Red Rock Ranch together.

Both of these books take the theme of eastern tenderfeet who come West to do one thing and end up doing another: sticking around. The women, who are strong cowgirl types, don't accept the men until they have shed their dude-like tendencies. This recalls Caroline Lockhart's Wallie Macpherson in *The Dude Wrangler*, written a decade earlier.

Hollywood made a few dude-related films in the late 1920s and early 1930s. *The Dude Cowboy* starred Bob Custer, a rodeo performer turned western actor, and it was released in 1927. Tom Mix made another film set on a dude ranch in 1930 called *The Big Diamond Robbery*. But after the success of the Krims and Grey novels, Hollywood decided to put more effort into making films in which dude ranching itself played a bigger role.

Studios reached further back for their first effort, releasing *The Dude Wrangler* in 1930, based on Caroline Lockhart's novel. It starred popular favorites Tom Keene and Lina Basquette, and silent film legend Francis X. Bushman. Critics praised the film's comedic aspects and especially enjoyed Keene's performance as the "pansy" cowboy.

In 1931 Paramount Studios released the film version of Milton Krims's book *Dude Ranch*. Future Hollywood powerhouse writers and producers Joseph and Herman Mankiewicz contributed to the script, and the film starred two screen favorites: Jack Oakie and Eugene Pallette. The story sticks closely enough to the original novel, but the female love interest is a visiting dudine, not the daughter of the ranch's owner. As with *The Dude Wrangler*, reviewers laughed at the contrast between the bumbling dudes and the stolid cowboys. Critics of the original novel felt the same way, often calling it a farce.

The way these films were written and reviewed shows how both the entertainment industry and society at large felt about dude ranches, and how Hollywood defined western movies. The dude ranch was a faux West and therefore had to be treated as comedy, even if the films did include some classic western elements: wide open spaces, cowboys, a strong but still-vulnerable female lead who falls for the unlikely hero (and who is not as independent as she is in the novels), and a good-versus-evil climax that affirms the western values of hard work and freedom on the open range. *The Dude Wrangler* and *Dude Ranch* were considered comedies, not westerns, despite their setting, and that was just how the studios wanted it.

This attitude changed in 1934 with the release of *The Dude Ranger*, based on Zane Grey's book. It starred George O'Brien, one of the biggest names in western films, who had also played the lead in a 1931 film version of *Riders of the Purple Sage*. Because the story is set on a cattle ranch and the only dude in sight is the visitor from back East, *The Dude Ranger* fit nicely into the western genre. A few comedic scenes lightened the mood, as there were some funny characters in the book, but they didn't rise to the level of silliness seen in movies in which the dude ranch and its guests were the focus of the plot.

Some critics praised the film as a modern western. "The 'dude' from the city is a hero, while the virile son of the west is the villain," read one review.[5] Marketing executives put Zane Grey's name on the posters and in movie ads in the local press, giving the film even more western credibility.

Two other films were released in 1934 that featured dude ranches in their story lines. *Rawhide Romance* and *Racketeer Round-Up* were solid B pictures, meant to follow the main or more popular film in a theater double feature. In *Rawhide Romance* the hero is a wrangler who falls for a visiting dudine, and in *Racketeer Round-Up* a reformed gangster running a dude ranch is killed for some loot he kept from a bank robbery, while his daughter's fiancé, the ranch foreman, is framed for the murder.

All of these films, and the books they were based on, include some element of crime and action-packed scenes in which the hero, who is either a native westerner or a former dude, fights the perpetrators and saves the ranch, the girl, and the day. The dude ranch provides the perfect setting for this formula because it has all the elements necessary for great drama and mystery: an isolated location, strangers with shady backstories, and a closed society with its own language and activities. Throw in horses, spectacular scenery, and cowboys and you have a setting worthy of a western.

◼

Box office receipts were one reason movie studios set films on dude ranches. But executives might also have noticed that ranches were opening up around California and had been since the late 1920s. Some started out as cattle ranches, like their counterparts in the Dakotas, because cattle were the backbone of California's economy before the upheaval of the Gold Rush.

Spanish and then Mexican settlers started bringing livestock into California in the eighteenth century. Regions like the San Joaquin Valley were later famous for vast herds prized for their hides and tallow, which were shipped out from California ports. New Englander Richard Henry Dana wrote about the grueling work of curing and loading the hides in his 1840 book, *Two Years before the Mast*.

After gold was discovered in 1848 and men poured into California, cattle were needed to feed the hordes of gold rushers. Distant Mexican ranchos saw huge profits at first, but when American cattlemen brought in midwestern livestock, the old rancheros found themselves without customers and soon without homes as their debt accumulated in the face of falling prices. Floods in 1861–62, followed by years of drought, were as devastating in California as the Big Die-Up had been in Texas. Larger operations survived and newer, smaller concerns started up, but the cattle business was no longer the economic driver it had been.

Some ranches had a long life in the livestock business and then added dudes to their lineup. And others served only dudes. The new Deep Well Guest Ranch, just a ten-minute drive from Palm Springs, was up and running by 1929. It advertised itself as a desert dude ranch, had a dietician on staff, and welcomed dogs.

The fairly new term "guest ranch," used by some advertisers and travel agents, was synonymous with "dude ranch" but signaled to potential vacationers that it wasn't overly horsey or cowboyish, something wealthier visitors to Southern California might have appreciated. Despite its history with cattle ranching, as well as its fine stables and a landscape perfect for filming western movies, most people did not think of California when they heard the term Wild West. Historian Robert Athearn agreed with them. He once said that he "would not let California into his West without a search warrant."⁶

Entrepreneurs did not let this perception stop them from opening ranches up and down the state. George Weston Pierson founded his Pierson Dude Ranch around 1930 in Wonder Valley, sandwiched between the Mojave and Colorado Deserts near Twentynine Palms. By the mid-1930s he made regular visits to Los Angeles to advertise his ranch, setting up a reservation center at the Roosevelt Hotel on Hollywood Boulevard.

In 1936 he brought a midget draft horse and a singing cowboy to his headquarters to entice people to book stays at the ranch. He also placed ads in newspapers in major cities throughout California, and a few in Washington and Texas. These were written with western slang in the voices of his guests, like this one from 1936: "We rode, swam, fished, hunted, hiked, and enjoyed a real ranch vacation. We cheered at an impromptu rodeo, learned to shoot a pistol, found out there are 'cowgals,' and devoured delicious grub."⁷

And because California has always been a place where the new is often also the weird, a woman in Pasadena opened a dude ranch for dogs in 1936. Gladys Shipman was inspired by the stories she read about dude ranching and decided to open a place for dogs in Big Bear Lake, about one hundred miles northeast of Los Angeles. Reporters took great glee in writing stories about the doggie dude ranch and emphasized its kitchen, daily activities, and even the maternity ward. Celebrities like silent film comedian and Saint Bernard owner Harold Lloyd regularly sent their dogs to the ranch. One writer said the only difference between Miss Shipman's dude ranch and the human version was that it didn't have a cocktail lounge.⁸

This is an interesting comment because dude ranches did not have bars in the 1930s. Ranch owners did not want to serve drinks to overstimulated dudes and end up being bartenders or bouncers, so alcohol was not allowed in dude ranches' public areas. However, some places allowed guests to bring liquor to drink in their own cabins.

One Northern California dude ranch began as the private home of a famous writer. Jack London, author of vigorous novels of both human and animal survival, died in 1916 on his Beauty Ranch in Glen Ellen, a few miles from Sonoma. London had also been famous for being a "scientific farmer," turning an overworked property into a small but prosperous livestock ranch. In 1934, his widow, Charmian, and sister Eliza Shepard kept the place going by revamping some of the living quarters for guests and opening the new Jack

London Guest Ranch. A fearless horsewoman herself, Charmian London emphasized the miles of available riding trails when she advertised the ranch, and guests were also allowed to bring their own horses.

Dude ranches started up in the Pacific Northwest in the late 1920s and early 1930s, which gave guests even more diversity in scenery, waterways, and fish species. This was good news for other western ranch owners, as they and the Dude Ranchers' Association believed that a rising tide lifted all boats.

In 1931 barmen and restaurateurs in Manhattan and Provincetown took notice of this popularity and opened nightclubs with names like "The Dude Ranch." Within a few years enterprising men and women founded dude ranches in Stony Creek and other locales in Upstate New York. There was even one in Florida, which announced its opening in the fall of 1928, promising visitors a stable of seventy-five horses, real cowboys, and roundups of cattle imported from Wyoming.

This irritated western dude ranch owners, who maintained that legitimate ranches could exist only in the West, where they could claim both heritage and longevity. But New York ranches, which grew in number as the decade progressed, were very appealing to easterners who wanted a horseback-riding, cowboy-themed vacation but didn't have the money to take the train out to Montana or Arizona. These places traded on the West in their advertising and were also featured in railroad company advertising.

They also had the occasional western problem: in February 1932, three buffalo, a cow, and a calf escaped from a dude ranch near Salamanca, New York, and a month later they were spotted meandering down the streets of Bradford, Pennsylvania, about twenty miles away. But before traffic officers could surround the animals, they took off into Allegany State Park and that was the last anyone saw of them.

The Dude Ranchers' Association wasn't aggravated by New Yorkers, or even Floridians, who opened ranches, and as long as they met the membership criteria, they could join the DRA. These were simple but nonnegotiable. Potential members had to take reservations for visits and could not take the "transient" trade, meaning people who just stopped by for a couple of nights' lodging as they did with the new auto courts and motels. Ranches had to offer the American Plan, where fees covered all expenses and, as mentioned earlier, they could not have cocktail lounges. And most important of all, they had to offer horseback riding. Most ranches had no trouble with the rules, as these were already the backbone of their business model.

In 1936, writer and former dude Lawrence B. Smith published the book *Dude Ranches and Ponies*. It's a guide to life on dude ranches, with an emphasis on the importance of horseflesh and the proper way to behave on a dude ranch. His list of "Don'ts" is six pages long and features advice such as "DON'T lie in bed mornings and then expect to get a ham omelet when you get to the grub-pile. If you are not well you will be taken care of, but don't get in the habit."[9] In the back of the book Smith listed all the ranches he could find, organized by region and the railroad lines that served them. In total, there were over four hundred, with just under one hundred of them active members of the Dude Ranchers' Association.

What's astonishing about these numbers is that the Depression was in full swing by the time Smith made his list and then published his book. And while some ranches went under during the 1930s, many survived by changing the way they operated: scaling back operations, offering longer stays for less money, even increasing their cattle herds, if they had them. Charmian London always said that she did not open her dude ranch in order to help keep the property afloat financially, but rather to offer her late husband's fans the opportunity to be close to where Jack London had penned so many of his books (it was probably a combination of both).

Tourism numbers tell an interesting story. In the 1934–35 season, dude ranches in Montana and Wyoming brought in about $13 million in revenue, and returns from Wyoming's gasoline taxes were 12 percent higher in 1935 than they were the previous year. The Santa Fe Railroad published a glossy brochure about New Mexico and Arizona dude ranches in 1935 and often advertised attractively priced rates for travel to ranch locations. The pamphlet also emphasized the "better places" among the dude ranches, and for a very specific reason. The people who normally went to dude ranches could still afford them. Dude ranching was an intentionally elitist vacation at this time, and however offensive that is to twenty-first-century travelers, it's one reason so many dude ranches survived the Depression years.[10]

Dude ranching got another boost in this decade, from a strange and socially fraught source.

In the early 1900s, Florida, Idaho, Arkansas, and Wyoming streamlined the divorce process by shortening the length of time people had to live in their state in order to get unhitched. The reason was economics, not morality. People wanting divorces would stay in hotels and eat restaurant meals for months, adding to local coffers.

Lawmakers in Nevada had the same idea, and in 1915 the state required a six-month residency before a divorce was granted. In 1927 this was reduced to three months, leading to a corresponding rise in part-time residents. But when the Depression took hold, this trend waned, partly because of the costs of long-term stays away from home. Nevada legislators went back to the drawing board, and in 1931 the state legalized gambling and allowed for divorce after a stay of just six weeks. Reno was the hub for the marriage enders, advertised as such because of its fine climate and many leisure activities, which now included gambling. These were necessary, because divorce seekers had to stay within Nevada's borders for the entire six weeks.

A few local dude ranches saw an increase in business from visitors who came to town to start the divorce clock ticking, while others opened up specifically as divorce ranches. There was a wide variety to choose from, depending on the guest's financial condition: everything from a tent cabin with a wooden floor, to a room in a sprawling ranch house with swimming pool privileges.

There were other privileges, too, and newspaper gossip columns were filled with tales of women who married the wrangler as soon as their paperwork came through. Lawrence Smith even addressed this in his "Don'ts" list. "DON'T (If you are a lovely female) go out to tie a couple of cowboy scalps to your belt just for the excitement; you may get fooled."[11]

Celebrity names like Consuelo Vanderbilt Smith also showed up in these columns. She was the granddaughter of James Fair, one of the "Bonanza Kings" who made a pile during the Nevada silver rush of the 1860s. She stayed at a Reno dude ranch to wait out her divorce in 1935. That same year Nina Gore Vidal, daughter of Senator Thomas Gore of Oklahoma, also spent six weeks in Reno after she and her husband, Eugene L. Vidal, split up (one of their children was the author Gore Vidal).

The appeal of staying at a dude ranch for women like Smith and Vidal was privacy. Far from the center of town with its hotels and newspaper photographers, prominent people could enjoy a measure of solitude. And columnists rarely if ever mentioned the name of the ranches where they were staying. Ranch owners knew they needed to keep this information to themselves if they wanted divorcées to recommend their place to friends.

The classic film treatment of the divorce ranch is *The Women*, from 1939. Based on a popular play written by Clare Boothe Luce in 1936, it's the story of a group of New York women and their marriage troubles. Three of them, played by Norma Shearer, Joan Fontaine, and Rosalind Russell, travel to a Nevada dude ranch to obtain divorces; Shearer and Fontaine meet Paulette Goddard and Mary Boland "on the train for Reno." Lucy runs the Double Bar T ranch and is played by the actress most known for her roles as Ma Kettle, Marjorie Main.

The short scene on the divorce ranch hits all the high notes. The ladies trade in their Adrian-designed gowns for denim pants and plain skirts or, in the case of Paulette Goddard, shorts, white leather boots, and fringed white leather gauntlets. Lucy talks with the twang and colorful language of the native westerner, but unlike her guests, she wears a sensible housedress and apron. She also gleefully shouts encouragement when Goddard and Russell engage in a brawl in the ranch's outdoor seating area, which features a fringed umbrella and the latest in Depression-era glassware.

The oldest of the women, and the one with the most divorces behind her, is Mary Boland's Countess De Lave, who wears ropes of pearls and a huge diamond brooch with her plaid shirt and jeans. She snags Buck Winston, the ranch's wrangler, marries him, and takes him back to New York. Fontaine's character, Peggy, is the only one who doesn't wear western clothing, and when she tells Lucy she hates Reno, Lucy replies, "You didn't come for fun!"[12] Everyone who saw this film understood the reference to being "Reno-vated" as well as the concept of the ranch itself.

Entertainment with a western flavor had to feature a very specific kind of costume. By this time, an immersion in the West, whether at a dude ranch, in a movie theater, or at a themed nightclub, meant that cowboy hats, bandannas, and boots made a regular appearance. Tourist and travel bureau brochures, as well as fiction writers and journalists, gave out advice to potential dude ranch visitors about the proper clothing to bring along. While blue jeans, wildly patterned shirts, and hats with elaborate decoration might come to mind when we hear "western wear" today, early dude ranch wear was simply what was best for horseback riding.

Photographs from the late 1920s and early 1930s show smiling riders wearing heavy khaki or corduroy jodhpurs tucked into tall, laced boots, and plain white shirts with a tailored riding coat on cool days. Many people had English-style equestrian wear on hand because they were already regular riders at home. The wranglers, on the other hand, wore jeans or sturdy pants made of a canvas-like material called duck, cowboy boots with higher heels, and serviceable denim or chambray shirts. The dude ranch owner might dress in a combination of all of these.

Cowboy clothing was practical and had been for decades. The first copper-riveted denim jeans were patented by San Francisco's Levi Strauss & Co. in 1873 and became the go-to trouser for cowboys by the early twentieth century, both by choice and by the company's intelligent marketing. Denim was tough enough, and yet it washed down soft enough, to make life in the saddle bearable. And just as all jeans were often called Levi's, all cowboy hats were often called Stetsons. John B. Stetson of Philadelphia created the "Boss of the Plains" in 1865, which, with modifications for function and fashion, has come down to us as the modern cowboy hat. The bandanna or silk neckerchief, colorfully known as a "wild rag," was used as facial protection and a sweat rag.

Cowboys wore all these items as their everyday workwear and didn't think anything of it. But when they started showing up as heroic types on screen and in fiction, a cowboy outfit became a lifestyle choice for tourists on dude ranches, with clothing serving as the closest approximation of the real thing.

Male dude ranch visitors turned to denim and simple cowboy boots earlier than women did. They were already used to wearing more practical garments when they were hunting and fishing. But women's leisure clothing tended toward the lightweight and sporty: tennis outfits, nautical tops and sailor pants, gingham overalls for working in the flower garden. These men and women were still, for the most part, from the monied classes and were in the majority as dude ranch guests. They could afford separate wardrobes for distinct activities.

Clothing companies took notice of the dude ranch trend and saw an opportunity to diversify, especially in women's wear. Levi Strauss & Co. was one of them, and in 1934 the company created the first jeans for women, called Lady Levi's. *Vogue* magazine took notice and featured the pants in its May 15, 1935, issue as part of an article about dude ranching. Titled "Boccaccio in Chaps," the piece was written by Bar B C owner Struthers Burt, who had published a memoir of his life as a dude rancher ten years earlier. Accompanying the text was an illustration of two very stylish women in very western clothing, with a caption designed to entice even the most clothes-conscious reader into taking a dude ranch vacation.

> True Western chic was invented by cowboys, and the moment you veer from their tenets you are lost. Your uniform for a dude

ranch or a ranch near Reno is simple-but-severe blue jeans or Levis . . . cut straight and tight fitting, worn low on the hips, in the manner of your favourite dude wrangler. With these jeans go a simply tailored flannel or plaid cotton shirt, or possibly a Brooks sweater; a plain silk kerchief knotted loosely; a studded leather belt; high-heeled Western boots; a Stetson hat; and a great free air of bravado.[13]

Note the coded language about "a ranch near Reno."

Articles like this, which appeared in all the upscale women's magazines, were intended as instructions for how to dress in alien territory. *Vogue* readers knew how to navigate the country club, the ocean liner, and the hotel tearoom, but sitting in a western saddle or on a log bench outside a pine-shrouded cabin were experiences for which they needed guidance. The social pages in big city newspapers also featured articles about appropriate dude ranch clothing, grabbing readers with headlines like "Go West, Young Woman—But Go Right!"[14]

Even wearing denim was revolutionary, and donning jeans gave women the "great free air of bravado" they didn't feel at home. Denim pants were very male and very working class, but Lady Levi's, and the others that followed, were cut for the female form and sewn with preshrunk, softer fabric. They signaled femininity even as the wearers themselves felt slightly uncomfortable for wearing them.

Although dude ranch owners gave their guests a list of appropriate clothing to pack, including jeans and cowboy boots, these weren't always available in New York, Newport, or Philadelphia. This was good news for merchants in places like Sheridan and Wickenburg, whose general stores and haberdasheries had stockpiles of jeans, Stetsons, boots, and wild rags for dudes to buy once they got off the train. Some of the larger ranches, like the Valley Ranch, had their own "trading posts," where dudes could buy the clothing they needed.

Locals in larger dude ranch towns also got in on the act. Caroline Lockhart encouraged Cody residents to dress in jeans, boots, and fancy shirts during the annual Cody Stampede, because visitors expected to see westerners when they came to town for the rodeo and the annual ball. Dressing for the dudes was good business.

Chapter 6

Good business was always the goal of the Dude Ranchers' Association. The men who ran the organization understood that many ranchers were just that: ranchers, not managers, and certainly not personnel experts. They knew how to run their cattle, keep their books, and pay their hands, but everything else about dude ranching was new. These men and women were also used to the independence that so many of them came West for in the first place, and they wanted to run their dude businesses their way. But the DRA helped them understand that cooperation and having some baseline standards would allow them to build on what they had started.

By 1931 seventy-four ranches had joined the DRA, with sixty-seven of them in Montana and Wyoming (the rest were in Colorado, Idaho, Texas, California, and an off-season ranch that the Eatons ran in Arizona).[1] Five years after its founding, the DRA knew it had a winning formula and that ranchers valued the support it gave them. To keep the momentum going, in the winter of 1932 the DRA debuted *The Dude Rancher*, a magazine devoted to the business of dude ranching.

The Dude Rancher was packed with articles about ranch life from the perspective of both the owner and the guest, practical advice about hiring staff, horror stories about unpleasant dudes, and at least one piece devoted to fish and game laws. Dude ranches that offered hunting and fishing had to keep in the good graces of rangers, game commissions, and state officials, especially those in Montana and Wyoming. Relations weren't always smooth, but like their government counterparts, dude ranchers knew that wildlife preservation and management was important not only to their business, but to the image of the West dudes expected to see. The DRA also had associate members who supported dude ranching but weren't in the business themselves, such as members of Congress, corporate leaders, and women's clubs. *The Dude Rancher* took in lucrative advertising revenue, too, and its ads reflected what both ranchers and guests needed: western clothing, banks, tack, and train schedules.

The DRA knew that travel to dude ranches would be a lot harder without the railroads, and *The Dude Rancher* had a transportation column in every issue. For that matter, railroads knew that if the dude business increased, so would theirs, and they regularly offered lower fares to cities near the larger ranches. They also continued to print and distribute brochures about ranches by region. The Northern Pacific, the Burlington, and other rail lines also threw a lot of money at dude ranching because they were nervous about competition. Not from other railroads, but from automobiles, which now had much better roads to drive on, thanks to something called the Good Roads Movement.

It began in the late nineteenth century when bicycle enthusiasts agitated for better roadways. New car owners took up the cause in the early years of the twentieth, and many states had their own Good Roads organizations by the 1910s. The most famous and one of the first national roads to benefit from the movement was the Lincoln Highway, which ran from New York to San Francisco. It was meant to encourage tourism, but the highway's popularity also pointed out the importance of federal assistance in road improvement. It worked: in 1916 President Woodrow Wilson signed the Federal Aid Road Act, which funded road paving in states that had their own highway departments. In 1925 a group of state and federal highway officials decided it was time to look at roads on a national scale, and in 1926 the National Highway System was born.

Fast action on road improvement was necessary because more Americans were buying cars. In 1900, about eight thousand automobiles were registered in the United States. Ten years later, residents of Sheridan, the nearest town to Eatons', owned ninety-five cars. In 1915, the year the first vehicle was allowed into Yellowstone National Park, there were over two million cars in the United States. By 1932, there were over twenty million automobiles on the road.[2]

Automobile clubs began to form in the 1910s, and many of them included dude ranch advertising in their brochures and membership materials, also coordinating their publicity with travel bureaus. Auto travel to ranches near improved roads meant more people could make a trip West under their own power. But even with their special lower fares for dude ranch visitors, railroads couldn't compete with the freedom offered by having one's own car, and train travel took a hit.

Advertising aside, the DRA and many ranchers did not think Americans taking vacations in their own cars was good for business. For one thing, entrepreneurs had started building camps and early versions of the motel to serve auto travelers, who could drive up, stay a couple of nights, and move on. This was the exact opposite of the dude ranch's hospitality model: make a reservation, spend your entire holiday at the ranch, and stay for at least a couple of weeks. No ranches took "transient" travel, though any that did would lose their membership in the DRA. Some guests arrived by car because it was convenient, after making the necessary reservations, and did enjoy their multiweek holiday. But many ranches saw a decrease in the length of stays when visitors got out of a Packard instead of a railroad sleeping car.

Dude ranchers also deplored the loss of wilderness areas when roads were improved or built from scratch. A pristine outdoor world was high on the list of ranch offerings, and asphalt roads did not add to the attraction. Even worse was the construction of huge billboards along the major roads and highways, a type of visual litter that people like Struthers Burt loathed. So did the American Automobile Association, which worked with Burt on its Committee for Roadside Development, opposing billboards for distracting motorists and destroying scenery.

Dude ranchers' irritation at how better roads and increased auto traffic led to shorter stays was about survival, of course. But there were many, like Larry Larom, who thought that something more intangible was being forgotten in the rush to get to the ranch, ride a few horses, and then take off with a squeal of tires. People came to dude ranches to relax, to give up the stresses of daily life, and to give themselves to the West. That could not be accomplished in just a week or two, which longtime dude ranchers knew very well.

Members of the Dude Ranchers' Association knew they couldn't do anything about the increase in automobiles, but they did not despair. Railroad travel was still the only way to get to some of the more remote ranches, and the DRA put articles about rail lines in every issue of *The Dude Rancher*. Individual ranchers also altered their reservation requirements to accommodate the short stayers.

The DRA wanted its magazine to benefit its members in ways that would help them increase their business and navigate the many challenges of dude wrangling. In December 1932 a new column debuted in *The Dude Rancher* called the "House Management Department," known in the newspaper world as the women's page.

Stereotypes about western women, and the categories they fell into, had been around since the nineteenth century and moved easily from dime novels, to books, to film: the schoolmarm, the sturdy pioneer, the rich rancher's haughty daughter, the mining camp laundress, the soiled dove. The dude ranch wife, as many called her, was something new.

Women ranchers had formed the House Management Department of the Dude Ranchers' Association during the 1932 convention. The chair was Mrs. Ralph Allan of Augusta, Montana, and the two secretaries were Mrs. Paul Van Cleve Jr. of Big Timber, Montana, and Mrs. C. C. Moore of Dubois, Wyoming. They identified themselves by their husbands' name and the location of their dude ranch, presumably because everyone knew who they were and the name of their ranch anyway. The Allans ran the Allan Ranch, the Van Cleves the Lazy K Bar, and the Moores the CM Ranch.

Mrs. Allan presented the goals of the House Management Department in her first column, which also spelled out how ranch women saw their roles. "It is good to see the interest house management has seemed to create as a very important part of dude ranching, making dude ranching a woman's game as well as a man's. One business the two could work out very successfully together. The outdoors and the indoors being so closely interwoven, one could not succeed without the success of the other."[3]

She also wrote that when she and her husband first started their ranch, she was at a loss about how to manage both place and people. She took a course in house management, which was probably like today's hospitality management, but she said it didn't help her with two of the most important aspects of running a dude ranch: pleasing the guests who stayed for weeks at a time, and the importance of personal contact. She said that dude ranchers' problems were different from those faced by hotel owners, so she turned to her sister ranchers for help. Out of this conundrum was born the House Management Department, which ran a column in *The Dude Rancher* magazine (under a variety of names) well into the 1970s.

The women understood that their role was a traditional one. They oversaw meal planning, housekeeping, hiring the domestic staff, and public relations. The column covered everything from how to organize food for a pack trip, to what to do about people who came late to breakfast, to keeping everyone entertained, to vermin control. All of these—and more—fell to the women.

House management was therefore both a support system and a stake in the ground to reaffirm just how essential the dude ranch wife was.

But not all female dude ranchers were wives. In 1930 the *Arizona Daily Star* ran a syndicated article about the popularity of dude ranching, with the eye-catching headline "Ranch Bosses Mainly Women." The reporter described life on a dude ranch and emphasized how women were visiting ranches in droves, as well as the astonishing number of them who were in charge of them. He said that of one hundred dude ranches in Montana and Wyoming alone, twenty-two were owned by women and that practically all ranches had women managing what he called the hotel end of the business. The article ended with this line: "They prove the modern theme song: 'If there's something new to be done, there's a place for women in it!'"[4]

One early woman ranch owner was Mary Shawver, who came out to Cody from Chicago to take a pack trip with Tex Holm, owner of the rustic Holm Lodge dude ranch. She returned year after year, even after Holm sold his place to packer and guide Billy Howell in 1914. Shawver, who was single and remained so, was such a fixture at Holm Lodge that Howell asked her to be his business partner in 1916.

Shawver was a gentle soul with strong opinions. Her personality and natural ability to make dudes feel welcome brought people back to Holm Lodge for years. She also knew what it was like to be a dude ranch wife, because those regular duties fell to her, and she embraced them. She also managed the wranglers, who loved her, and went along on pack trips. One winter she was alone on the ranch when an unexpected snowstorm marooned her for three weeks. She had fuel and food, and one of the Yellowstone rangers managed to get through a couple of times to check on her, but she was candid about the experience in her memoir, *Sincerely, Mary S*. One night, her fire went out and the cold was too fierce for her to go outside to get more wood. "Had I been warned of this no-slumber party, I would have been weak with dread and fear. Having my full quota of strength, I survived and suffered no ill effects."

She was also more tuned to the desires of the young women who came to Holm Lodge and tried to gently persuade them out of their romantic notions about cowboys and life in the West. To those who wanted to marry their "Virginian" (a nod to Owen Wister's novel), Shawver gave this advice:

> They do not foresee long winter days alone, while he looks after stock, very often not his own. They do not know that in many

places during the winter, mail days are few and far between. They do not realize that because they have lived such widely different lives, they do not have enough in common to keep their interest in each other alive indefinitely. Too many unforeseen circumstances are conducive to "cabin fever" which may develop to a state too acute for the marriage to be a success.[5]

The list of women dude ranch founders and owners also includes Helen Brooke Herford, who was born on her family's ranch near the Musselshell River north of Billings, Montana. The family was well off and sent Helen to school in Massachusetts and Germany, but she came back to Montana to teach and work on the ranch. In 1929 she and her cousin Helen Underwood Wellington formed a partnership and opened the Swinging H dude ranch near Limestone, in Stillwater County south of Billings.

Helen Herford was an outspoken, fearless woman who worked right alongside her hands fixing fence, cleaning ditches, and halter breaking colts, in addition to leading trail rides and multiday pack trips. She wrote promotional essays about what it was like to run the ranch, especially as a woman, and she especially enjoyed writing about the girls who visited the Swinging H.

In one essay, titled "With Only One Woman," she described taking a group of socially prominent young women in her car on a muddy, treacherous road to visit a sheep camp. She also enjoyed watching them exchanging their eastern clothes for jeans and spending their days riding, visiting nearby dude ranches, fishing, writing letters, and shooting with both a gun and a camera. They told her that they'd had the best time of their lives.

Helen understood the importance of wearing the right clothes on the ranch, and in April 1934 she wrote to Levi Strauss & Co. in San Francisco, suggesting they make jeans that would fit women. She had worn men's jeans all her life but knew that a more feminine style would appeal to her nonwestern guests. She also wanted a better-fitting product for herself.

The national sales manager responded to her letter and said that they were already working on a women's version of the overalls—the old name for jeans—and would send her a pair once they came out of the factory. The Lady Levi's arrived in June, and Helen made a few comments about the fit in a series of lively letters she sent to the company over the course of 1934. The firm sent her another pair in November, and she wrote back to say that she liked the pants very much, except for one thing. "Have heard much praise for the women's overalls and only one complaint. That they have not as many buttons on placket as mens."⁶

Katherine Chaves grew up on her family's ranch at Cowles, New Mexico. She opened the Los Pinos guest ranch on the property around 1923, and in 1929 one notable guest was J. Robert Oppenheimer. He was just about to start his professorship at the University of California, Berkeley but had been diagnosed with tuberculosis. He went to Los Pinos to get the rest and fresh air he needed and spent many hours on horseback with Chaves.

Dr. Caroline McGill first stayed at the Buffalo Horn Creek Resort in Montana's Gallatin Canyon in 1911. She was taking a break from treating tuberculosis patients at a hospital in Butte, and she returned to the ranch many times whenever she needed to get away from the demands of her practice. She began to visit even more frequently, and in 1936 she bought the ranch from the owners, snatching up an additional adjoining parcel. The two properties added up to 320 acres, and she renamed her place the 320 Ranch. She was famed for her toughness and once had to walk twelve miles in the snow to get to the ranch after her car broke down.

On the surface, these women and others who owned their own dude ranches had very little in common. Herford and Chaves were born into ranching families. McGill grew up on a farm in Missouri before working her way through medical school. Herford and McGill never married. These women also started up their ranches in the late 1920s and 1930s, when dude ranching was surging in popularity but was still a seat-of-your-pants type of business, subject to less regulation by local governments. They were also operating in the West, where nearly all states had granted women full or partial voting rights before the passage of the Nineteenth Amendment in 1920. This was a nod to their worth in developing the West, at least on paper. Attitudes toward women still took strange turns, though, and sometimes took them on dude ranches.

In 1930 Al Croonquist, vice president of the Dude Ranchers' Association, announced with glee that high-country ranches in Montana and Wyoming would be offering their female guests a new kind of souvenir to take home. Some Montana papers carried his announcement with the headline "Sun Brands Will Mark Women Tourists Returning East from Season Spent on Dude Ranch."

According to Croonquist and officials at the Northern Pacific Railway, people got deeper suntans when they rode at high elevations, and this gave the men an idea. Ranch owners should put a piece of adhesive tape in the shape of a ranch's brand on the back of female riders. Then, during their time on the sunny trail, they would tan around the tape, leaving a patch of paler skin in the shape of their dude ranch identity.

Croonquist and the railroad men made quite a few assumptions when they thought up this publicity stunt. One, that the women owned and/or wanted to wear a halter top or some other kind of blouse that exposed their backs and could lead to sunburn. Also, that they didn't mind becoming decorative objects or walking advertisements for dude ranches, when men were not. The one thing Croonquist and others could be sure of, at least in this decade, was that all riders were white.[7]

Dude ranches were not cookie-cutter operations. Each ranch offered guests something unique, whether it was the architecture, the food, the scenery, or the activities. Some of the larger ranches had polo grounds. At the smaller ones, guests often pitched in to help with chores. Some places had main lodges with dining rooms, stores, and living rooms, with individual cabins for guests, while others housed everyone in one big building that included the dining room and office. A ranch's individuality was its strength. But all ranches had the one thing that dudes wanted, and without which they could not join the Dude Ranchers' Association.

Horses.

Visitors to dude ranches from the East in the early twentieth century were used to riding horses but did not rely on them for transportation as much as westerners did. Dude ranches, ranches, homesteads, and even towns could be miles away from each other over bad roads, and horses were essential to getting around. Fewer people rode as automobiles became more popular, but they expected to get on a horse when they booked their dude ranch vacation. They were temporary westerners and wanted their cowboy experience. Cowboys were magicians on a horse, and for a few weeks of a Rocky Mountain summer, or a comfortable southwestern winter, dudes wanted some of that magic for themselves.

In dude ranching's early days, visitors rode whatever horses the ranch had on hand, no matter what they were used for. This led to unpleasant and sometimes dangerous situations. Draft horses had often been crossed with saddle stock and were not suited for riding, and as noted earlier, many horses had been sent to Europe during World War I, so the animals left behind were even less useful for a pleasure ride.

What saved the American horse, and the dude ranch, was the US Army Remount Service. Remounts were horses or mules chosen to replace those that had been injured or killed. Even before World War I, members of the War and Agriculture Departments realized that American riding stock was far inferior to its European counterpart and testified before Congress about the importance of good horseflesh. They suggested the government set up a breeding program to solve this problem.

Wealthy horsemen also came to the rescue. August Belmont Jr. was a second-generation financier and breeder. The Belmont Stakes was named for his father, August Belmont Sr., and his stables bred Man o' War, one of the world's most famous racehorses. In 1911 Belmont offered to loan two of his best Thoroughbred stallions to the Army Quartermaster Corps for a new remount program. About fifty mares were bred with the stallions, and the program was revived after 1919 to provide horses for ranches and farms, repopulating stocks that had been lost to the war.

In 1923 the remount board shipped 279 stallions to horse breeders in nearly every state in the union, with the largest percentage going to ranchers. Another program involved loaning government-owned stallions to ranchers, with remount centers buying the colts. The West was crucial to the success of this program, which was administered mostly in California, Wyoming, Missouri, Colorado, Utah, and Texas.[8]

This was good news for dude ranchers, who soon had much better stock to choose from. By the postwar years they realized they had to keep a variety of mounts on hand for the varying riding skills of their dudes. Owners and wranglers had to evaluate guests before their first ride and ask questions about their experience. Only then could they choose the horse best suited to each one, and dudes generally rode the same horse for their entire stay.

However, it was not unusual for embarrassed guests to exaggerate their riding skills in order to look less dude-like, and it did not take long for the wranglers to realize that those people were on the wrong horse. Sometimes a guest just didn't like a horse, and sometimes riders improved so much in the saddle that they could graduate to a more spirited animal. Matching a rider with his or her horse was the kind of skill that made wranglers even more valuable to dude ranchers.

The right saddle was also essential to a good dude experience, and many people who were used to riding on the English "pancake" saddle were a little flummoxed when they first sat on the western version. Mary Roberts Rinehart thought the cowboy saddle was the best one for dudes.

> It has a horn in front which the nervous one may clutch, it has a high cantle at the back, and its stirrups go straight down instead of being swung forward, as in the English saddle, and afford a broad and steady support for his feet. Small wonder that after his first day or two he begins to demand more action and asks for a horse with more life in it. Which, by the way, he will not get until he is fully qualified.[9]

Rinehart, like many wealthy women in the 1910s and 1920s, still rode sidesaddle at home, which was not an option on a dude ranch. Western women had long adopted the "cross saddle" or "clothespin" style of riding, which was much better suited for their work and the landscape. Dudines who were nervous about straddling a saddle soon discovered how liberating it was, though they didn't always take easily to what they sat on. In the 1939 film *The Women*, Rosalind Russell's character shows up at the Reno divorce ranch carrying an English saddle, which ranch owner Marjorie Main calls a dude contraption. Russell announces that she refuses to learn to ride "one of those Western things," to which Main replies, "Did you ever see a horse laugh?"[10]

Dude ranch horses often had snappy western names that appealed to their riders and also reflected how much ranchers loved the animals. Mary Shawver put a partial list of Holm Lodge's horses in her memoir, and it included the names Zephyr, Windsplitter, Six Bits, Maverick, Speedball, Moon, Calico, and Guts.[11]

Riding horses in the great outdoors was healthful exercise, something that dude ranchers wanted their guests to enjoy. Brochures and in-person meetings with potential visitors emphasized how well they would sleep, what good food they would eat, and all the fresh air they would breathe, but nothing about making them well if they were sick. There was a very specific reason for this language. Dude ranchers wanted to distance themselves from something the West was famous for but that they wanted no part of.

People with illnesses like tuberculosis had been coming West for decades, especially to the Southwest and California, because they thought the mild climate and drier air would help them get well. Sometimes they did, but not always, but that did not prevent the desperate from heading westward by the trainload.

Ranch owners were not worried about those who showed up fatigued or worn out by overwork. And ranches continued to be a refuge for people who wanted to stop drinking, if only temporarily. When guests went home tanned and smiling, they were walking advertisements for the benefits of spending a few weeks at a dude ranch. But tuberculars or others with contagious and possibly life-threatening illnesses were not welcome.

In the early part of the century a few ranches did take in the ill, but that was by design. The Bear Tooth Dude Ranch near Cody opened around 1909 and advertised how quickly guests would regain their health. Tuberculosis patients thrived in the balsam-laden air, and tourists had the time of their lives. There were very few places like this, however. In 1935 a teenager looking for a job put this advertisement in the *Arizona Republic*: "BOY 16 wants any kind work on stock or dude ranch. Not T.B."[12] Real estate agents touted remote properties as being suitable for either a sanatorium or a dude ranch, since the business model for both relied on being far from cities or towns.

Sometime before 1910 the Valley Ranch opened near Pecos, New Mexico, about twenty-five miles east of Santa Fe. At first glance, its brochure looked like a typical dude ranch handout, with photos of flowing streams, far-off mountains, beautiful architecture, happy people on horses, and information about local tourist attractions. But there was very clear language about the ranch's purpose: it was not a sanatorium, just a cheerful, homelike resort where people could get away and restore themselves if they were run down, or recovering from an operation. Testimonials from doctors and letters from previous guests also filled the pages, but the word "dude" was never used.

The 1931 brochure listed the variety of accommodations available, from single rooms to suites with private baths, and instructions about where to take the train. By the 1940s improvements in public health and the costs of running a resort with a full medical staff forced the next generation of owners to convert the Valley Ranch into a real dude ranch.

Ranchers knew from experience that guests did get sick and sometimes got injured, so they had supplies on hand to solve simple medical problems (more serious injuries meant a possibly long ride to the nearest town). Dudes who wrote memoirs about their first season on a ranch usually included a self-deprecating section about how green they were, especially after their first time on horseback. In *French Heels to Spurs*, Connecticut native Loraine Hornaday Fielding described her condition after day one of a long pack trip. "Camp! And—ouch! Oh, oh, ouch! How could I ever get out of that saddle? And how could I stand after I did get out?"[13]

Companies of all kinds had started to realize the consumer value of dude ranches and their guests. One of them was W. F. Young, Inc., of Massachusetts. They had developed a horse liniment in 1892 that farmers started putting on their own sore muscles, so the firm created another version for human use, which they named Absorbine Jr.

In 1939 W. F. Young was represented by the J. Walter Thompson advertising agency. In June of that year they sent two hundred sample bottles of Absorbine Jr. to Larry Larom at the Valley Ranch to give out to his dudes and to sell in his Trading Post, and they also mailed out more samples the following year. Each bottle came with a preprinted letter from "Bill," which was illustrated with a line drawing of a cowboy in hat and bandanna. Bill touted the benefits of Absorbine Jr. in western language as perceived by a PR man from a New York advertising agency. And it was aimed at dudes only, not dudines: "You bet you can be a tough 'ombre. We ain't no softies neither. We've rode 'em tough and mean, but us old hands find this Absorbine Jr.'s a pretty good bet after forkin' a mean cayuse or ridin' herd all day. It jest seems to oil up them jints and shy off the cricks any feller can get."[14]

Chapter 7

Dude ranch owners wanted their guests to have an authentic western experience. This was not difficult to do, because the men and women who hosted visitors were real ranchers who hired real wranglers to manage the dudes, as well as their livestock. But many guests also wanted to see the cowboys' counterpart: Indians.

This wasn't always possible, because most places were nowhere near reservations or populations of the Native Americans who worked on cattle spreads or in small towns. Dude ranchers who brought Indians to their places to talk to guests or entertain them saw that it was good for business and sometimes good for the native peoples. Not surprisingly, dudes brought their preconceived notions about indigenous people with them.

The dudes at Eatons' in Wolf went to the Sheridan County Fair in October 1913 and were so thrilled to see a realistic performance of Indians attacking a stagecoach that they wanted to ride in the stage themselves. Many ranches had their own stores where guests could buy clothing, snacks, and souvenirs. And many of them, like the one at the Valley Ranch, were called the Trading Post, a name that recalled the days of mountain men trading furs for bags of flour and sugar at remote forts, and Indians bringing in their own goods to barter.

Larom was fascinated by Indians, and from his earliest days in dude ranching he brought members of the Crow Tribe to Valley Ranch to interact with his guests. He led pack trips for teenagers starting in the 1920s, and part of the post-trip celebration was the visit of a group of Crows who were camped nearby and rode to the ranch to demonstrate traditional dances. They returned in the evening and drummed as painted performers danced around a campfire.

One of the native men who came to the ranch in 1923 was a local activist named Robert Yellowtail. In 1917 he and Crow chief Plenty Coup worked with other tribal leaders to stop the government from opening their reservation to homesteaders. Two years later Yellowtail went to Washington, DC, to lead the fight to pass the Crow Allotment Act, which protected the tribe against future land grabs. He spent the rest of his life fighting to preserve his tribe's rights and culture.

Despite his apparent respect for his Crow neighbors, Larom had no qualms about buying up their cultural objects and displaying them at the ranch. Indians and their material culture were, and would remain, something to be viewed. They were living, dancing artifacts of the Old West, and not just in Wyoming. In 1925 Navajo tribal members in traditional clothing danced in the parade marking the midwinter rodeo in Tucson.

Indians on dude ranches got fictional treatment in 1921 with "Dude-Puncher Steve," a short story by Fred Copeland. The narrator is a visitor to a Wyoming dude ranch where he has taken vacations for a number of years. The ranch's owner, Steve Lawson, has a daughter, Olla, whose mother was Sioux and who spent two years at a girls' school in Chicago.

One day a man named Steve Graydog arrives at the ranch, and his beaded moccasins and long braids cause Lawson to blurt out, "Where'd you es-c-a— Did you come over from the Crow reservation?" Graydog's perfect English startles the narrator and causes him to think about "Carlisle"; this was the Carlisle Indian Industrial School in Pennsylvania, one of the infamous schools that took native children away from their families in order to turn them into good white citizens.

The narrator rides along with Phil, one of the hands, when he picks up a load of dudes at the train station, and on their way to the ranch they see Graydog on his pinto off in the distance. One of the dudines, a schoolteacher, shrieks, "It's a real Indian!" and wants to get closer, but Phil tells her she'll see him a lot because "he ranges right here on the ranch." Which makes him sound like one of the livestock, not one of the workers. Everyone from Lawson to his cowboys laughs at Graydog's first "dip in the pool of dude-ranching," but he proves his worth. The dudes are thrilled to learn horsemanship from an Indian, and he rescues some of them during a thunderstorm.

As the story progresses, we discover that Olla and Graydog have met before and are attracted to each other, but nothing comes of it until some Canadian guests take the girl with them to their home in Montreal. Soon afterward, Graydog disappears from the dude ranch. Lawson and the narrator hurry north, where they find the couple rowing in a canoe on the Ottawa River. The Indian's braids are gone, and even in a boat he's wearing a finely cut suit.

Lawson gives up on retrieving his daughter when he learns that Graydog owns property in Montreal and sees that at least he dresses like a white man. He also knows Graydog will never come back to his dude ranch.[1]

Travel brochures also treated Indians like tourist objects. In the 1930s the Burlington Railroad printed a multipage guide to dude ranches in Montana, Wyoming, and Colorado, with the title "Dude Ranches Invite You to a Typically American Vacation in the Glorious West." Each page is devoted to the sights, activities, and amenities of dude ranching. One paragraph is headed "Wildlife and Redskins" and reads: "Indian bucks, squaws and papooses are common sights throughout this country. Many ranches adjoin Indian reservations where the wild days before the coming of the White Man are often re-lived at tribal ceremonies."

This is followed by another paragraph about the wild animals and beautiful flora available to avid photographers. The illustration for this section is a photograph of a kneeling Indian man in full eagle-feather headdress beating a drum, flanked by two young boys in what appears to be traditional clothing. Here, the "Indians," unidentified by their tribe, are classed as a category of nature. Like antelope.

In the 1931 film *Dude Ranch*, Eugene Pallette's character plays the movie version of an Indian "chief," with beaded buckskin pants and moccasins, and sporting a feathered headband. He is part of the troupe of actors hired to entertain the bored guests and is the only thing close to a Native American to appear in a dude ranch–themed film until later in the 1940s. Hollywood had noticed how popular these vacation destinations were and started to release more dude ranching films as the 1930s progressed. Studios put their biggest western stars in these movies, which meant that a dude ranch story had both box office appeal and good receipts.

In 1935 Ken Maynard, Indiana-born expert horseman and fan favorite (though not so much with his costars), starred in *In Old Santa Fe*, along with his equally famous horse Tarzan. Reviewers thought it was a breezy drama and better than the usual run of western yarns. The plot involved yet another story about the potential for crime on a dude ranch, and the film is probably best known today for featuring the musical debut of a future megastar: Gene Autry. That same year, George O'Brien led the cast of *The Cowboy Millionaire*, whose story revolved around mistaken identity and romance on a dude ranch, ending on the streets of London.

A new generation of western stars showed up in dude ranch films near the end of the 1930s. Hopalong Cassidy was born William Boyd and grew up poor in Oklahoma. He made his way to Hollywood during the silent era and had some success as an actor but didn't break out until his first Hopalong Cassidy film in 1935, based on the character created by novelist Clarence Mulford. By the time he starred in *Sunset Trail* in 1938, he was a genuine film phenomenon.

Early in this film one of the lead characters actually "invents" the dude ranch. Ann Marsh's husband is killed and his money stolen during a stagecoach robbery, leaving Mrs. Marsh and her daughter unable to run the family's cattle ranch. She expresses her fears to the superintendent of the stage company, who suggests a solution to her financial problem, as well as a way to get her money back. A lot of people in big cities would love to visit the beautiful country where her ranch is located, he says. They'd like to experience the western thrills they read about and would pay for it, too.

"Suppose you start a—umm, what shall we call it?"

"A dude ranch?"

"Splendid! I think you've coined a new phrase there Mrs. Marsh."[2]

The superintendent knows the famous cowboy Hopalong Cassidy, who fights for justice all over the West. He advises Mrs. Marsh to hire Cassidy to be one of her dudes, so that he can smoke out the robbers, whom she suspects are among her ranch hands. Cassidy's portrayal of a dude, called William Harold Cassidy, is hilarious. He wears fussy, almost feminine clothing, doesn't like to ride, and allows himself to be ridiculed by the real cowboys. He figures out who the culprits are while still in his dude persona and returns to his real identity and western clothing in the film's final scene. The ranch is not only saved but has proved to be popular as a dude ranch, which it remains.

Dude ranching achieved cultural icon status in film at the end of the 1930s, when studios released movies starring celebrities who had not come up from the ranks of the western. One of them, whose later fame would be in western films, was Randolph Scott. Known for being the leading man in both dramas and light comedies, he starred in *The Road to Reno* in 1938, a comedy about misplaced romance on a divorce ranch.

Men were always the focus of these dude ranch films, but in 1939 the movie *Maisie* debuted with Ann Sothern in the title role. Her career in light comedies took a leap in this film. She plays a burlesque dancer who gets stranded in

Wyoming and ends up on a dude ranch, where she tangles with unlikely cowboy Robert Young. The language in some of the press materials played up the contrast between the slightly disreputable eastern woman and the aw-shucks cowboys she meets: "A Blonde Fan Dancer Marooned on a Dude Ranch!"[3] "Marooned" is an interesting choice of words and sets up the viewer for comedy. *Maisie* was an unexpected hit and was followed by nine more films featuring the title character.

The Judge Hardy series of movies, starring Mickey Rooney as the perpetually-in-love son Andy Hardy, took a western turn in 1938 with *Out West with the Hardys*. It's set on a real Arizona cattle ranch, not a dude ranch, but the plot pays homage to dude ranches by showing the contrast between the city folks and the ranchers. Everyone but Mrs. Hardy changes into cowboy clothing upon arriving at the ranch, which is owned by old family friends.

Daughter Marian wears a fringed buckskin riding skirt with a vest, simple shirt, and cowboy hat. She falls for Ray, the widowed ranch foreman, whose tomboy daughter Jake doesn't like her, and takes on the cooking and cleaning chores for them as a sort of trial marriage. It doesn't go well, especially after she ruins Ray's boots. She finally realizes she isn't cut out for the life, and when she breaks up with Ray she howls that she isn't a tough western girl.

Andy Hardy goes full movie dude: fluffy angora chaps, satin shirt, cowhide vest, and oversized hat. Jake calls him a Monkey Ward cowboy, meaning the kind that looks good until he gets on a horse.[4] Andy is the comic figure in the film until he turns into the hero, and his clothes get less outlandish as his character matures. As in all the Hardy family films, everyone learns something new about life and themselves.

Movie stars continued to go on the record about their enthusiasm for dude ranching, and newspapers reported that men such as cowboy stars Jack Hoxie, George O'Brien, Joel McCrae, and even swashbuckler Errol Flynn had plans to open dude ranches of their own. This list also included Bela Lugosi, who had shot to movie fame in 1931's *Dracula*.

Sometime during the summer of 1935 Lugosi filled out a biographical questionnaire for Cameo Pictures Corporation, which created the publicity for Lugosi's next film, *Murder by Television*. Under the "Present Ambition" category, the star wrote "Dude Ranch." This tidbit was picked up by the press, and at the end of July a number of newspapers featured an article with the headline "Vampire to Retire to Dude Ranch."

Over the course of multiple paragraphs, this article revealed that Lugosi had no intention of retiring to a haunted castle in the mountains of his native Hungary. Rather, he wanted a home on the range, preferably a dude ranch, "where all the midnight shrieks, if any, will be from guests whose digestive systems have disagreed with the ranch fodder." He had allegedly purchased property in Northern California's Gold Rush country, near the ranch of his friend, movie cowboy Buck Jones, and was planning a lodge-pole style of ranch house, not the typical stucco and red tile of most Hollywood homes.

According to the actor's son, Bela Lugosi Jr., his father and mother never mentioned that they had visited a dude ranch or had spent time on one, and to his knowledge, his father did not own property anywhere near Buck Jones's ranch. Bela Lugosi's granddaughter Lynne Lugosi Sparks added, "My grandfather was an interesting person and I believe he could have thought a dude ranch was a good idea. He really loved the outdoors and especially enjoyed hiking and taking walks."[5]

One star did have the credibility to claim an interest in dude ranching. Montana-born Gary Cooper spent summers on his family's cattle spread outside Helena, and in the late 1920s his father, Judge Charles Cooper, opened a string of ranches and turned one of them into a dude ranch named for his son, now famous for films like *The Virginian*. By the mid-1930s this venture failed, possibly because visitors expected to see the star himself when they got off the train.

Cooper believed in what dude ranches were trying to accomplish, or at least his publicity manager did. The January 1937 issue of *The Dude Rancher* published an article titled "To the Dude Rancher," allegedly written by the star. In flowery language evoking western novels, Cooper praised the work of dude ranch owners, who supplied a refreshing contact with something real to weary vacationers. After mentioning his latest film, Cooper ended the article by saying, "And running a dude ranch is my idea of a great occupation. I've tried it once and may have another fling at it one of these days."[6]

Hollywood's publicity machine was always tuned to what was culturally relevant. Nothing said more about the increasing importance of the dude ranch than having movie stars claim they wanted to own one, truthfully or not. In modern terms, this is akin to celebrities who tell their social media followers they plan to open a restaurant.

Newspaper comic strips started to feature dude ranching in the early 1930s, the decade that saw the comic pages expand from daily gags to multiweek story lines with strips such as *Popeye, Blondie, Terry and the Pirates, Dick Tracy*, and *Superman. Tailspin Tommy, Slim & Tubby*, and *Winslow U.S.N.* were among the comics that sent women into peril on dude ranches or saw important people disappear on them. Dashiell Hammett, already famous for his novels *The Maltese Falcon* and *The Thin Man*, debuted a strip in 1934 called *Secret Agent X-9*. The main character is a cross between a spy and a private detective who, like Hammett's Continental Op, is never named. In strips from the fall of 1934, X-9 rescues people held at the Skull Dude Ranch in Sagebrush, Wyoming.

Short story writers regularly placed stories in syndicated newspapers that ran in serial form over the course of a few days or weeks. Mark Plum's "The Dude Ranch Mystery" appeared between April and June 1932 and told the story of a dude ranch cowboy trying to solve the murder of a visiting geologist, while also romancing a visiting dudine. Hidden identities and squabbles over options on open land place this tale firmly in the West.

Some stories took up only a couple of columns. One of these was "Wrong Crowd," from 1938, syndicated by the Associated Press. It's the story of a haughty dudine named Leona who shows up on an unnamed dude ranch with her crowd of equally snooty friends. She is attracted to the foreman, Jeff Winslow, who ignores her until she proves that she isn't like the people she came to the ranch with. He then takes her into his manly arms and professes his love for her. This well-worn plot works well in a dude ranch setting but could easily have taken place at a suburban country club.

The same can be said for *Death on a Dude Ranch*, published in 1939 by Francis Bonnamy, the pseudonym of Audrey Boyers Walz, who wrote a series of mysteries featuring her detective, Peter Shane. The book has all the hallmarks of a good murder mystery but could have been set anywhere. Bonnamy gives the story a western flavor with lots of horseback riding and a gunfight at the end.

Short stories and novels often featured plots in which men (always) took on new personas for either a noble or sinister purpose when they were on a dude ranch. This happened in films, as well; Tom Mix's turn as a doctor in *Hard-Boiled* is one example. Perhaps it was because people got the chance to be someone else when they went to a dude ranch. At home, they would never wear denim or cowboy hats. If they rode, they sat on an English saddle and didn't spur their horses along rocky desert trails. Their cook didn't serve them hearty meals made with simple ingredients. A dude ranch holiday was about temporary transformation into something rougher and yet also finer, reflecting the spirit of the cowboy, the knights of the West. Writers and filmmakers also knew their impostors could only play at being cowboys. Real cowboying couldn't be faked.

Dude ranches were so popular in the 1930s that anything remotely related to their activities ended up in both local and national newspapers.

Sorority and fraternity get-togethers often featured dude ranch themes. The Chi Omega sorority at the University of New Mexico in Albuquerque held a dinner party for rushees in 1932. Guests were told to wear cowboy or "Spanish senorita" costumes, and the initiates had to play the dudes.

Humor was often the theme of a news item. One syndicated column told the story of a young woman from the East who was on vacation at a Wyoming dude ranch. One day she noticed a cowboy coiling a long rope and asked him what he used it for. "I use it to catch cows with, ma'am." To which the perplexed guest replied, "Well, what do you use for bait?"

Even serious topics about dude ranching got the funny treatment. In 1934 the University of Wyoming began to offer a bachelor of science degree in recreational ranching through the College of Agriculture. Ranch owners and workers had to understand the care, feeding, and life cycles of livestock, know how to cultivate crops and use the proper machinery, and be familiar with the local flora and fauna. These courses were already part of the agriculture college's curriculum, but they were supplemented by classes in bookkeeping, food purchasing and cooking at an institutional level, and even public speaking. Every aspect of dude ranch management was part of the program, which was heartily endorsed by the Dude Ranchers' Association. Although the number of students who took this track toward their degree was not large, they were enthusiastic. The 1936 class formed a Dude Ranch Club on campus, and the university offered the recreational ranching bachelor's until the 1942–43 school year, when World War II pulled people away from both ranches and colleges.

A reporter for the *Independent-Record* in Helena, Montana, took a satirical view of this idea. He wrote that officials in Montana should not let Wyoming get a jump on them, because there were more dude ranches in Montana and they offered more than just sagebrush and sand dunes. "Our State College at Bozeman would be the place to organize courses, not only in dude ranching, but in the domestic science of hot-dog serving; the care and feeding of tourists; the mechanics of getting a 250-pound woman up a Montana mountain without over exertion. . . . Let us educate visitors not to accept a hamburger unless the cook can show a diploma."

The Girls' Industrial Institute in Sheridan, Wyoming, was an educational institution of sorts, but only for what were termed "juvenile delinquents." In old movie parlance, it was a reform school. In 1933 the state legislature debated about changing its name to Wyoming Girls School, to reflect the fact that not all the girls were "bad"; some of them just needed a helping hand. Worth Garretson, representing Medicine Bow, thought this was a ridiculous idea, not only because the discussions took up valuable time but also because "Industrial Institute" perfectly described what its purpose was. He made his point by concluding, "We'd just as well change the name of the penitentiary to the Wyoming dude ranch."

Crime and dude ranching sometimes intersected. In 1930 Hugh Ingersoll, who ran a dude ranch north of Helena, Montana, was convicted of grand larceny for stealing a calf owned by William Steinbach of Wolf Creek. This was the second time Ingersoll had been tried for the same offense, because the first time his case went to the jury they were deadlocked and the judge declared a mistrial.

Mrs. Rush Swayne, who owned a dude ranch near Santa Fe, New Mexico, reported that two of her cars were stolen in the summer of 1933: a Chevrolet and a Nash. The Chevy was recovered, though it was badly damaged. The Nash was never seen again.

One notorious criminal started a dude ranch of his own in Colorado. Chicago gangster Leland Varain, known by the alias Diamond Jack Alterie, had been accused of burglary and murder, among other crimes, but was never convicted. He was part of both the Dion O'Banion and Al Capone organizations and decided to get out of the line of fire in the late 1920s. His wife was from Colorado, so the couple moved to a ranch at Sweetwater Lake, north of Glenwood Springs in Garfield County.

He told people and the press that he just wanted a quiet western life, and he held rodeos at another ranch he owned near Denver. A reporter for the *Daily Sentinel* newspaper in Grand Junction took another view of Alterie's motives. He said Alterie had left Chicago because he decided that Colorado ranching was better for his health than beer running.

In the summers, he ran the Sweetwater place as a dude ranch. He dressed like a movie cowboy, and many who saw him strutting around Denver compared his getup and swagger to Tom Mix. His Chicago cronies visited the ranch during deer season, and Alterie used guns against a fisherman who boated onto Sweetwater Lake. The ranch was a private place for his friends rather than for the general public, though it's easy to imagine that many people would have enjoyed spending time around a famous gangster, as this was the era of Bonnie and Clyde. He went to Chicago occasionally and in 1931 was in court testifying about Al Capone's financial dealings, though his answers were vague and he was charged with perjury.

Rumors abounded that the dude ranch was actually a firearms-filled hideout, and given that Alterie was charged with assault against the aforesaid fisherman, this was not hard to believe. But Alterie's days as a dude rancher—which is how he was described in local papers—came to an end in 1933. After someone beat him up at the Hotel Denver, he went on a drunken rant and shot two bystanders. The courts found him guilty of assault with intent, and the judge gave him a choice: five years in prison, or leave Colorado.

He chose the latter, and even as he was getting ready to close down his ranch and depart, authorities in Denver went on the lookout for him in connection with a local kidnapping, but that didn't stick. He eventually moved back to Chicago and was gunned down in 1935. His dude ranch passed through many owners, who operated it mostly as a hunting and fishing lodge. Renamed Sweetwater Lake Lodge, it burned down in 1955.[7]

◼

In July 1935 the organizers of Cheyenne's annual Frontier Days announced the names of the entertainers lined up for the multiday western extravaganza. The one who got the biggest headlines was Sally Rand.

She was a Missouri-born aspiring actress, but she took her talents in a different direction. She was among the first and one of the most notorious fan dancers of the 1930s. She crashed the first day of the 1933 Century of Progress Exposition in Chicago, (un)dressed as Lady Godiva on a white horse, and was immediately hired to perform for visitors. Her dances were just short of obscene and within legal boundaries for burlesque, and the

Frontier Days committee hired Rand knowing that her appearance would add to their coffers.

A Casper, Wyoming, reporter took note of her addition to the program and said this in the *Star-Tribune*: "With Sally Rand and her dancers coming to Wyoming for Frontier Days, now is the time for somebody out our way to go the resorts one better and start a nude ranch."[8]

And that's exactly what she did.

In June 1936 she debuted a show at the Fort Worth Frontier Centennial, which she called "Sally Rand's Nude Ranch." A large exposition building was devoted to the ranch, with the name displayed in large letters made of wood with frontier-style carving. The first *d* in the word "dude" was crossed out and the letter *n* placed above it. For twenty-five cents visitors could go through the doors and watch girls in boots, hats, and gun belts twirl lariats and play badminton.

Three years later Rand brought her Nude Ranch to San Francisco. The city put on a world's fair to celebrate the opening of the Bay Bridge and the Golden Gate Bridge, building Treasure Island in San Francisco Bay for the Golden Gate International Exposition, held from 1939 to 1940. Everyone had heard of the Nude Ranch by this time, and it was constructed in the Gayway, an extravagant midway known as "Forty Acres of Fun."

On opening day, February 18, 1939, a line over a block long formed outside the Nude Ranch, which protected its cowgirls behind glass panels. This time, the structure was made to look like a southwestern dude ranch, with adobe walls and a roof of red Mexican tiles held up by rough beams, which shaded the entryway. The famous wooden sign with its crossed-out letter *d* was on full display, as were the forty "rancherettes," who wore a G-string, bandanna, boots, belt and holster, and ten-gallon hat.

Rand's show quickly became part of popular culture. A poet writing for a Palm Springs newspaper wrote some short verses about the people who walked around town on Sundays, and how they were dressed. The poem ends, "Eleven A.M. until five / A mixture of dude ranch / And Sally Rand's nude ranch / On Sunday on Palm Canyon drive."

San Francisco was the Nude Ranch's last appearance, though many of the performers traded on their time with Rand for future careers in burlesque. Rand had found her first husband out West. She met Red Lodge, Montana, champion bronc rider Turk Greenough at the Cheyenne Frontier Days in 1935, and after he divorced his wife, they were married in 1941. They told reporters they planned to open a dude ranch at Red Lodge after Rand finished some theatrical engagements and Greenough performed at a Denver rodeo. The couple did buy a ranch near Wyola, Montana, but it was their home, not a dude ranch. Their marriage did not survive World War II or Rand's risqué career, and they divorced in 1945.

Rand kept on dancing until nearly the end of her life; she died in 1979 at the age of seventy-five. Although in private she was a devoted mother to an adopted son, she had a notorious public persona that she didn't mind trading on. She looked at the world in ways that others didn't and took the West in a titillating direction for a short, sweet time in the years before World War II. When Rand wanted to put on a burlesque-type show in Texas she took the dude ranch and flipped it on its head. This says everything about the place of dude ranching in the popular imagination.

Whatever individual dude ranchers thought about the Nude Ranch, they kept it to themselves.

Chapter 8

Dude ranching was a very mainstream vacation, and deliberately so. Society's outliers were not encouraged to visit, though if they had the right credentials, they could pass the reservation test. (It's tempting to wonder how visitors would have reacted if Sally Rand had showed up at their dude ranch.) But some outsiders went to dude ranches because they had learned how to hide who they were.

Gay men, lesbians, bisexuals, and transgender people had long lived double lives in the United States. Their very existence was criminalized, and these men and women either burrowed deep into the closet and found their communities in the margins, or openly defied the myriad laws against them. These laws dated back to America's colonial days, when "sodomy" was punishable by death in some states. By the early nineteenth century most states punished homosexual behavior with long prison terms, and within a few decades, laws against obscene publications and entertainments were also on the books, as well as prohibitions against cross-dressing. Many state and local governments had their own laws against sodomy, which was an *act*. The concept of homosexuality as an *identity* did not crystallize until the mid-nineteenth century, and this did nothing to slow down the discriminatory statutes and cultural hatred LGBTQ people endured.

Homosexuality was not confined to cities, and scholars have started to uncover gay history in the West, specifically among men, because men were frequently alone in the western landscape, and this includes the cowboy. (Information on the lives of transgender people is much harder to track.) Here again, it's important to distinguish between acts and identity. When there were no women around, men turned to each other for sex and there was no shame attached to it. There were true homosexual cowboys, who did have to hide their desires and relationships, but out on the range, at the ranch, and in all-male small towns, sex was just what you did, even if it was with another cowhand.

Homosexual couples who wanted dude ranch vacations together registered as "friends" and shared their cabins, with apparently no one the wiser. Gay men and lesbians learned early to be discreet and to "pass" as straight. Or perhaps no one cared what their relationship was. It's difficult to know how hard or easy it was to keep same-sex relationships a secret because dude ranch records and correspondence are scanty, and so is the personal correspondence of men and women who went to ranches and wrote to friends back home.

One gay man, Philip H. Cummings, went alone to the Valley Ranch in Cody in 1932, but not as a guest. He was a teacher at Larry Larom's Valley Ranch School, which had opened in 1922.

The idea that wayward young men could be remolded by spending time in the West spilled over into education in the 1920s. Educators started to open schools in remote western places, believing that if youths could study away from the temptations of the city, they would benefit not only intellectually but also morally. Schooling in the mountains or the desert, which also involved physical labor, would prepare them for leadership. Many western schools were preparatory institutions, where students studied the topics they needed in order to take the College Entrance Examination Boards.

Larom's Valley Ranch School was one of these, and his students came from the same elite families who booked seasonal vacations each year. Both Larom and Winthrop Brooks had gone to prep schools themselves before entering Princeton and Yale. So, they not only knew the appropriate curriculum but also understood the character-building function of these institutions. The school opened on October 1, 1922, with three teachers called masters, and eight students, though there were eleven by the time the term ended in June 1923. This was an important source of income for Larom, who did not offer vacations for dudes during the winter months. He did have a problem in the late spring when the term was over, because the Valley Ranch School was accredited as an examination center after 1925, and both the students and an examiner lived in cabins that should have been cleaned out and made ready for dudes. But Larom enjoyed the prestige of being a College Board test site and made adjustments, even though it cost him money.

Students took classes in English, various foreign languages, algebra, geometry, trigonometry, physics, and both US and ancient history. The boys also played polo, and Larom made sure he had horses on hand to give the students good practice in the sport that many of them already played back home.

The school was very successful and more students signed up each year. Few of them left records behind to express how they felt about spending nine months on a Wyoming ranch forty hard miles from the nearest town, however. They published a yearbook each term with photographs and information about themselves, and it's not hard to pick out the boys who were having a good time and those who weren't.[1]

Philip Cummings began teaching at the Valley Ranch School in the fall of 1932. Born in 1906 in Vermont, he was a poet and sophisticated world traveler in addition to being a teacher of modern languages, which was his specialty at Valley Ranch. In 1928 Cummings met the Spanish poet Federico García Lorca in Madrid, and the two were instantly attracted to each other. They spent a vacation together in a cottage in Vermont in 1929, and a year later Cummings saw Lorca again in Spain after the poet had returned to his homeland. But political turmoil, which later led to the Spanish Civil War, forced Cummings to go home, and he was devastated when he heard of Lorca's assassination in 1936.

Larry Larom used his eastern connections and the manager of the ranch's New York office, Julian Bryan, to find masters. Cummings heard about the Valley Ranch School through a teacher-placement service and was hired for the 1932–33 academic year, pleased to see that the salary was generous and the position came with room and board. Cummings did not meet Larom until a few days into his term, as Larom had been in the hospital when he arrived at the ranch. When they did meet, Cummings probably did a good job of hiding his sexual orientation, because Larom made it very clear to everyone that he did not hire sissies.

Larom had reviewed Cummings's application and praised his credentials and appearance in a letter to Bryan. "He is six feet tall, weighs a hundred and eighty pounds, and his photographs look as if he has plenty of energy." He asked Bryan to meet with Cummings in person and then compared him to another master who had applied for a job, whose name was Bullion. Cummings, Larom wrote, "looks more like an outdoor man than Bullion does. I am inclined to think the latter has some 'sis' characteristics."[2]

Cummings promised his mother and aunt that he would keep a journal to document his western adventure, and he was true to his word. He typed an entry every day he was at the school, and by the end of the term in June 1933 he had over four hundred single-spaced pages.

He was a talented observer of people, landscapes, and his own feelings about his first visit to the West.

People here wear blue denim overalls which are very tight on the leg. The high heeled shoes . . . are designed to help you keep your foot in the stirrup . . . [and] make my low oxfords seem most ridiculous. Next comes the hat, ample, broad-brimmed, and high-crowned. I must seem a dude, and the term makes me far too sensitive. I'll get over it, and bit by bit I shall acquire the articles to make me presentable to western eyes. But the inquisitive looks which are NOT unfriendly are a little disconcerting.[3]

Cummings presented himself as thoroughly heterosexual, but there were occasional cracks in this facade. Some of the boys suspected he wasn't what he claimed to be and teased him about it, and there is some evidence he had a relationship with a man in Cody. But hints and innuendo did not endanger his teaching career, and Cummings was hired again for the 1933–34 term. Unfortunately, the Great Depression caused even the most affluent families to educate their boys closer to home to save money, and Larom had to close the Valley Ranch School in June 1934.

Cummings went back East and continued to teach. Like many gay men of his era, he needed to fit into society in order to further his career, and he married in 1938, though he continued to have relationships with other men. He became a popular lecturer and news analyst, and only near the end of his life did he come out about his orientation, when he told a Spanish poet about his relationship with Lorca. By this time Cummings was widowed and in declining health. He spent his final years in a nursing home suffering from dementia and died in 1991 at the age of eighty-four.[4]

Larry Larom regularly invited photographers to come to the Valley Ranch to shoot images of his dudes, dudines, horses, ranch buildings, and himself. Some of these photos were used in his promotional material or sent to the railroad companies for their brochures. Many other photos simply went into the ranch's own files. Among them are two photographs from the late 1930s, taken by Chicago photographer Stan Kershaw, which hint at the presence of a same-sex couple at the ranch.

Kershaw had come to Cody at the invitation of Mary Jester Allen, Buffalo Bill's niece, who was the driving force behind the creation of the Buffalo Bill Museum in 1927. She wanted to create an art colony much like the Taos Society of Artists and invited six artists to come to town in 1936, including Kershaw. Larom hired him to take photographs at the Valley Ranch, and the owners of Sunlight Ranch, northwest of Cody, and Eatons' in Wolf, also booked him to document their operations.

Two of the Valley Ranch images picture the same two women: one perhaps in her forties, the other a bit younger. They wear similar leather skirts, fringed jackets, hats, and fancy stitched cowboy boots, and the older woman has a pin of some kind on her jacket. In one shot they are posed by a corral looking both shy and amused, while the other image looks candid and unstaged. The women sit close to each other on a bench outside one of the cabins. The older woman smiles as she looks at the younger one, who seems to be laughing, and Kershaw captures the obvious affection between them. To modern eyes they look like a couple, and it's very possible they are: they wear the same ring on their left ring fingers.

Another Wyoming photographer was also a dude rancher. Charles Belden was born in San Francisco in 1887, and on a European jaunt in 1908 he met Eugene Phelps, whose father owned the Pitchfork Ranch near the Greybull River in Wyoming's Bighorn Basin. After working for a couple of years, Belden visited Phelps and fell in love with both the area and Phelps's sister Frances. They married in 1913, set up housekeeping at Pitchfork, and the following year they started to take dudes at the ranch.

Belden had taken photographs while touring Europe years earlier and started to document life at Pitchfork; everything from livestock to landscape to cowboys. He sold his work to magazines ranging from *The American Hereford Journal* to *National Geographic* and wandered around Wyoming looking for subjects. His photographs of cowboys met all the expectations of a national audience, though many of them were posed for the correct effect. Belden knew what would make a good photo, whether it was the scenery or the subject matter. In the summer of 1934, he took photographs of Amelia Earhart.

The famous aviator and her husband, George Putnam, had booked a stay at the Double Dee dude ranch near Meeteetse, Wyoming, which was opened in 1931 by Montana native Carl Dunrud. He had taken Putnam on Yellowstone pack trips the decade before, and Putnam wanted his wife to experience the glories of the high country. Earhart drove cross-country to the Double Dee by herself, and Putnam joined her later.

Belden, hearing that Earhart was at the dude ranch, drove the twenty-something miles from Pitchfork and took a number of photos, which, although obviously choreographed, are both charming and poignant. In one image, she sits by a corral while Dunrud pretends to cut her hair with sheep shears. She posed with one of the dude ranch dogs, and with the Dunrud children, and Belden also captured her looking pensive leaning against a corral wearing side-zip denim pants, a checked shirt, and men's two-tone low-heeled oxfords.

Earhart loved the area and filed a claim at the former mining village of Kirwin a few miles away. She also told Dunrud she wanted to have a cabin of her own at the Double Dee, which he started working on in 1936. Around this same time, she sent Dunrud a few things to store for her until she could return to Wyoming, including a buffalo coat that movie star William S. Hart had given her, along with a flight jacket.

On May 21, 1937, Earhart took off on her around-the-world flight. Two months later she and her navigator vanished from the sky.

Dunrud was heartsick at the loss of his friend, and though he invited Putnam to return to the Double Dee, he never came back. The ranch closed during World War II, and in 1966 Dunrud donated Earhart's two coats to the Buffalo Bill Center of the West.

Charles Belden became a celebrity for his photography and for his multiyear project to rescue the pronghorn, whose numbers were dwindling in Wyoming. He and Frances divorced and Pitchfork gave up hosting dudes in the 1940s. Belden took his life in 1966 after he developed Parkinson's disease and was no longer able to take photographs. His work fills museums, private homes, and dude ranches to this day.

Photographers were essential to dude ranch advertising. Regional railroads showcased their work in tourist brochures, and men like Larry Larom and Dick Randall used photos of their ranches to boost interest when they went East to give talks and meet potential guests. The Dude Ranchers' Association also used photography to good effect in *The Dude Rancher*, including photographs of the ranchers themselves, which put a face to the industry.

By the mid-1930s more ranches had opened in the eastern states, forcing the owners of places in Wyoming, Montana, Arizona, and New Mexico to put more of the West into their advertising. They used familiar images: cowboys silhouetted against a sunset, happy dudes in fancy clothing clustered around a wrangler doing rope tricks, a row of dudines sitting on a corral. Native

Americans were still shunted off to the side as decor for the most part, with a few exceptions.

A member of the Crow Tribe, Max Big Man, wrote an article for the June 1933 issue of *The Dude Rancher* titled "The Buffalo Plunge, The Buffalo Roundup." He was an honorary member of the Dude Ranchers' Association and a former worker on the Burlington Railroad. The article introduced him as someone who was interested in expanding tourism in the West, and who had also traveled throughout both the East and Midwest. He wrote about a thoroughly Indian topic—buffalo—but used his article to foreground native people in the present, though he admitted to readers that he was not an experienced rider (even so, he was photographed for the article on horseback, garbed in traditional clothing). This countered everything dude ranchers and their guests thought about Indians, and he used his article to appeal to dudes and westerners alike to respect native culture. He straddled a line between advertising and advocacy and was useful to the Dude Ranchers' Association in bucking up the image of the *real* dude ranch.[5]

Big Man had a lot of cultural assumptions against him, though strangely not in the movies. While images of the noble savage (male) and Indian squaw (female) made it into silent films, by the 1930s Indians were rare on the celluloid frontier. The native stereotypes that lasted for decades and found their way onto early television westerns started appearing mostly in the 1940s. However, characters like Eugene Pallette's "Sioux" in 1931's *Dude Ranch* ended up on the screen because they first appeared in popular books.

One woman took the character of the Indian and worked it into an unusual artistic career that touched briefly on dude ranching. Helen Howe was born into a cultured and literary Boston family in 1905, went to Radcliffe, but then found her calling in the performing arts. She had a gift for satire and began to write short, often hilarious sketches of the people she knew in New York, where she studied theater. She parlayed these into monologues that she gave around the city and then around the country by the early 1930s. Described by the press as a "monologist," Howe turned her satires into short dramas, set around a loose unifying theme.

During the summer of 1935 Howe toured New Mexico and after returning to New York wrote a monologue titled *Mañana: A Drama of Escape in Five Scenes*. She went back to New Mexico two years later and performed her piece in Santa Fe and Albuquerque. *Mañana* is set on the Aislado dude ranch, owned by an unnamed hostess who is also the narrator. Her guests include the typical characters with which writers and filmmakers usually populate a dude ranch: a woman whose Reno divorce just came through and whose lover is waiting for her at the Aislado; a female journalist whose health has broken down; a couple of "aesthetic" young men; and a middle-aged woman looking for her second youth.

Also in residence is an Indian, "Squatting Hokum," who drinks whiskey and sits silently by while the hostess talks about him in the third person. "In exchange for my paltry gift of board and lodging for his lifetime he is admitting me to some of the inmost secrets of his tribe—the true symbolism of the dum-dum dances, the esoteric meaning of the sacred bull."

On the surface, *Mañana* is a send-up of the dude ranch, but it soon becomes something darker. The people who show up at the Aislado aren't there for vacation, but for escape from something in their lives they can't shake. Howe then introduces another character: an old woman named Maggie Fernley, a local eccentric who guards a mine that she and her late husband had worked and owned for many years. Howe reveals her own view of the West in Maggie, who ends up shooting the lovers because they aren't strong enough to stand up to life on the harsh frontier.

A reporter for the *Albuquerque Journal* also revealed local prejudices against dudes in his review of Howe's performance in April 1937. "Her [Maggie's] remark after the killings that the country was 'not for little people who are running away from themselves but for big people, conquerors' found an echo in the hearts of her audience, most of them intelligent and intellectual representatives of a community where little of the backwash of typical 'New Mexico tourists' troubles its daily life."[6]

That disdainful audience was made up mostly of transplants from the East and Midwest who were probably called dudes when they first showed up in Albuquerque or Santa Fe. Now long-term residents, they could sniff at the visitors who chose to spend their time on remote ranches rather than in the city's fine hotels.

Dude ranchers still worried that their westernness was being appropriated by ranches opening up in New York and Florida. Journalists and writers continued to bemoan the loss of the Wild West and felt contempt for movies, radio, and dude ranches for trying to bring it back and failing. The Dude

Ranchers' Association, the railroads, and individual dude ranchers did not take this lying down. During 1936, after a number of articles about western artificiality and dude ranching in Florida hit newspapers, other articles began to appear about the authenticity of dude ranch vacations.

Wayne Farley, of United Press International, published an article in May with the intriguing title "'Waddies' of the West Accept Dude Ranching but They Won't Observe East's Cocktail Hour." "Waddie" originally meant a thief or cattle rustler, much as the word "cow-boy" was defined before novelists and movie makers made cowboys respectable. The term then evolved to mean any sort of hired hand. The theme of Farley's article was the work and personality of dude wranglers, who were not effeminate swillers of cocktails but tough boys who took their red-eye straight.

He then went on to describe the authenticity of dude ranches, which did not have golf courses or heated swimming pools. His source was Larry Larom, whom he quoted near the beginning of the article. "If we try to compete with the de luxe accommodations of the East, we won't have what the dudes want—novelty. We'll lose the lure of the West and we might just as well get rid of the big hat and the care-free attitude associated with the cowboy."

Franklin Snow, writing for the *Brooklyn Times Union*, published a piece in July 1936 titled "Dude Ranch Life Is Ever Pleasant: Patrons Return to West Year after Year for Vacations." This article has everything: flowery language about wanting to play cowboy for a few weeks, the carefree life of hunting and fishing available on dude ranches, the delightful ranch names, the simple daily routine, and the colorful clothing that dudes wear. The article sounds as if it was written by the Dude Ranchers' Association, but Snow doesn't mention it.

Other pieces were published throughout the summer with titles like "Romance of the Old West Is Revived at Dude Ranch." All these articles served the purpose of the individual ranches as well as the trade organization. The dude ranch was the real West, visitors could play cowboy in comfort, people liked dude ranches so much they came back year after year, and no one had to dress for dinner. The Northwestern Pacific Railroad advertised fourteen-day dude ranch vacations for the rock-bottom price of $105, equivalent to about $2,000 today.[7]

The Dude Ranchers' Association easily balanced the needs of both high-end ranches and small family operations and used the pages of *The Dude Rancher* to do it. One striking feature of the magazine was its continuing focus on women. It frequently ran articles about women who took dude ranch vacations, as well as columns written by women dude ranchers themselves about how they managed the quotidian details of their business, regardless of who their clientele was.

Lora Hale was a writer and future associate editor of the tony *Town and Country* magazine and took occasional trips out West to write chirpy travel articles. On her first visit to a dude ranch, in 1934, she earned the respect of the wranglers for the way she handled her horse (she had spent time on horseback as a child in Nebraska and Colorado). She went to Ox Yoke, the OTO, and Eatons' that summer and returned on a second trip where she visited the Valley Ranch. The magazine sent her back to Wyoming in the summer of 1936, and she wrote a long article for *The Dude Rancher* titled "My Impression of a Dude Ranch."

On this trip she went to a jaw-dropping nineteen ranches, where she interviewed ranchers, guests, and cowboys. She also took photographs that appeared in *Town and Country* and in an exhibition at New York's Radio City Music Hall in the spring of 1937. The editors of *The Dude Rancher* were no doubt thrilled that this influential easterner concluded her article by saying, "A ranch vacation is the one kind of which I shall never tire."[8]

The page on which Miss Hale's article is printed also includes advertising, as do many of the other pages of the magazine. Next to Hale's photograph, which shows her in a sprightly print shirt, patterned scarf, and man's fedora, are ads for Dude Duds at the Frank Clothing Company in Livingston, Montana; Jonas Bros. taxidermy in Denver (where hunters could get their trophies mounted); and Sawyer's Groceries, Feed, and All Ranch Supplies, which was apparently so well known that its location wasn't in the ad.

These businesses could also join the Dude Ranchers' Association as associate members, and they were listed by city when new ones joined up. In April 1936, the associate members in the town of Sheridan, Wyoming, included City Furniture Co., the Palace Café, Superior Laundry, D & D Hardware Co., and the Sheridan-Wyo-Rodeo. Supporting the DRA was good business and could bring in custom from guests as well as ranches. Clothing stores were always in the "Associates" column.

The Dude Rancher's editors had contacts with higher-end magazines back East like *Town and Country*, and its pages occasionally piqued the interest of New Yorkers who had heard about dude ranches from friends. The April 1936 issue of *The Dude Rancher* contained the following small ad: "YOUNG WOMAN WANTS JOB ON DUDE RANCH. Tired of six years' editorial work on important magazine. Could do dude wrangling, secretarial or publicity work, willing to fill in as cowhand, truck-driver, or errand girl. Healthy, intelligent, energetic, twenty-six years old, with some ranch experience. Remuneration of secondary importance."

Women did work as wranglers, but they were usually ranch owners' daughters, or local girls who grew up on a family ranch and knew their way around livestock. It's doubtful any dude rancher hired the above Young Woman as a cowhand or wrangler, but it would be nice to know whether she did manage to get out West away from the stresses of magazine work.[9]

Dudines were still a different breed, and writers for the women's pages in newspapers wanted to make sure they didn't come in for ridicule when they showed up at a dude ranch. A photo of actress Kay Sutton, wearing khaki pants and a striped shirt and posed with a horse at a dude ranch, accompanied a syndicated column written by Betty Clarke in 1939. The picture was captioned, "Take to your dude-ranching with as little make-up as possible—as Kay Sutton, movie actress, does it." Clarke took six paragraphs to instruct women about the proper beauty products to take to a dude ranch.

"City slickers who show up with make-up kits and bottles amuse the old hands," she wrote. She then told her readers to make sure to bring lip pomade [today's ChapStick] and suntan oil, as the women would be spending a lot of time outdoors. Hand cream was also essential, but dudines did not need to worry that they would be teased for wearing gloves to protect their hands while on trail rides, because even the cowhands wore gloves when they handled the reins. And finally, Clark suggested that women sew an elastic strap to the hem of their blue jeans to hook under their boots. This was to keep the legs from riding up (a fashion faux pas) and prevented chafing.[10]

Men didn't need any advice about what to bring to a dude ranch. Their casual clothing was already suited to outdoor life, though it was a bit fussier and a lot cleaner. Cowboy wear was easily imitated, but when worn by the wranglers it was part of their gear, a set of fabric tools for work and sometimes just for everyday living. These tools also came in handy when cowboys participated in a traditional sport that larger ranches started to offer their guests as entertainment.

Rodeo.

Railroads created special brochures to lure tourists to dude ranches in the 1920s and 1930s. Collection of the author.

Dude ranch advertising took many forms. This is an "ink blotter," made of special paper that blotted the ink left behind by fountain pens. Blotters were a popular gift with purchase for decades, and this one dates to the 1940s. Collection of the author.

The women on the cover of this 1950s guide to dude ranching are wearing the popular "squaw dress." Collection of the author.

Every state had its own dude and guest ranch trade organizations that published pamphlets and brochures. The tagline in this piece from the 1950s is "East is East but the West is Wonderful." Collection of the author.

Eatons' was one of the first dude ranches to create postcards for its guests to mail to friends and family. This card, from October 1917, was addressed to a man in England and reads: "Frontier Days at the Ranch. Bill Eaton roping three horses at once." Collection of the author.

Curt Teich published a collection of funny dude ranch postcards in the 1950s called "C. T. Dude Ranch Comics." Curteich-Chicago, C. T. Art-Colortone. Collection of the author.

Music played at dude ranches made its way onto record albums and into western-themed parties. Adolph Hofner and His San Antonians recorded this album in 1950. Collection of the author.

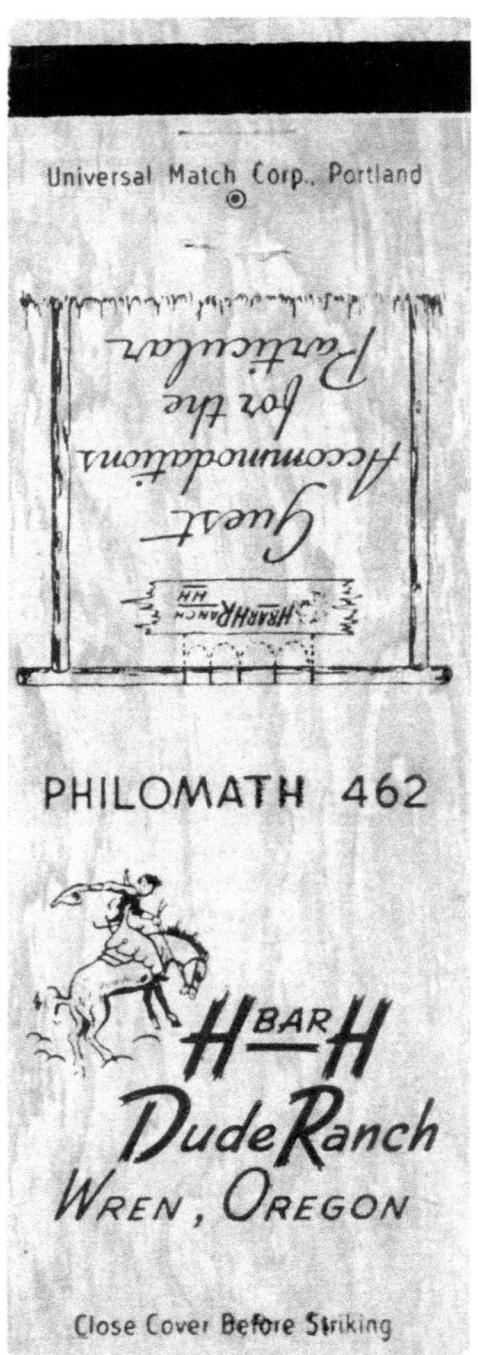

Matchbooks were a popular and inexpensive way to advertise anything, including dude ranches. Collection of the author.

Philanthropist Phoebe Apperson Hearst's palatial home east of San Francisco was converted to a dude ranch and renamed the Old Hearst Ranch in 1940. Collection of the author.

Some dude ranches created special souvenirs for their guests to take home, such as this album from the Jack & Jill Ranch in Montague, Michigan. The album has a collection of ranch photos and a place for dudes to include their own. Collection of the author.

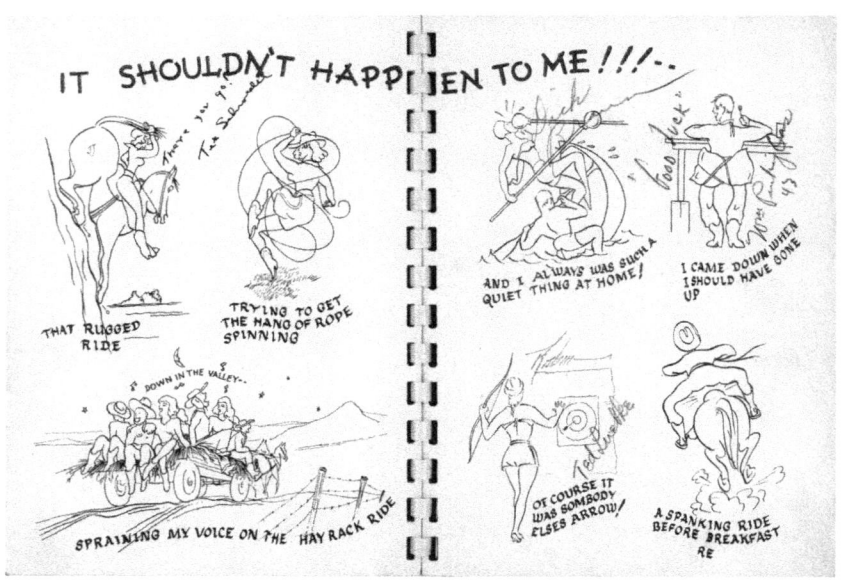

Airlines competed with railroads and automobiles for the dude ranch business in the 1950s and 1960s. Collection of the author.

New York's Adirondack region was home to many dude ranches beginning in the 1930s. This postcard was sent in 1943. Collection of the author.

In the early years, dude ranchers ferried guests from railroad stations out to the ranch in horse-drawn wagons but switched to automobiles, trucks, or early versions of the station wagon as soon as they could. This ranch vehicle dates to about 1915. Collection of the author.

Dude Ranch brand preserves filled supermarket shelves around the West from World War II to the 1960s. Collection of the author.

George Pierson, founder of Pierson's Dude Ranch in California, had a long correspondence with writer Earl Clemons, who wrote a profile of the ranch for *Pacific Sportsman* magazine in 1930. Collection of the author.

Sally Rand's "Nude Ranch" was the hit of the 1939 Golden Gate International Exposition in San Francisco. Collection of the author.

Arizona's Y-Lightning Ranch used both photos and artwork on the postcards it created for its guests, beginning in the 1920s. Collection of the author.

Railroads touted the value of train travel to dude ranches, as in this advertisement from the 1940s. Collection of the author.

This rare cowboy hat–shaped postcard was created by the chamber of commerce in Wickenburg, Arizona, in 1950. Collection of the author.

The Wyoming Commerce and Industry Commission published this guide to the state's dude ranches in 1951, illustrated with each ranch's brand. Collection of the author.

This Wyoming dude ranch cabin has all the decorative western features the dudes loved. From the collections of the American Heritage Center, University of Wyoming, Laramie.

Larry Larom poses with guests at his Valley Ranch near Cody, Wyoming, in the 1920s. From the collections of the American Heritage Center, University of Wyoming, Laramie.

Actress Gladys McConnell wears dude-inspired clothing on the set of the 1926 silent film *The Devil Horse*. McConnell starred in the picture, which was shot at the Morris Ranch near Cody, Wyoming. MS599-Max Wilde Collection, P599.04.05.075, McCracken Research Library, Buffalo Bill Center of the West, Cody, Wyoming.

Dudes enjoy a picnic on Wyoming's Pitchfork Ranch between 1930 and 1939. MS003-Charles Belden Collection, PN.67.089d, McCracken Research Library, Buffalo Bill Center of the West, Cody, Wyoming.

Two women, possibly a same-sex couple, chat on a bench outside a cabin at the Valley Ranch, Cody, Wyoming. MS-014, Irving H. "Larry" Larom Collection, P.14.234, McCracken Research Library, Buffalo Bill Center of the West, Cody, Wyoming.

The Cherry Ames series of novels included this entry from 1953. Collection of the author.

Many restaurants adopted a dude ranch name or theme as a way to draw in customers. This menu is from the Dude Ranch restaurant in Long Beach, California, in the early 1940s. Collection of the author.

In the 1940s, the makers of children's paper dolls produced books containing a wide variety of dude ranch outfits. Collection of the author.

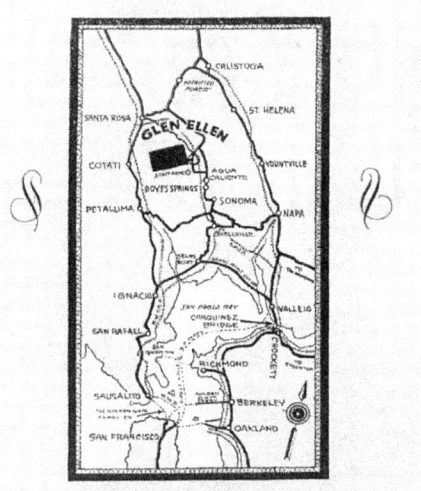

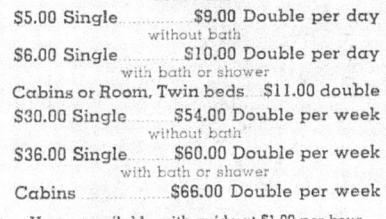

Charmian London, widow of writer Jack London, converted their Beauty Ranch in Glen Ellen, California, into a guest ranch, which was open from the early 1930s through World War II. Special Collections Department, Sonoma State University Library, Rohnert Park, California.

Levi Strauss & Co. introduced Dude Ranch Duds in 1938, a line of clothing specifically for the dude and dudine trade. Levi Strauss & Co. Archives, San Francisco.

Chapter 9

The first organized contest of cowboy skills was held in Deer Trail, Colorado, in 1869, where all the best riders in the area gathered for a "bronc busting" competition. No one seemed to mind that an Englishman won the prize, because he stayed on a horse named Montana Blizzard for a jaw-dropping fifteen minutes.

Other American cities held similar events, but until the late 1910s, these contests were not called rodeos. They were bucking and roping contests, or championship meetings, but a rodeo was something else: a roundup of calves for branding in the spring, and then again in the fall to ship to market. The word could also refer to collecting wild horses to be broken for ranch work. Rodeos were regular events in cattle country, and an interesting spectacle for new residents. Newspapers regularly published information about the days and times for roundups. "The annual Spring rodeos are now being held in various parts of the county, furnishing novelty and amusement for our Eastern visitors. Every vehicle in town was in service to-day to attend the rodeo at Soledad," ran one notice in 1875. And this, from 1887:

> Yesterday was a lively day at Huachuca Siding. The fall rodeo or round up of stock met here with several thousand head of cattle, and the Arizona cow-boys, with their chapereras, broad sombreros, riates and big spurs, were a sight to the special palace car occupants, consisting of Senator Cameron and party, laying here for a few days.[1]

Cameron was a Pennsylvania senator, and he and his entourage were no doubt thrilled at the displays of cowboy mastery. Other articles from this period refer to rodeos as cattle roundups only, and any mention of cowboy competitions calls them just that.

This 1887 story holds a clue to rodeo's origins and busts one of its biggest myths: that rodeos began as informal contests between cowboys during downtime when they weren't busy herding, roping, or branding. This likely did happen in a small way all over cattle country, but what drove the creation of formal competition, which is now the juggernaut called National Finals Rodeo, came from somewhere else. The clue is in the language: *rodeo, chaparrera, sombreros, riatas.* Rodeo began in Mexico.

In fact, much of what we consider cowboy culture can be traced to the vaqueros of Mexico. "Vaquero" comes from *vaca*, or cow, and the English word "buckaroo," so beloved of novelists and screenwriters, is an anglicized version of "vaquero." *Chaparreras* became chaps. *Riata* became lariat. And "rodeo" itself comes from the Spanish *rodear*, to surround or encircle; interestingly, it is one of the few cowboy terms still used in Spanish. It can be pronounced ro-DAY-o, as a Spanish speaker would, or, more commonly for English speakers, ROE-dee-o; the pronunciation depends on where you live and how the people around you pronounce it. Another term still used in the original is "bronco," from the Spanish for "rough," usually shortened to "bronc."

Rodeos in Mexico began as *charrerías*, equestrian contests that included steer and horse roping, bull and bronc riding, and bull wrestling. These get-togethers were held in conjunction with festivals and fairs and often included a bullfight. Cattle ranching was big business, easily traced back to sixteenth-century Mexico, and charrerías were a reminder of life in Spain, home of the fiesta. By the early eighteenth century, cattle ranching had expanded to Texas and California, and American ranchers were stunned by the horsemanship and skills of the Mexican vaqueros who also came north to work.

One thing historians do agree on is the influence of Buffalo Bill's Wild West on the emergence of American rodeo. His cowboys competed against each other in roping and riding, and although no one knows where Cody got the idea to make a contest out of everyday cowboy activities, the idea took off. He also acknowledged the contributions of Mexican vaqueros by featuring performers like roper Vicente Oropeza, who later taught Will Rogers how to work a lariat. Posters for the Wild West showed dignified (if fancily costumed) "Mexican Hidalgos," and all these efforts went a long way toward removing the stereotype of the Mexican *bandido* from the minds of audience members.

As a result, between 1883 and 1920, cities all over the West started to hold similar gatherings: Pecos, Texas; Payson and Prescott, Arizona; Cheyenne, Lander, and Cody, Wyoming; Pendleton, Oregon; and Salinas, California.

Dude ranchers took notice of rodeo's popularity, and by the 1920s many of them held informal rodeos on their ranches or took their dudes to local towns where they could see the cowboys compete. Some ranches and even big city rodeos held tame events so dudes and dudines could participate. Peggy Thayer's wild ride at the Jackson Hole rodeo in 1920 was supposed to be one of these nonlethal events, but it didn't turn out that way. Other dudes had the same experience.

William Rosenthal, son of Julius Rosenthal, president of Sears, Roebuck and Company, was staying at a dude ranch near Broadus, Montana, in 1922 and terrified everyone (especially the ranch's owner) when he jumped into the chute where a bronc awaited its turn at the bucking event. Before anyone could stop him, an official opened the gate, the dude's mount pounded into the arena, and "the ranch host prepared to telegraph young Rosenthal's family of the horrible details."

But the young man surprised the crowd by staying on the horse for longer than anyone expected. Papers did not report how long he remained in the saddle, but the horse eventually flipped Rosenthal into the air and he landed on his back, dazed but grinning. He told reporters he wasn't hurt at all and only regretted that the promoters wouldn't let him try the stunt again. An article about his ride ended, "Broadus doesn't think much of tenderfeet ordinarily, but young Rosenthal can come back any time he wants to. Broadus likes a good sport."

On July 4, 1929, the Lone Wolf dude ranch near Billings, Montana, held a rodeo to entertain guests and locals, with less excitement but more safety. The *Billings Gazette* announced the event, and the dude ranch sent out announcements written in cowboy lingo and illustrated with pen sketches of bucking horses, steers, and other rodeo themes.

In June 1933 George Pierson held a rodeo on his Pierson Dude Ranch and booked some of the biggest names to wow his dudes. Earl Thode showed up to demonstrate his skill as a "bronco-buster." He was a professional rodeo competitor who won many saddle bronc riding competitions, including the coveted championship at the Cheyenne Frontier Days. Sam Garrett, who organized the events, was a champion trick roper and All-Around Champion at multiple rodeos. He showed off his roping skills for the locals and the dude ranch guests.

And Pierson did not forget the ladies: he also brought in Bonnie Gray, Rose Smith, and Paris Williams, some of rodeo's most famous cowgirls. Gray was a trick rider who also had a degree in music, a career as a tennis champ, and a legacy of nursing Native Americans during the 1918 influenza epidemic. By the 1920s her most famous stunt was jumping over an open car with passengers still in its seats. Rose Smith was a champion bronc rider who won large purses at events in places like Madison Square Garden. Paris Williams was also a fearless trick rider.

Pierson held his event at the same time nearby Visalia held its own rodeo, and he cooperated with the local chamber of commerce to offer a week's stay at his dude ranch to the winner of the Sweetheart of the Rodeo contest. Peggy Daniel, famed local horsewoman, won the riding events that gave her the title and earned her a trip to the even more famous Salinas Rodeo.

In April 1939, Godshall's C Bar G dude ranch, about a two-hour drive from Pierson's, held an intercollegiate rodeo on its grounds. College students had started to compete in rodeos in the early 1920s, and the ranch decided to hold its own contest to help local kids gain experience and bring the C Bar G some much-needed publicity. Men's events included steer riding, calf roping, team roping, bareback riding, and saddle bronc riding. Women could compete only in cow milking, bareback and saddle riding, and the rescue race. In this timed competition, one person stands by a barrel at one end of the arena. Another one rides in from the opposite side toward the barrel, picks the person up, puts her on the horse, and takes both of them back to the starting point. The student winners of these events were hailed in newspapers all over Southern California.[2]

Dude ranch wranglers also competed in local rodeos, earning prizes for skills they usually showed off only to dudes and dudines. In June 1938 New Mexico's Valley Ranch hosted a calf-roping rodeo for its guests and the guests at other nearby ranches. All the contestants were dude ranch wranglers and came from Valley Ranch, Brush Ranch, K Bar, and Forked Lightning. A few weeks later, these four held an interranch rodeo at Valley Ranch where the wranglers entered contests in bareback bronc riding, saddle bronc riding, steer riding, calf roping, and team roping. This was the first of many rodeos in New Mexico's Pecos region, which was gaining fame for its cluster of dude ranches, especially the Forked Lightning. The rodeo was founded in 1925 by a famous promoter, Tex Austin, who put on big events in New York, Chicago, London, Berlin, and Paris.

Dude ranches also entered contests at the parades that usually preceded big rodeos. The Circle Z dude ranch in Patagonia, Arizona, had its own arena and held a regular rodeo for its guests. In 1935 it won first prize for the best dude ranch entry at La Fiesta de los Vaqueros, the big midwinter rodeo in Tucson. Its entry was a pair of buggies and a large contingent of well-mounted riders, whose leader wore silver-cloth chaps.

Black contributions to the history of the West, and to ranching and rodeo, match those of Mexico's vaqueros. Everyone knows about the Buffalo Soldiers, the troops that fanned out across the West and fought in some of the most violent conflicts in the region, from the Indian Wars to bloody cattle-ranching clashes in Wyoming. Among the first Black men in Arizona Territory, for example, were soldiers posted at the forts that had been established in the wake of Anglo confrontations with indigenous tribes. They were soon joined by miners eager to cash in on the gold and silver that was first discovered during the Civil War years.

Before 1900, over 40,000 men were employed as cowboys on cattle drives, and between 5,000 and 6,000 of them were Black. Among the 25 to 30 percent of nonwhite cowboys were Native Americans, as well.[3]

Black and indigenous men competed in early rodeos, though their presence was not always welcomed. These men had to truly excel in order to be taken seriously, win prizes, and make it into publicity pieces. Nez Perce cowboy Jackson Sundown competed at the Pendleton Round-Up in Oregon in 1911 as a bronc rider against a Black cowboy, George Fletcher, and a white competitor, John Spain. Sundown placed third in the contest, but the crowd booed the results because they thought he had earned first place.

Jesse Stahl was another famed Black bronc rider, but the most celebrated and influential was Bill Pickett, the inventor of bulldogging, in which a mounted competitor leaps off his horse onto a running steer and wrestles it to the ground. Pickett's trademark maneuver was biting the animal's nose as they collided.

Native American and Black men were rarely if ever employed as wranglers on dude ranches, certainly not on the bigger spreads near large cities, where the amenities were more attractive and the prejudice more acute. And until the 1970s or even the 1980s, dude ranches did not demonstrate much ethnic diversity in their guest lists, a function of long-ingrained attitudes and prejudices, marketing, and fear.

Dude ranches were white spaces, though there was diversity in the domestic staff, if not the bunkhouse. Black, Latinx, and Asian men and women sometimes filled the roles of cook, housekeeper, gardener, and so forth at dude ranches, much as they did in hotels and motels. In 1938, for example, the Nevada State Employment Service advertised for a "Colored Houseboy for Dude Ranch." It also placed ads for a Dude Ranch Stableman and Dude Ranch Handyman, though everyone who read the ad knew these jobs were for white men.[4]

Even during the Depression years, families still took vacations, and this also applied to families of color, especially when the price of an automobile came into reach for the middle class. A road trip was different for Black families. They had to carry everything they would need in their car because service stations, hotels, and other places open to white travelers were both forbidden and dangerous. Then, in 1936, Victor Hugo Green, an entrepreneur from Harlem, founded *The Negro Motorist Green Book*, and the first issue was published the following year.

He was inspired by the guides published for Jewish travelers, who found many of the same restrictions against them when they went on the road. His book was a physical and emotional road map to safe places for Black individuals and families.

The Negro Motorist Green Book grew in popularity, influence, and importance, and the list of approved stopping points for Black travelers also grew in geography and description. Hotels, nightclubs, garages, barber shops and beauty parlors, restaurants, and tourist homes filled the pages; tourist homes were private houses that rented rooms and sometimes provided meals, offering a homier version of the more impersonal hotels and motels. Dude ranches, however, did not make the *Green Book*, and no one was surprised.[5] However, in the late 1930s a Black couple from Apple Valley, near Victorville, California, made the dude ranch idea a reality for travelers eager for the western vacations they were denied.

Apple Valley skirts the southern portion of the Mojave Desert, about a two-hour drive from Los Angeles. Racially skewed covenants kept the best real estate out of reach for Black home buyers. A civic club for Black members, called the Forum, started to encourage families to buy land in Apple Valley, and homesteading began in 1914, though prominent residents retained their connections to Los Angeles and the Forum. One of them was Arthur Cook, who was good friends with a married couple named Nolie and Lela Murray. Nolie Murray owned a billiard parlor and cigar store, and Lela was a nurse. Her health was delicate, and life in Los Angeles was hard on her. Cook wanted to bring good people out to Apple Valley, so in 1922 he sold the Murrays forty acres of his own land.

The couple cared deeply about the welfare of children and began to build a collection of bungalows, stables, and chicken coops on their property so that they could offer a country home to at-risk young people. They worked with the California courts to send unprivileged, homeless, and abused children to the ranch to live in the open, eat good food, and do character-building chores. About a dozen children were usually on hand at one time, some of them staying as long as seven years.

But after the Depression hit, the Murrays had trouble keeping the ranch afloat, even with the money the courts gave them to care for the children. Their own savings were running out and they had run up debts. They lived near the town of Victorville, which had become well known for its many regional dude ranches. So, they decided to change their business model and convert the place into a first-class dude ranch to get on a better financial footing. It was called Murray's but was dubbed the Negro Dude Ranch by others. It limped along for a couple of years, and then the Murrays caught a break that changed their lives.

In 1934 the Victorville Chamber of Commerce started sponsoring amateur rodeos, and by 1937 attendance had gone from a few locals to around ten thousand people, including celebrities like singer Tex Ritter, movie cowboy Hopalong Cassidy, and silent film vamp Clara Bow and her husband, western movie icon Rex Bell.

The Victorville rodeo, held that October, also caught the attention of recently crowned heavyweight boxing champion Joe Louis. While wandering around and accepting accolades from fans, he heard about Murray's and decided to pay a visit. A crew of photographers from *Life* magazine were also in town reporting on the rodeo, but they knew they would get a better story if they followed Louis. The result was a two-page spread in the November 15, 1937, issue.

The article begins with a photograph of a very relaxed Louis sitting outdoors in a woven wooden chair, chatting with Leon Washington Jr., the founder and publisher of the *Los Angeles Sentinel*, an influential Black newspaper. Washington is dressed for the West in a satin cowboy shirt, white cowboy hat, jeans, boots, and spurs. Louis wears riding jodhpurs with English riding boots, a black shirt, and a white cowboy hat with a wider brim. In another photo, Nolie Murray holds a horse's bridle while Louis settles himself in the saddle for a photo op. Lela Murray is shown wearing all white, with a bandanna around her neck, in work boots and a white Stetson, carrying her Brownie camera as the ranch's official photographer. The rest of the images show happy guests enjoying themselves.

Louis's visit and the *Life* publicity brought more people to the dude ranch and helped the Murrays pay off their debts. The white owners of other nearby dude ranches helped promote the Negro Dude Ranch, realizing that however strange it was to have people of color taking vacations nearby, publicity for one place helped everyone. Local businessmen felt the same way. In October 1939 the Victorville Chamber of Commerce hosted a dinner at Murray's for members of the Army Corps of Engineers, who were surveying the Mojave River for future flood control operations.

In February 1939 Joe Louis returned to Murray's to train and to get in some relaxation before his match against Jack Roper in April. As soon as he checked in, Louis went on a horseback ride and told reporters that he planned to ride, hike, and play softball. He stayed for a couple of weeks, then moved on to his Los Angeles gym to continue his training. Louis and Roper met in the ring on April 18, and the dude-ranch-relaxed Louis handily defeated his rival in a bout that lasted only two minutes and twenty seconds. Three months later, Louis returned to Murray's for a short stay to ride and learn how to rope.[6]

Black celebrities also flocked to Murray's: Lena Horne, Hattie McDaniel, Louise Beavers, and Bill "Bojangles" Robinson, among them. Middle-class Black families could afford the five-dollar nightly cost and were thrilled to have a chance to ride, or just learn how to sit on a horse. Nolie and Lela made the cowboy West available to members of a community that had contributed to its history for a century but could never participate in its recreations.

One potential visitor put this issue succinctly in a letter he wrote to Lela Murray. "I am a bachelor. I like to ride horseback very much. I have always wanted to spend a few weeks on a dude ranch. Being colored, I doubted that I would ever have the chance. I was happy to learn about your ranch. Please let me know the cost of a vacation with you."[7]

The North Verde Ranch was another dude ranch in the Victorville area, and movie history was made there in 1940. Orson Welles sent screenwriter Herman Mankiewicz to the ranch to write the first draft of the screenplay for *Citizen Kane*. Mankiewicz, suffering from a broken leg and too much alcohol, wrote the script while staying at North Verde, which, like all dude ranches, did not allow alcohol (he did manage to go to Victorville bars, however). *Citizen*

Kane is the barely concealed story of the colossal publishing magnate William Randolph Hearst, who had his own links to dude ranching.

His father, miner turned millionaire George Hearst, owned a piece of property in Pleasanton, about forty miles east of San Francisco, where he had a hunting lodge. After his death in 1891 his widow, Phoebe Apperson Hearst, added to the property and turned it into one of her homes. After she died in 1919 her son kept the place but then moved many of the antique furnishings to his grand home in San Simeon. He sold the property in 1924 to a group of investors who turned it into the Castlewood Country Club, which lasted until 1940.

As Mankiewicz struggled with his script at the North Verde, the Hearst property up north was sold to a man named John Marshall, who owned a dude ranch in Pyramid Lake, Nevada. He converted the imposing home into a high-end guest ranch later named Old Hearst Ranch, which was a popular getaway for wealthy Californians for nearly fifteen years. In 1952 Marshall sold it to another group, which turned it once again into a country club.

Phoebe Hearst herself, the West's greatest philanthropist, helped save the town of Cody, Wyoming, in 1896, when she invested money in a venture called the Cody Canal Company. Conceived and financed by entrepreneur George W. T. Beck, the idea was to create an irrigation and reclamation project to build up the town, and another early investor was its namesake, Buffalo Bill. But the company began to hemorrhage money, and when Beck turned to family friend Phoebe Hearst for help, she bought $30,000 worth of bonds, which kept it from going under. The project survived, development of Cody continued, and its future as a center for dude ranching was secured.

Beck was a transplanted Kentuckian. He came out to Colorado in 1877 as a young man, eager to see its glories and get in on the potential for riches in its mining regions before moving on to Wyoming. Years later he wrote a memoir about his many adventures, both exciting and terrifying, and summed them up this way: "The West was not going to let a dude down."[8]

The Negro Motorist Green Book was just one of many travel guides published in the 1930s. Among President Franklin D. Roosevelt's New Deal initiatives was the Works Progress Administration, and under this umbrella lived the Federal Writers' Project (FWP).

First organized in July and August 1935, it was one of a number of programs that focused on culture and the humanities; others included the Federal Theatre Project, the Historical Records Survey, and the Indian Arts and Crafts Board. The FWP employed 6,686 writers, researchers, historians, editors, and art critics. Altogether this disparate group created more than 1,700 local histories, children's science books, and deeply researched works of history, including oral histories with former enslaved people. The FWP is best remembered today for the American Guide Series, sturdy books about all forty-eight states plus the District of Columbia, Alaska, and Puerto Rico. Each volume included information about history, culture, and detailed tours by geographic region, along with compelling photographs, and the guides are regularly reprinted to this day.[9]

Dude ranches were always included in the guides, and depending on who the writer was, their descriptions ranged from basic to almost lyrical. Here is the introduction to dude ranching from the 1939 Montana guide:

> Increasing tourist trade and a growing dude ranch industry have Montanans think of themselves as hosts, and has added a certain smoothness to the simple good-fellowship and bluff hospitality of older times; but, among themselves, they remain informal and respect few artificial conventions. Hospitality, as proud a tradition West as South, has come down from the days when a rancher's home was everyone's castle, and a good citizen never locked his door, knowing that a cold, tired, and hungry rider might need to enter and cook a meal.[10]

The Nevada guide, published in 1940, had a surprising amount of information about the divorce trade, and a smattering of sentences about dude ranches, but did not link the two. The New York guide stated that dude ranches provide "active (but not too strenuous) outdoor life, with real horses and synthetic cowboys, [and] have become popular in the southeastern Adirondacks." Western dude ranchers were no doubt pleased with the use of the word "synthetic" in front of "cowboys."[11]

Dude ranches weathered the Depression years by sticking to what they did best: adapting to circumstance. Not all ranches survived; some that had only just started up as the stock market crashed could not get their footing and went under quickly. The ones that did come out on the other side took in fewer guests, relying on their own gardens and livestock for food, and were not afraid to invest in infrastructure when possible, hoping for recovery. Cattle ranches continued to take in dudes to add to their bottom line.

By 1935 the Dude Ranchers' Association reported that business had exceeded that of 1929 and 1934 (two especially prosperous years) by 50 percent. Travel bureaus estimated that dude ranches welcomed over 20,000 people over the summer of 1937. Another advantage in being able to stay afloat was the class of clientele, especially at the larger and more established dude ranches. Wealthy families from places like New York, Philadelphia, Washington, Chicago, and other major cities could still afford dude ranch vacations, and with the war news in Europe beginning in 1939, many travelers decided to stay within America's boundaries.[12]

Dude ranchers valued all their employees, from dude wrangler to housekeeper to groundskeeper (if they had one). But the most valuable worker, perhaps even more important than the cowboys, was the cook. It didn't matter whether guests ever got the hang of riding, or whether their preconceived notions of cowboys were met. If they didn't eat well, they were not happy and would not hesitate to tell everyone back home about how much they did not enjoy their dude ranch experience.

Sometimes the cook was the co-owner, meaning the dude ranch wife. If ranchers could afford a cook, he or she had to be willing to work seasonally and perhaps in a very remote location, with few opportunities to go to town to see a movie or do some shopping. Occasionally, a cook was a college student who had summers off and spent that time earning some money and gaining a few job skills from June to September.

Preparing food for groups of people at a dude ranch was not the same as cooking for hotel guests. Far-flung ranches had to keep large stocks of supplies on hand because it was too difficult to run into town to get additional bags of flour or cans of coffee. Stores could be hours away, even in a fast car. And meals had to be planned around guests who might be staying for a month or more, so variety was paramount. The kitchen was also a place where racial prejudice sometimes took a back seat to good food.

Dora Randall, who owned the OTO with her husband, Dick, had many trials with cooks over the years. One early employee was Chinese American, and though his meals were always delicious, he insisted on cooking lettuce instead of leaving it raw and putting it in salads. Randall tried hiding the heads of iceberg, but that didn't work, and they parted company. Another chef had a sullen personality and made watery mashed potatoes. When Randall tried to tell him how to make proper potatoes he quit on the spot, and she had to take over in the kitchen to serve the seventy-five dudes in residence. She also employed two Japanese American chefs over the years.

The women of the Dude Ranchers' Association understood the importance of a ranch chef better than anyone. The kitchen was their domain, whether they did the cooking themselves or supervised the one who did, and food was always one of the main topics at meetings and in correspondence. By 1940 their discussions and their most successful recipes went into the "House Management Department" column of *The Dude Rancher,* so that everyone could benefit.

Mary Shawver wrote the lead article in the July 1941 issue and began with a lament: "Cooks, cooks, who has the cooks? Have they all vanished to no one knows where? With all the cry about unemployment, why does no one want to cook?" The reason for her concern was not just continued job losses and the perpetual troubles of finding a good chef, but worries about the United States possibly entering the European war. Would potential guests, old and new, see their sons go into the service? And if so, how could they plan a last vacation together? And would ranchers be able to hire good cooks to serve them? Shawver pulled herself and her readers together and wrote that all they could do was continue to buy and prepare food for the guests they had and keep friends and former visitors in their thoughts.

With that in mind, Shawver printed articles exclusively about food in the House Management Department column in this issue. Mrs. May Ford, of the F and H Ranch in Darby, Montana, had recently sent her their recipe for chili, one of the dudes' favorite suppers, which they requested more than any other. Perhaps guests at the F and H did not eat chili or see it on the menus of their favorite restaurants back home, and the novelty and simple ingredients appealed to palates unfamiliar with traditional western cuisine.

Mrs. Ford's recipe included only round steak, white onion, butter, canned kidney beans, canned tomatoes, and Worcestershire sauce. She served her chili with "green corn off cob," which is sweet corn whose kernels are soft and just ripe, and she heated it in butter, salt, and pepper for five minutes. She also served Norwegian rye bread, a yeast bread made with both rye flour and rolled oats, and for dessert there were fresh strawberries with sour cream.

Another article in Shawver's column was titled "Farm Diets Rate Best in All Regions of U.S." Members of the Bureau of Home Economics had surveyed the diets of representative groups in the country, from corporate presidents to laborers, and although they ate very different foods, the economists came to a surprising conclusion. Farm families had better diets than city families, thanks to the simple foods they were able to supply themselves: milk, butter, eggs, fresh vegetables, and fruits. The point of running this piece was to reassure members of the DRA that their equally simple meals were not only delicious but healthy, another benefit of spending time at a dude ranch.[13]

In the summer of 1940, Mary Frost, of the Lazy 6-V Ranch near Cody, put together a list of early New Year's resolutions and published them in *The Dude Rancher*. The list included "Not let the cook stare me down when asked to try out a tricky new recipe," "Never try out a tricky new recipe," and "Not let my heart sink to my boots when the cook sends word she wants to see me... chances are it is about a new way to fix potatoes, and not that she is quitting."[14]

Another important staff member was the head housekeeper, usually in charge of the girls (always) who cleaned rooms, did laundry, and served meals. At the 1940 Dude Ranchers' Association convention, the members of the House Management Department discussed the value of having a housekeeper. Most women felt they were helpful in taking charge of meal planning, inventory, and staff management. Others thought they were a nuisance and preferred to do that work themselves.

They also discussed the topic of what staff members did when they weren't working. Many ranch owners let young female staffers ride horses when they were off the clock, and some even gave a waitress or cabin girl a horse at the end of the season as part of her pay. Girls who came to the ranch by car could take their vehicles and run into the local town but needed to get permission first. These conversations centered mostly around the female staff, which was of course under the purview of the dude ranch co-owner/wife. They were happy to let the men deal with cowboy problems.

There weren't that many, but of course cowboys could be rowdy. Wranglers were often young men, and though it was forbidden, they often got into romantic entanglements with the female guests. Alcohol was also an issue. No spirits or wine was served at meals, though dudes could still bring their own to enjoy privately. Bottles made their way into the bunkhouses where the wranglers slept, with predictable consequences. For example, a wrangler from an unnamed dude ranch in Southern California was arrested for drunk driving in February 1933. When the Highway Patrol officers pulled him over, he told them he could handle a horse, but a car was different.

Incidents like this one were rare and did little to tarnish the image of the cowboy for either dude ranch guests or the general public, especially fans of cowboys in the movies. On the screen, heroic horsemen were still iconic figures. And before the 1930s were over, some of them would show their fans that they had an untapped talent.

They could sing.

Chapter 10

Every region in the United States has its iconic musical tradition. The West has cowboy songs about driving cattle, riding horses, and whooping it up in saloons. And, as with most things cowboy, the origin of this music has often been mired in mythology.

The most well-known story has cowboys settling nervous cattle at night on long trail drives by singing to them: folk songs and hymns from back home, or old tunes with new words. Jack Thorp, a cowboy himself who began to collect and write western songs in the late 1880s, had this to say about crooning cowhands: "I have stood my share of night watches in fifty years, and I seldom heard any singing of that kind . . . just some old hymn tune, like as not—something to kill time and not bad enough to make the herd want to get up and run."[1]

While he didn't hear the men singing specifically to the lowing cattle, he did hear the occasional song around the evening campfire, sometimes accompanied by a guitar or harmonica. Men who worked in isolation, wherever it happened to be, always found a way to make music to stave off boredom, fear, and loneliness. Railroad workers, sailors, lumberjacks, miners, and cowboys always brought song traditions from their homes into new places. They took familiar childhood or regional songs and gave them new lyrics specific to how and where they labored. The familiar ballad "Bury Me Not on the Lone Prairie," for example, was taken from a sea chantey called "The Ocean Burial." And the melody for the equally familiar "Streets of Laredo" goes back to eighteenth-century Ireland.

Jack Thorp published the first collection of cowboy songs in 1908, which contained the words (but not the music) to twenty-three tunes. He had compiled his list while taking a 1,500-mile horseback trip through Texas and New Mexico between 1889 and 1890. His book was reprinted a few times, and he also wrote magazine articles about western life.

One of the biggest names in folklore was John Avery Lomax, who grew up in Bosque County, Texas, alongside one branch of the famous Chisholm Trail. He could hear the cowboys sing at night, and when he was in his teens, he started writing down the lyrics of their songs. He went to college at the University of Texas, where his professors rolled their eyes at his interest in cowboy music. In 1906 he won a scholarship to Harvard, and there he found two scholars who shared his enthusiasm. They helped him advertise a project to collect and record western songs, and he went back on the road with a notebook and a wax-cylinder recording machine. In 1910 he published *Cowboy Songs and Other Frontier Ballads*. Lomax's son Alan became even more celebrated as a folklorist and ethnographer and recorded all kinds of American music for the Library of Congress.

Cowboy music impressed English writer J. B. Priestley when he and his family took multiple vacations to the American West in the mid-1930s. The author spent a couple of winters at the Remuda dude ranch in Wickenburg, Arizona, where the owners built him a special shack so he could have privacy to write. Priestley wrote frequently about cowboys in his American memoir, *Midnight on the Desert: A Chapter of Autobiography*. The first ones he met were wranglers at the dude ranch, and he noted how they frequently broke into song.

> When not at work, they practice for forthcoming rodeos or entertain themselves, and you, with that melancholy music, those long lugubrious strains, for which all men who lead an active open-air life seem to have a strange passion. . . . The cowboy, who is a man of tradition, keeps the traditional tone in song, an odd and rather nasal little tone, which would drive any singing master mad but somehow pleases the rest of us.

Priestley was perceptive enough to realize that the cowboy had created a music specific to his personality and his place.[2]

Music of some sort had been part of the dude ranch guest experience from the beginning. By the 1920s, dude ranch owners took extra steps to provide this benefit to their visitors.

Larry Larom welcomed guests with musical experience so they could entertain everyone in the evenings. Finding musicians to make the long trek to Valley Ranch was difficult, so he relied on his dudes and encouraged them to bring instruments with them. But things didn't always go smoothly.

In March 1923 Larom wrote to his secretary Elizabeth Phillips about a friend of hers, a classical musician who wanted to come out to the ranch. She could be persuaded to perform for the guests but she did not like dance music. Larom told her another guest with classical music skills had already booked a stay, and he was worried that the two might clash over who got more time in the spotlight, so he suggested that Phillips put her friend off. He also thought that no one would be particularly interested in that kind of music, anyway.

A week later, Phillips wrote to Larom that she knew a saxophone player who wanted a gig at the ranch and would charge fifty dollars a month, plus living expenses. Larom did not respond to this letter, so it's likely the sax player didn't make it to Valley Ranch.

C. F. Doyle, who had opened the Deep Well Guest Ranch outside Palm Springs, placed an ad in the *Los Angeles Times* in 1929: "COWBOY—I can use a good looking banjo playing, singing, lying, one right now on new dude ranch. Chuck a few dimes to entertain guests next 6 wks." Clearly, he expected that a cowboy who could sing and play his own instrument would also be the "lying" kind who could tell a good story in song.

Sometimes musical dude wranglers had reputations outside the ranch. Wyoming Jack O'Brien and Weldon Hawkeye Fowler had entertained the guests at the Tepee Lodge in Wyoming during the 1934 season and were then hired to work at the Y Slash P dude ranch for the upcoming season in 1935. Before taking up their new jobs that summer, they toured women's clubs and fraternal organizations in cities around the Midwest.

In February 1935 they sang at the meeting of the Minneapolis Optimist Club, and their appearance garnered a hilarious article in the local newspaper. Under the headline "Montana Dude Ranch Manager Suffers during Song" was a photo of the two wranglers with a couple of the club members, dressed head to toe in dude duds, singing along to "Bury Me Deep on the Lone Prairie." Fowler suffered in silence as they massacred the song, while another club member aimed his six-shooter at the singers, wondering whether he had enough bullets in his gun to fulfill their request.[3]

Throughout the 1930s amateur singing groups performed cowboy tunes and songs about dude ranch life. New ensembles and bands also formed during this decade and played at places with catchy western names. Rodeo Ray Hinkson's Dude Ranch in Camden, New Jersey, featured Curly Mack's band. The Dude Ranch String Band performed at the Dude Ranch nightclub in Visalia, California. The newly opened Dude Ranch Club in Bakersfield offered entertainment and dancing to the music of the Dude Ranch Wranglers. And the Old Heidelberg Inn in Billings, Montana, hired the Hines Brothers Orchestra to lure local dude ranch guests to the club. The Hines Brothers were known for their "Old-Time and Cowboy Numbers," and the inn also hired an expert caller for an exhibition square dance.[4]

Local and national radio shows began to feature dude ranch–themed programs at the same time. In 1936 the NBC network had a dude ranch segment in which Jim Braddock, foreman of a fictional ranch, told stories about rustling, robbery, and romance. A musical interlude followed, during which Louise Massey and the Westerners sang cowboy songs. Woody and Dean, the Dude Ranch Boys, sang regularly on radio station WJBL in Decatur, Illinois, in 1938. And the following year, the famed *National Barn Dance* show announced that it would vary its "he-mannish background by going on a dude ranch party" but would still feature songs like "I'm an Old Cowhand" and "Little Grey Home in the West."[5]

Dude ranches inspired the musical careers of two men whose lives and work intertwined at the start and then ended up in very different places.

The first was Romaine H. Lowdermilk, born in Kansas in 1890, who spent time in New Mexico as a teenager recovering from an unspecified illness. He went back home, but he had been charmed by the western landscape and returned West, this time to Arizona. He homesteaded 160 acres on the Hassayampa River in Wickenburg in 1909 and started a cattle ranch that he named Kay El Bar: the KL was for his mother, Katherine Lowdermilk. In 1914 he built an adobe house as the ranch headquarters and bunkhouse for the wranglers. He started taking paying guests in 1918, and by 1926 the operation was a full-time dude ranch.

Lowdermilk was a natural entertainer and would pull out his guitar and sing cowboy songs for his guests whenever he had a free moment. He taught himself how to twirl a lariat and would sometimes perform rope tricks while balancing on a wire. He was also good friends with the other dude ranchers, especially the White brothers, who worked at the Remuda Ranch and later opened their own place, the Monte Vista.

Bob and Luke White had another brother named John, who was famed at the University of Maryland's glee club for his fine baritone voice. He went out to Wickenburg to visit his brothers in the summer of 1924, and there he met Lowdermilk, who would inspire the next phase of his life.

White had brought a ukulele with him, and he and Lowdermilk often played music and sang together, trading the cowboy songs they both knew. Those were the best days. "As we sat around the corral or in the shade of the mesquite trees, we amused each other trading ballads. [Lowdermilk] also introduced us to a dog-eared copy of the first John A. Lomax anthology, *Cowboy Songs and Other Frontier Ballads*. Greatly impressed, I purchased one at the earliest opportunity. I also resolved to acquire a guitar the minute I returned home."[6]

White returned East and enrolled at the Columbia University School of Journalism, and in 1927 Lowdermilk sold the Kay El Bar and eventually opened a few more dude ranches, earning him the nickname "The Father of Arizona Dude Ranching." He spent time with the Eaton brothers when they opened their own winter place in Arizona, and he entertained the rich guests at the Biltmore hotel in Phoenix. He also had a knack for writing pulp western stories and hilarious send-ups of both cowboys and easterners. He then cemented a national reputation when he began singing on radio station WLS, home of *National Barn Dance*.

Writers who were fascinated by the new popularity of cowboy music often wrote about Lowdermilk and credited dude ranching for the interest in western tunes. "Most picturesque of the entertainers doubtless is Romaine Lowdermilk. . . . He knows all the good yarns the waddies spin, and all the songs they sing. Now he waxes fat financially by twanging a guitar and singing of range vagabondage and generally snorting around in cowboyish fashion among the Easterners who are Wild Western pro tem."[7]

John White never forgot the few weeks he spent in Lowdermilk's company that dude ranch summer in Wickenburg. He worked at the *Washington Star* newspaper, and one day when he met an old friend who was a professional radio singer, he asked the man how to get on the radio. At that time, all you had to do was walk in the door and do a quick audition, and that's what White did. He went to New York and performed for the owners of radio station WEAF, who hired him on the spot to sing cowboy songs with his own guitar for fifteen minutes a week. They didn't pay White for his time, but someone at station WOR heard him and offered him twenty-five dollars to sing on one of its shows.

He loved it, but the money wasn't enough to live on, so White took a job at General Drafting in New Jersey. His managers had no objection to having a radio singer on the payroll and let him take time off each week to record his songs. Producers and music executives came his way, and in 1930 he joined the cast of a new show called *Death Valley Days*. Each episode featured a collection of tales from the Wild West, and White, who eventually took the stage name "The Lonesome Cowboy," sang cowboy ballads in between the stories. He stayed with *Death Valley Days* until 1936, and after his marriage and the birth of a daughter, White began to write and record songs as well as write books and historical articles about western music.

He kept in touch with Lowdermilk for the rest of his life. White retired from General Drafting in 1965 and no doubt mourned when his musical mentor died in Arizona in 1970. In 1975 White published the influential book *Git Along, Little Dogies: Songs and Songmakers of the American West* and dedicated it to Lowdermilk.

As White and Lowdermilk plied their musical trade on the radio, other cowboy singers moved into films, with dude ranching still playing its part. Western movies had started to feature musical acts as the 1930s began, with singers like Johnny Mack Brown, Len Slye and Sons of the Pioneers (before Slye became Roy Rogers), even John Wayne as Singin' Sandy Saunders.

George Gershwin linked dude ranching and song in 1930 with the musical *Girl Crazy*, with a story written by Guy Bolton and John McGowan. The play follows spoiled rich boy Danny Churchill, who is exiled to his family's Arizona ranch to toughen up and dry out. There, he falls for a down-to-earth postmistress named Molly, turns the ranch into a dude ranch, and decides to make the place his permanent home.

The play was a smash, and in 1943 it was turned into a film with Mickey Rooney and Judy Garland in the lead roles, though the setting was a boy's prep school and not a ranch. Rooney puts on a pistol-packin' western music show to save the school from bankruptcy, fronted by famed bandleader Tommy Dorsey in complete cowboy getup.

But the man who personified the singing cowboy, and who traded on the dude ranch experience many times in his films, was Gene Autry.

Born in Texas in 1907, he grew up around both horses and music. Autry started singing early in his life and kept it up while he worked for the St. Louis–San Francisco Railway in Oklahoma. His friends and family—and, according to legend, humorist Will Rogers—told him he had a gift, and in 1927 he pulled enough money together to go to New York. Music producers were encouraging but told him he needed more experience before he could make a real career in music. He practiced and honed a personal sound that included yodeling in the style of the incandescent Jimmie Rodgers, "The Blue Yodeler." Autry joined the *National Barn Dance* radio show and was tapped for the musical interlude in the 1935 film *In Old Santa Fe* because star Ken Maynard couldn't sing. Autry's debut also included his once and future sidekick Smiley Burnette.

In the midst of the film's action, which involves a rigged horse race at a dude ranch along with a blackmail scheme, Autry and Burnette entertain the dudes in an after-dinner show. Autry does the calls for a square dance and then sings "Wyoming Waltz" and "In Old Santa Fe," to which all the guests sing along. Autry wears tight gabardine pants, a satin shirt with contrasting piping, and a big cowboy hat as he plays his guitar, a version of the personal performing uniform he would wear for the rest of his career. Burnette, in more subdued clothing, plays the accordion.

Autry and Burnette were not credited in the film, but their performance got a lot of attention in Hollywood. The following year Autry was the star of *Oh, Susanna!* along with Burnette. The story of mistaken identity and robbery takes them to the Mineral Springs dude ranch, and the assembled guests give Autry and Burnette the opportunity to display their talents. They are backed up by the better-known band called the Light Crust Doughboys; one of their early members was Bob Wills, who had left the group two years earlier to form the Texas Playboys and would go on to be deeply influential in the development and popularity of western swing.

In 1938 Autry starred in two other musical films with dude ranch story lines: *Western Jamboree* and *Gold Mine in the Sky*. As in the other movies, the dude ranch is almost a prop, but an important one. In a dinnertime scene, the dude ranch owner brings out a trio of attractive young women with a harp, a cello, and a violin, but when they start to play classical music, the guests turn restless. Autry and Burnette watch in horror, and Autry says, "Say, I don't think they like this. They want cowboy music. Let's go get the boys."

As the guests stand up and start to leave, Autry and Burnette walk back in singing "Dude Ranch Cowhands," accompanied by J. L. Franks' Golden West Cowboys. Delighted, the guests sit back down, and even the classical female musicians start to sing along.

The music performed on fictional movie dude ranches was far more professional than what guests heard at real ranches. Occasionally a ranch owner might be able to bring in a well-trained singer or piano player, but the big sound of a swing band and a strong lead singer existed only in the minds of scriptwriters. Did dude ranch guests feel they weren't getting their money's worth if the occasional entertainment did not live up to Hollywood standards? Or did they enjoy Autry's films even more because they had sat in a dude ranch dining room themselves, dressed in satin shirts, denim pants, and tooled cowboy boots? Even if they didn't have their own singing cowboy experience, they could imagine themselves into the movies where he appeared.

What began as a musical break in the plot of *In Old Santa Fe* became the point of the story by the time Gene Autry starred in *Gold Mine in the Sky*. Setting these and future films on dude ranches allowed for the full display of Autry's soaring popularity. After all, he needed an audience to sing to, and he could find no more appreciative audience than a room full of dudes.

Another star was on a parallel track with Autry, but he had a very specific fan base.

Herb Jeffries was known as the Bronze Buckaroo, and he was the first Black cowboy star. He had loved western films since childhood, but there was no one on the screen for him to relate to. As he grew up and started singing with performers like Earl "Fatha" Hines, he would go to movies in the towns where they toured, though he and his friends weren't allowed in the white theaters. He wanted to see Black actors on horseback like the white ones on the screen, so he decided to make the movies himself.

With the help of a Hollywood producer named Jed Buell, he came out with *Harlem on the Prairie* in 1936, described as a novelty musical western. *Two-Gun Man from Harlem* followed in 1938, with *Bronze Buckaroo* and *Harlem Rides the Range* in 1939. He needed a western setting for his stories and approached the Murrays about filming at their ranch. They were thrilled, and the exteriors of Jeffries's movies are some of the only remaining views of their Negro Dude Ranch. Jeffries went on to a stellar career in westerns and was also the first Black singing cowboy, known for infusing classic cowboy songs with notes from jazz and blues.

In November 1939 the cast and crew of a new Jack Benny film, *Buck Benny Rides Again*, spent time shooting in Victorville. Benny, who had a long career in vaudeville and radio as a violin-playing comedian, first made the move to films in the 1920s. *Buck Benny* is a send-up of the classic story of an eastern doofus who tries to impress a woman by pretending to be a real westerner. The dude ranch in this film is a Nevada divorce ranch, adding a little extra spice to the plot. Along for the ride is Benny's Black valet, Eddie "Rochester" Anderson, known to fans simply as Rochester. When the film crew located to Victorville and stayed in local hotels, Rochester stayed at Murray's dude ranch, where he received an enthusiastic reception. He no doubt had the opposite experience at hotels in Victorville.

In 1938's *Cowboy from Brooklyn*, Dick Powell, one of Hollywood's most popular crooners, plays a desperate Brooklyn entertainer who finds himself on a dude ranch in Wyoming and can make money only by pretending to be a real cowboy singer named Wyoming Steve Gibson. Based on the play *Howdy Stranger* by Robert Sloane and Louis Pelletier, and originally titled *The Dude Rancher*, the film also stars Pat O'Brien, an actor not known for westerns. The cast also included an actor who would later be photographed frequently on a horse, and not just on the screen: Ronald Reagan. The film parodies the dude ranch, its owners, its guests, and the clothing they wear, but gently. Powell's dude tendencies (he's afraid of animals) are played for heartier laughs.

As the 1930s came to an end, the movie version of the dude ranch had regular stock characters and visuals. Wherever the ranch happens to be located, the landscape is always of the "wide open spaces" variety. The guests are in full dude clothing: jeans or tight riding pants, plain or plaid shirts, wild rags, big-brimmed hats, and fancy boots. The actual westerners are in similar but more subdued clothing, for the most part. The women are spunky and usually play the ranch owner's daughter or are part owners themselves. There is often one predatory female guest out to snag the eastern dude. And someone is always singing.

The men and women performing cowboy tunes in nightclubs, on the radio, or at fraternal and social club events wore the snazzy western clothing inspired by the increasing popularity of dude ranching and the fashion world's adoption of the newfangled duds it was seeing on movie screens.

During San Francisco's Market Week in 1939, store buyers were amazed to see the variety of dude ranch–themed women's sportswear available for them to carry on their racks. Many of them credited the Golden Gate International Exposition for the "yippee tone of the recreation garb," and so did reporters, who said that dude ranching and the exposition's upcoming Fiesta Days were responsible for bringing Wild West attire to San Francisco streets. "There were fancy boots and belts, rakish hats and cowboy shirts and jackets adorned with printed slogans in bunkhouse jargon, with cattle-brands and lariats." No one mentioned Sally Rand's Nude Ranch, however.[8]

Companies vied with each other to create authentic western clothing to meet the increasing popular demand. H. D. Lee called its blue jeans "Lee Cowboy Pants" and advertised heavily in *The Dude Rancher*. The company used language and imagery to entice dudes to choose its products. The Cowboy Pants had a "Saddle Crotch" and a "Hot-Iron Branded Hair-on-Hide Label." Drawings that accompanied the text in the full-page advertisements showed men in the denim pants, holding a cowboy hat, wearing a plaid shirt, and often talking to an attractive dudine on a horse.

Levi Strauss & Co. began to position its original blue jeans as cowboy wear in the 1920s and made them the signature product in its first western wear collection in 1938, called Dude Ranch Duds. Along with the jeans for both men and women and a classic denim jacket, the company offered satin "Rodeo" shirts with contrasting piping, gabardine riding pants (side zip for women), and plaid or checked flannel shirts. "Authentic" dude ranch clothing as defined by designers, store merchandisers, and dudes themselves was reluctantly embraced by dude ranch owners. They were happy for any publicity, especially the kind that made it into the newspapers.

In the winter of 1938 the head of costume design for RKO Pictures, Edward Stevenson, was vacationing at either a resort or a dude ranch near Phoenix. He was fascinated to see how many of the other guests wore western clothing and described them as "costumes worn in lavish pictures that concern fantastic ranch romances."

In April 1940 actress Ellen Drew was photographed for a newspaper fashion column called "Tomorrow's Styles-Today" wearing a fringed divided skirt of brown suede, a white crepe tailored shirt, dude ranch boots, gauntlets, and a ten-gallon hat. She is shown leaning against the rail of a corral, staring into the distance, holding the hat with a star-emblazoned gauntlet. Drew was then starring with Jack Benny in *Buck Benny Rides Again* and wore similar cowgirl clothes in her role as Joan Cameron, one of a trio of singers who perform at the dude ranch.

Designers went crazy for western clothing that spring of 1940. One syndicated fashion column said that dude ranch clothing had been functional but now featured more feminine details such as trim and softer fabrics.

A fashion writer named Vera predicted that dude ranch clothing would be "the big noise in vacation toggery this summer from coast to coast." She wanted to get a firsthand look at what all the excitement was about, and since she lived in Tucson, she traveled to a variety of local ranches to see what people were wearing. What she found was akin to a uniform and included blue denim overalls, "a ten-gallon felt hat tricked up with a fancy band of some sort, the loudest cotton shirt to be found, gobs of sterling silver jewelry, a bandana, and sturdy boots that come well over the ankles." While silver jewelry inspired by Native American designs was a southwestern feature, no doubt the women who visited dude ranches in the Rocky Mountain West wore similar clothing. Some home-decorating companies even created wallpaper with dude ranch designs.[9]

Films set on dude ranches with singing cowboys, fancy clothing that wasn't really suited to the outdoor life, and cowboy music with touches of jazz might not have reflected real dude ranch life, but their owners didn't care. New ranches were opening, and guest lists were increasing. By 1940 the Dude Ranchers' Association reported that there were 350 dude ranches in the United States and Canada, though those were self-described, and not all were DRA members. The eastern dude ranches, which now had their own trade organization, were also thriving and traded on their proximity to their customer base.

An estimated 25,000 people took dude ranch vacations in the summer of 1940, including visits to the nearly fifty ranches in New York, Pennsylvania, New Jersey, and Connecticut. Costs were still on the high side and not within reach of every family, averaging about $50 per week, which included lodging, meals, and the use of a horse (about $1,000 today).[10] Writers as well as filmmakers took notice of their popularity, and in the spring of that year, popular novelist Peter Kyne published the book *Dude Woman*.

The story resembles some of the film plots of the 1930s, in which a soft-edged male easterner goes out West and after many misadventures becomes a man and a permanent western resident. *Dude Woman* turns this premise around. The main character is Mary Sutherland, a rich, confident young woman from New York who decides to take a vacation at the Wagon Wheel dude ranch in Yavapai County, Arizona. When she arrives, she discovers that the ranch is out of business, and on a whim she buys the majority equity in the ranch and starts it up again. Mary already knows how to ride a horse and shoot, and she earns everyone's respect, including that of a local cowboy with whom she slowly falls in love.

Reviewers praised Kyne for the authenticity of the setting. He likely had been to—or at least knew about—one dude ranch in Wickenburg, Arizona, which was over the border in Maricopa County, and it shows up throughout the story. The former owners of the Wagon Wheel ranch were named "Burdan"; the "Burden" family ran the Remuda Ranch in Wickenburg, the place where J. B. Priestley had spent time a few years earlier. The Wagon Wheel was near Congress Junction, a former mining town about fifteen miles from Wickenburg. The town and its river, the Hassayampa, also make the occasional appearance.

Kyne perfectly captured life on a dude ranch, though some of the Wagon Wheel's characters had an attitude toward dudes that no real employee, much less a dude ranch owner, would ever reveal out loud. "Every time I see a mess o' dudes, all dressed up like movie picture cowboys an' cowgirls, with more color on 'em than a Chinee pheasant, an' follerin' the dude wrangler like sheep foller a billy-goat, I say to myself: What is Arizona a-comin to?"

Readers and reviewers also liked the spunky Mary and praised her for keeping her femininity despite her strength of character in facing the harsh realities of the West. She was perfectly believable as an easterner who molded herself to the vivid West, so much so that she was able to shoot a cattle thief without batting a mascaraed eyelash.[11]

While 1940 was proving to be a good year for both profits and publicity, ranchers kept a nervous eye on events in Europe. That spring the concept of the dude ranch collided with current events.

A Santa Fe resident named Mercedes Wheelon received a cartoon from a friend who was serving in the British Army. It showed a bucking horse in the corral of a dude ranch, and sitting on the horse, about to be pitched into the dust, was Adolf Hitler. A sign on the corral read "Double Cross Ranch," and her friend had inked in the words "Santa Fe" underneath it. No doubt anyone who saw the cartoon thought it was very funny, but the reality of war would soon hit dude ranching with the force of a runaway bronc.

Chapter 11

On December 8, 1941, the day after the Japanese attacked Pearl Harbor, newspapers around the country published an article titled "Dude Ranch Saddle Horn May Go for Emergency Duration." Officials at the Denver headquarters of the Office of Production Management, a government agency created in January 1941 to coordinate federal procurement programs, reported that the nickel, bronze, and brass used in the manufacture of saddle horns might have to go straight into tanks, guns, and ships.

The design of the western saddle owes much to early Mexican versions, and saddle horns had been standard equipment for centuries. Strangely, whoever wrote the article assumed that the saddle horn was an innovation exclusive to dude ranch trail riders. The writer also said that saddle makers were going to be pressured to make a hornless saddle for dudes. Stories like this spread quickly in the early years of the war.

Dude ranchers did have reason to worry about one thing, though: a shortage of horseshoes. Older ranchers who had lived through the privations of World War I knew that metal was precious and feared that the government did not understand the importance of horseshoes to their business. Larry Larom, now in his fifteenth year as president of the Dude Ranchers' Association, put it bluntly: "No shoes would mean no mountain horseback rides and probably a stoppage of the dude ranch industry." Although the government reduced the amount of metal that nonwar industries could use, the feared horseshoe shortage didn't happen, though it cropped up in conversation and the media throughout the 1940s. In 1944 an unnamed humorist published a piece of newspaper filler suggesting that if dude ranches couldn't get shoes for their horses, perhaps the ranch owners could just install a merry-go-round.[1]

But the war footing put other strains on the dude ranch industry. Automobile tires and gasoline were heavily rationed, and since many dudes now arrived at ranches in their own cars, this meant that they could not take long motor trips. Trains were still available for travelers and went to many dude ranch locations, but railroads were not allowed to carry the volume of tourists they had seen before the war.

At the 1942 Dude Ranchers' Association annual conference in Billings, Larom urged ranchers to compile data about the amount of food they produced themselves, thereby demonstrating to local and national governments that they and their dudes were not consuming food meant to go to soldiers and war workers. But business was falling off fast, and although the DRA was worried about its future, the members voted unanimously to keep their organization going and to support each other. They all shared the same worries but also remembered how they had faced threats to their business in the past: by being creative, adaptable, and tough.

One of the biggest challenges was the lack of ranch workers and wranglers. Young men signed up with the military or reported when they were drafted, leaving ranches bereft of not only good employees, but the very men their dudes wanted to spend time with. Some ranchers filled the gap by putting the dudes to work, creating a ranch vacation that also helped the war effort. This was not a new idea, but it had worked for years because some dudes wanted to rough it on ranches and not just take tame trail rides. Mexican men also took jobs at dude ranches, though they did not interact with the dudes as wranglers.

As the war progressed, overstressed business and government executives took time away from their desks and stayed at dude ranches, where spending time outdoors and just relaxing prepared them to go back to their demanding jobs. People kept indoors by the many hours of work in defense plants also benefited from a short time at a dude ranch. Larry Larom, who was always thinking about how to get more people out to Valley Ranch (and dude ranches in general), created a program for young people in the summer of 1943 called the Victory Vacation. Teens and college-age boys and girls came out to the Valley Ranch and stayed for six to eight weeks, which included a week-long pack trip to designated camping sites all over the region. The cost was lower than that of the usual dude ranch vacation, and the fees could be kept down only if the kids pitched in and helped around the ranch.

They had to "cooperate with the Ranch in its effort to increase war production, by devoting several hours each day to helping in the vegetable gardens, potato patches, hay fields, corrals, etc., and caring for their own cabins." The system worked and the Victory Vacation ran for the duration of the war. After 1946 the pack trip participants were renamed the Range Riders.[2]

Ranches that had once run cattle but then turned to dudes when times were hard found themselves being encouraged to raise cattle again, as the demand for beef was higher than it had been for years and the price had also gone up. Most ranches had no problem running both cattle and sheep, as long as they had the acreage to do so. Some ranchers, anticipating the war, started to take on more livestock even before Pearl Harbor.

Paul and Helen Van Cleve, of the Lazy K Bar in Montana, bought a second band of sheep in the fall of 1941, though during the spring lambing season of 1942 every member of the family had to pitch in because many of their workers had enlisted. And to some ranchers, running cattle was patriotic. Irving Corse, who had bought out his partnership with Struthers Burt at the Bar B C near Jackson Hole, turned his energies to cattle by the middle of 1942. As he told *The Dude Rancher*, "If it takes more beef to win the war, the Bar B C will try and furnish more beef."[3]

Dude ranches made a lot of these changes during the first year of the war, but visitor numbers were still down. Some ranches experienced a downturn that was worse than what they had seen during the Depression, and those that could not change their business model had to close, sometimes permanently.

The Dude Ranchers' Association worked hard to get publicity for its members and to demonstrate how dude ranching contributed to the war effort. Food production and recreation opportunities were at the top of the list, especially after Franklin and Eleanor Roosevelt said publicly that it was still important for Americans to engage in sensible recreation. Officials who oversaw the distribution of ration books and stamps made sure that dude ranches that regularly had children among their guests got the full number they were entitled to.

Larry Larom floated an idea to DRA members in early 1942. He queried them about their ability and willingness to stay open year round in order to bring in needed revenue. His focus was on the Rocky Mountain region, where ranches closed during the winter. However, he and the ranchers realized that the cost to install a heating system for a ranch in the snowy states would eat into any meager profits it might have made over the previous summer. He apparently didn't worry about ranches in the Southwest and Southern California, some of which did stay open all year. However, the blistering summers in places like Arizona, where the only relief from the heat came from evaporative or "swamp" coolers, made vacationing there as difficult as a winter sojourn in Wyoming. Larom's concept looked good on paper but didn't go anywhere.

Ranchers also hosted more locals than they had in previous years. With gas and tire rationing, people in Wyoming, Colorado, California, and Arizona couldn't travel far for vacations, if they could take them at all. So, a nearby dude ranch was the perfect solution: something different to do that wasn't too far away and, with a reduction in costs, not too expensive.

In early 1943 the government began to look at dude ranches as possible locations for setting up infirmaries for returning soldiers and sick civilian war workers. Not only would the ill and injured be able to recover in a beautiful setting, but the income would help out the ranches that were struggling to keep going. As one official stated, they were "ranches first and resorts incidentally," because many had their own water plants and electricity and raised much of their own produce, not to mention beef cattle. Their spacious lodges and individual private cabins could house both patients and medical staff. Records are spotty, but apparently this idea didn't go any further than government reports.[4]

A couple of places did benefit from the country's war preparations. The Tamaracks, a dude ranch run by Maude and Henry Turner at Seeley Lake near Missoula, hosted between twenty-five and forty army aviation cadets each weekend during June and July 1943. The men trained at nearby aviation schools and enjoyed all the ranch's amenities on their weekends off, including the hearty meals ranches were known for. Maude wrote about the visiting young men for *The Dude Rancher*. "Found out first-hand that the army can (and does) eat. We were able to get extra points from our ration board for feeding them—but don't think the board expected forty boys to consume thirty-five pounds of leg of pork at one sitting! Lucky the family likes eggs."

In December 1943 four women "Air-WACs" from the Marana Army Airfield north of Tucson spent their three-day passes at the nearby Flying V dude ranch. "WAC" stood for Women's Army Corps, organized in May 1942 so that women could serve in the military, though only in clerical, medical, food service, or driving jobs. Air-WACs supported the air force and worked as teletype operators, clerks, weather observers, dispatchers, and photographers.

The young women who went to the Flying V got a ride into Tucson, where they were met by a wrangler driving the ranch station wagon. They then changed into western garb and joined all the activities, some of which were new to them, such as riding and calf roping. At the end of their stay one of the women told the ranch owner that she now had something to write home about. Perhaps clerking at a wartime air base wasn't the thrill she had expected it to be.[5]

Maude Turner, Helen Van Cleve, and the other female ranch owners supported each other through personal letters and via articles in the pages of *The Dude Rancher*. They all faced the same restrictions, challenges, and terrors of operating a unique business in the middle of a world war.

Getting people to come to the ranch was high on this list. Mary Shawver of Holm Lodge was still in charge of the "House Management Department" column of the magazine and always had something pithy to say in her monthly editorial. In July 1942, for example, she wrote about what the dude ranch could offer to people already feeling the pressures of the war's first few months. "If people in the coast cities could realize how peaceful our inland ranches are compared to the tense atmosphere elsewhere, they surely would come flocking to us. Particularly the nervous people and the young folks."

When guests did come, they proved to be valuable for more than just the fees they paid for food and lodging. Most of them didn't mind pitching in to clean their cabins, or even helping out in the kitchen and dining room. Sometimes they took their trail rides only when it was convenient for another staff member to take them, because the wranglers had gone to war.

The Turners regularly hosted a group of doctors and their families at the Tamaracks, and they still showed up during the war. They also jumped in to help, even going beyond the ranch to offer their services. With many doctors serving overseas, small towns were left without their regular physicians, and travel to larger cities was sometimes impossible, especially in an emergency. During the summer of 1943 two of the doctors at the Tamaracks made house calls at nearby homes, and another stitched up one of the ranch's horses that had an eighteen-inch gash in its side, saving a trip to the vet sixty miles away, and the horse's life.

Food, of course, was also a constant worry. Sugar was rationed in May 1942, followed by coffee in November, and then meats, canned meats, fats, cheese, and canned milk the following March. Mary Shawver recalled that ranches had voluntarily cut back on sugar in 1917–18 during World War I and remembered what a relief that was for the cook, who didn't have to plan a different dessert every night.

By January 1943 Jessie Spear, who ran the Rafter Cross Bar Ranch in Montana with her husband, Phil, was secretary of *The Dude Rancher*'s House Management Department. Spear's editorials were titled "Ranch Life in War Times," and in this issue she suggested that ranch women form their own organization called "R.W.W.—Ranch War Wives," to reflect how much they contributed to the war effort.

Under her guidance, women sent in more articles about food, rationing, and their wartime recipes. In April 1943, Frances Allan of the Allan Ranch in Augusta, Montana, wrote about a woman on the radio who cheerily advised housewives to make trips to their local store to buy lettuce, strawberries, and other produce to augment the canned foods they served their families. Spear, in an editor's note, had this to say: "I wonder if any of these persons who make the plans and rules governing food rationing ever thought of having to snowshoe thirty miles for supplies?"

Guests also got a closer look at the day-to-day operations during the war. A woman named Eda M. McKnew wrote a letter to *The Dude Rancher* in 1943 about her visits to the Pitchfork Ranch in Wyoming over the previous seven years. She had now rented out her house in Washington, DC, and taken a job at the ranch. She was intrigued by how the ranch wife made her own butter, cottage cheese, and liverwurst, and the magic of making a cake at high altitude.

Spear asked her readers for popular recipes, and in addition to traditional items such as nut-date bread and rhubarb pie, there was the occasional nod to life with rationing. A recipe for tomato juice cocktail (which sounds like the makings for a Bloody Mary) could also be heated up and served as soup on cold days. Cottage cheese, inexpensive and easy to make, could be dressed up at mealtime, and many women noted that the dudes liked the homemade version better than what they could buy back home. The April 1943 issue of *The Dude Rancher* listed seven recipes for this staple, from fried cottage cheese balls to cheesecake.

Some recipes dated from previous decades and were not always familiar or appetizing to contemporary eaters. But they could be inexpensive to make. A few dude ranchers continued to serve a traditional boiled pudding made with suet, sorghum (a cereal-based sweetener), brown sugar, eggs, dried fruits, nuts, and spices like cinnamon, nutmeg, and cloves. Baking the pudding was easy, if time consuming. "Steam for four hours in a flour sack submerged in boiling water. Or fill two-pound coffee cans one-half full of batter, cover tight and steam in boiler." Served with hard sauce, which was simply whiskey, butter, and sugar, this was a hearty and long-lasting dessert. And just in case it didn't sound appealing to ranch guests, *The Dude Rancher* suggested giving it a new name: Cowboy in a Sack.

One aspect of dude ranch life didn't change: the perennial difficulty of finding a good cook. If anything, it was harder, because so many women could get good factory jobs, making better money in less out-of-the-way places. The House Management Department's columns were filled with the same horror stories of a decade earlier. Jessie Spear wrote about this problem in one issue. "Our last treasure departed in a huff about a week ago, and I half expected to see her throw her suitcase at Phil, who was taking her back to town, rather than into the car. . . . And, oh how she could cuss."

In 1944 Mary Shawver was in charge of the "House Management Department" column of *The Dude Rancher* again, but the name had been changed to "Women's Page" earlier that year. The new masthead included a simple ink drawing of a fashionable woman's profile. Her short hair was curled in a style more popular in the 1930s, and she wore long, dangling earrings. And while some dude ranchers did try to look smart and professional, they would never have had the time to create this sleek hairstyle. They might have worn fancy earrings in the evenings, but never while doing their chores.

So, what was the point of having a woman who looked nothing like a "dude ranch wife" illustrating a column devoted to ranching issues? The articles in the column were as practical and occasionally complaining as usual, and there was nothing in the subject matter that made the women look less strong or more stereotypically feminine. Whoever made the change didn't explain it, but if anything, the woman on the new masthead looked exactly like a mature eastern dudine.[6]

While the ranchers themselves struggled with wartime privations, the outside world saw dude ranches differently. They were places of escape, of humor, and they propped up the weary for the duration.

In February 1942 Gladys Shipman's dude ranch for dogs at Big Bear Lake in California took in some evacuees from Pearl Harbor: dogs and other pets belonging to servicemen who wanted them out of harm's way as the war began. Nearly one hundred animals were shipped to San Francisco to be picked up by the soldiers' families on the mainland, but the dogs that did not have anyone to care for them went to Shipman's ranch.

The following year a tourist told the local press around Tucson how much he had enjoyed his recent dude ranch vacation, which he took only because his usual resorts had been appropriated by the military. "It's hard to believe there's a war on, with guns booming and shells screaming, when you ride peacefully along cattle trails near Tucson. . . . From now on I dude it when I take my Winter vacation!"

There's a lot going on in this story if you read between the lines. How old was this man, and why wasn't he in uniform? He was probably too old for military service, or the reporter would either have called him out for it or mentioned it in the article. Also, anyone who says he takes a winter vacation implies he also takes one in the summer and is therefore a person of means. He was the ideal dude ranch guest, who spent more than just a couple of weeks on the ranch because he could easily afford it.

Dude ranches got a boost from an unexpected place during the war. Brooklyn-born William C. Burghardt was known to his friends as "Montana" Bill. After leaving high school, he took a job as the ski coach at the University of Montana in Missoula. He taught skiing at the Double Arrow dude ranch at Seeley Lake in 1939, when the owners were trying to get through the Depression by offering their guests some nontraditional activities. He also cowboyed at the nearby Gordon Ranch and may have entered some local rodeos.

Burghardt enlisted in the army in March 1941, and when war was declared he was sent to North Africa, where he served in a tank battalion. In March 1943 he was declared missing in action. A month later his relieved parents learned he had been captured by the Italians, and he was eventually sent to Oflag 64, a German prisoner-of-war camp in Poland. He was allowed to write only a few letters, and his correspondence went mostly to his parents. But in July 1944, he sent off a note to the Dude Ranchers' Association in Billings, which at this time was simply the home of whoever was the organization's secretary. In this case, it was Al Croonquist.

In his letter, Burghardt asked the DRA to mail him brochures about Montana dude ranches so he could pass them around to the other officers in the prison camp and drum up postwar business. Newspapers were tickled by the young man's enterprise.[7]

And in the spring of 1943 a new brand of jams and preserves debuted on store shelves: Dude Ranch Pure, from Southwest Food Products Co. of Long Beach,

California. The line included apple jelly, peach preserves, orange marmalade, apricot jam, and grape jelly. The products were made well into the mid-1960s, but their appearance during the war is interesting. Many women were making their own jams and jellies, but if they couldn't get apricots or peaches, they turned to their local stores, which didn't always have a big selection. The new collection of preserved fruits was probably very popular.

But why would the company choose the name "Dude Ranch Pure"? It was probably just good marketing. The name evoked the West, where American values still reigned. Dude ranches were places where these values could be acted out, perhaps in their purest form, and not incidentally they were also places where tired tourists could get good American food. A jar of jam thus became something patriotic and soothing to war-weary families, even if they didn't know much about dude ranches.

The attractive western aura of the dude ranch also inspired Hollywood studios to make more films with dude-related plots during the war years. These continued a trend that had started in the mid-1930s. Prior to Gene Autry's first singing appearance in *In Old Santa Fe* in 1935, dude ranching movies were typical western stories, set in serious places with sometimes deadly characters. But with the introduction of Autry as a fancily clothed crooner at a dude ranch, however authentic a cowboy he might be, ranches became places where very unserious things happened. Between 1942 and 1944 dude ranch films and short subjects reflected the dudes more than the westerners.

Autry's *Heart of the Rio Grande* was released in 1942, featuring a plot about spoiled eastern girls, a feud between dude ranch foreman Autry and his predecessor, and drama at a cattle roundup. Autry includes "Deep in the Heart of Texas" among the songs he sings in between the scenes of action and romance.

Two other films came out that year, and they began to move the dude ranch into sillier realms. *Dudes Are Pretty People* was one of Hal Roach Studios' "Streamliners," films that were longer than a short subject but shorter than a feature. In this movie, the cowboys are muddle headed and the dudines are suckers for them, though the main female character discovers that she loves the fiancé she left behind, after all. *Ride 'Em Cowboy* has a familiar plot about a fake cowboy who goes West to follow the true cowgirl he met when she was vacationing back East. She and her father run an Arizona dude ranch, and the dude cowboy proves his mettle and wins the girl. But what turns this standard story into slapstick are the antics of Abbott and Costello, who hide out at the dude ranch and end up saving the day.

Chatterbox, *Riding High*, and *Take It Big*, released between 1943 and 1944, also use the dude ranch to comic effect. The men start off as weaklings but, as usual, find a way to toughen up after being tested by the West. The women are all down-to-earth local gals and give their hearts to the dudes once they have proved themselves. *Riding High* and *Take It Big* also feature musical numbers, sung by Dick Powell and Jack Haley.

Movies about singing cowboys, with goofy plots set at a dude ranch, served the same purpose during World War II as Shirley Temple's films had done during the Depression: an escape from bad news, the uncertainty of the daily meal, and real sacrifice. And if dude ranchers were irritated at how their businesses were portrayed on the screen, they never said anything about it in public. Larry Larom and the other officers of the Dude Ranchers' Association were probably thrilled.

In early 1945 Walter C. Nye, the new secretary of the DRA, noticed that the organization had started to receive a number of requests for information from men serving in the navy. In January a naval lieutenant commander in the Pacific wrote to the DRA saying that he wanted to get as far away as possible from what he was seeing and hearing. Three months later a seaman first class who had wrangled dudes on ranches in Montana before the war also wrote to Nye and asked for brochures about local dude ranches to give to the servicemen and officers on his ship. As the summer began, the Dude Ranchers' Association placed ads for wranglers, guides, and packers in papers around the Rocky Mountain West. With men being discharged from the service and now needing work, the DRA wanted to grab the qualified ones before they got away.[8]

A year earlier, in August 1944, officials of the American Express company had taken the long view of dude ranching and its place in the tourist industry, especially during the war. "Today, the dude ranches are building their greatest attendance around the three R's—rest, recreation and romance. City people near Western cities, who formerly ignored the dude ranch appeal, see in the dude ranches the ideal facilities which fit war vacation needs."

The DRA thought this approach would also work when the conflict was over. At its annual meeting in Missoula in November 1945, three months after World War II ended, 150 members listened to officers and fellow ranchers predict a surge in guests for the following summer. Rail and air restrictions would soon be lifted, and with gasoline and tires no longer rationed, travel to ranches would be easier than ever. The Great Northern Railway was already planning to put "ultra-modern" trains into service by June 1946, and the Northern Pacific was improving its tracks to make way for new high-speed rail. More people would take the long visits of previous years, instead of only the short hops they were able to afford during the war, and many vacationers had been saving their money instead of traveling and so had cash to spare.[9]

There was a lot to be hopeful for, which the women of the DRA wrote about in *The Dude Rancher* as the war news started to look sunnier that spring. They felt pride in having faced hardships with fortitude. In the summer of 1945, which many ranchers rightly believed would be the last one of the war, Marion Moore, of the CM Ranch in Wyoming, wrote an editorial for the "Women's Page" about one way that dude ranchers could reward themselves for their hard work and prepare for better times again.

She suggested that ranchers become dudes themselves: go for daily rides, do some fishing, loaf in the sun along with the guests as much as possible. "We all know that the dude ranch spirit, the intangible thing that brings the dudes back . . . is found in the hearts of the men and women who run our ranches, and it functions the same for one as for fifty. The thought of having someone to share your home spot, is what makes the fun in our way of life. This summer, let's relax and enjoy it with them. We will probably make better dude wranglers in the days to come, for having duded a bit ourselves!"[10]

Chapter 12

On August 10, 1945, the Japanese empire offered its surrender to the Allies, and deliberations to end the war began. Barely two weeks later, Walter Nye set off on a tour of western dude ranches to assess their condition and future needs. He predicted a bright future for 1946, but the prospects for peace had already brought out the dudes.

Some ranchers were surprised at the number of people who made reservations for the summer of 1945, and they weren't always prepared for the hordes: unbroken colts filled corrals, ditches weren't completely cleaned out, and fences barely stood their ground. But none of this mattered. The dudes still had fun, and plenty of former soldiers would be coming back to find jobs and take on the undone chores. The ranchers had good reason to be optimistic. Plenty of weary former GIs and their families needed the peace and relaxation of a dude ranch vacation to prepare them for postwar life. But changes were coming.

Dude ranches had been on a path to growth and expansion as the Depression ended, but the war years interrupted all forward movement. Even though gasoline and tires were no longer rationed after the war was over, there were still shortages of both for quite a while, and the same was true for foodstuffs. It would be months or even years before people could buy what they wanted at a service station or grocery store.

And something else was happening in the West. Many men and women had come out to the western states for work during the war, and they liked what they saw. Natural beauty and vistas of unbroken land appealed to those who were not anxious to return to crowded cities. The individuals and families who could choose where they wanted to live began to put down permanent stakes in places like California, Colorado, and Arizona. Employment in the service industries in the western states grew five times faster than the national average between 1940 and 1960, and the West received significant sums from the government to spur prosperity.

Americans also got into their cars and hit the road, some of them taking their first vacation in four years. Auto courts and motels refurbished and added to their accommodations to prepare for the increase in customers, but this was worrisome to dude ranchers. They still operated solely by reservation and for stays longer than just a night or two. This made them unique in the hospitality industry, and they did not want this to go away. For one thing, the mystique of the dude ranch would fade if guests were not immersed in the western lifestyle they offered. Dudes were guests of the ranchers in their homes, not guests of an anonymous manager who surfaced only when they paid their bill. And on a more practical level, accepting overnight, on-the-road tourists would reclassify dude ranches and make them subject to laws governing the hotel trade, forcing them to accept anyone who wanted a room.

The Dude Ranchers' Association helped its members stick to their guns and run their businesses as they always had. And prospects were bright enough for some states to see an increase in ranch openings in the late 1940s, especially in Colorado, Arizona, Montana, and Wyoming.

Ranchers continued to advertise their places much as they had done before the war. When possible, they went East to speak at clubs and glad-hand at trade shows to encourage potential guests. Regional dude ranch organizations, which had started up in the previous decade, also increased their outreach. Members of the Colorado Dude and Guest Ranch Association, for example, had always gone to Chicago to drum up business, and in big numbers. They started up again after the war, shipping horses by rail and putting on a parade, delighting residents who weren't used to seeing livestock near the Magnificent Mile.[1]

Government officials and entrepreneurs thought that dude ranches could serve different functions in the postwar years. As early as June 1945 citizens who lived near Camp Bowie in the central Texas town of Brownwood formed a committee to sponsor what were called "redeployment" activities for returning soldiers. Among the suggestions that came from Mrs. J. W. Trapp, president of Daniel Baker College, was the creation of a special dude ranch just for soldiers, which unfortunately did not happen.

Some military properties were no longer needed once the fighting stopped, and municipalities had to come up with creative solutions for these installations. The government had a surplus real estate disposal program, and in January 1947 it held a conference in Phoenix to discuss pressing issues. Colonel J. A. Read, the head of the organization, visited the former glider and power aircraft training airfield in Wickenburg and was pleased with what he saw. The buildings were in good shape and the plumbing still worked, and he deemed it above average in condition. He thought it could be sold for a school, a military academy, or a dude ranch. None of these ideas were adopted, but the military obviously thought dude ranches were important to postwar recovery.

Then there were the sillier solutions. A group called the Dallas Bonehead Club met for lunch once a week and discussed "zany doings." They came up with four suggestions for the peacetime use of the North American Aviation plant in Dallas. At the top of the list was converting it into an indoor dude ranch, with no mosquitoes and no sunburn.

In the postwar period Americans became more aware of what the advent of the atomic bomb meant for their lives and their future. One dude ranch reached out to the men who worked at the Los Alamos facility in New Mexico, where J. Robert Oppenheimer had led the Manhattan Project. Rancho Rio, near Santa Fe, placed this ad throughout 1948: "LOS ALAMOS WORKERS—Come join us at the dude ranch. Accommodations for 25 men. Twin beds, private baths, good food, recreation room. Strictly high class. Room and board—$25 a week."

Walter A. Schelden, a realtor in California's Lucerne Valley, offered sixty-eight acres for sale in Horse Thief Flats, near Victorville, in the summer of 1948. Schelden's sales pitch tapped into the new age of atomic anxiety, as well as the continuing popularity of dude ranching. "Wild, rugged, picturesque—a miniature kingdom.... Will make an unusual dude ranch, and a safe retreat from atomic warfare."[2]

This language also made its way into the pages of *The Dude Rancher*. In the fall of 1946 Mary Shawver, still the head of the House Management Department, which published the "Women's Page," wrote about the exhilarating and exhausting summer. "It was an atomic cyclone that whirled and roared twenty-four hours a day all the summer.... People came from everywhere, brought their friends, relatives and in-laws. They over-stayed their time and then wanted to stay longer."

Shawver and the other ranchers were happy for the crowds to return, but the first season after the war, they often had to take on new and inexperienced employees, as their regular wranglers and other hands had not all been discharged from the service. But Shawver, at least, was pleased that the summer passed at her place, Holm Lodge, without any serious injuries.[3]

One summer guest came out to a Montana dude ranch from Michigan for an unusual reason: allergies.

Molly Wilson was a fun-loving eighteen-year-old from an accomplished, educated family in Ann Arbor. Her mother was a freelance writer who worked for the Red Cross during the war, and both her brother Ted and her father served in the navy. Molly went to boarding school and had worked as a counselor at summer camps, where she learned to ride and was also a strong swimmer. But as much as she loved the outdoors, she had one problem: she was seriously allergic to ragweed, which grew everywhere in Michigan, spreading its pollen from summer into early fall. She suffered so much that her parents sent her to Beaver Island in Lake Michigan for a few years, where the plant didn't grow. Then, in the summer of 1946, a family friend named Hank Burgess told them about a place called the Bones Brothers dude ranch, run by his good friends out in Montana.

The "Bones" brothers were actually the Alderson brothers: Floyd, Allen, and Irving, who were born at the family homestead on Hanging Woman Creek in Montana's Tongue River Valley in 1895, 1898, and 1900, respectively. As soon as they were old enough, the boys went to work at the nearby Three Circle ranch, owned by one of their relatives. They wrangled horses, helped the cook, and did heavy chores like chopping firewood.

They got their unusual nickname from the cowboys at the Three Circle. Floyd, the oldest, was so skinny they called him "Skin and Bones," or just Bones. Allen was the opposite, a husky kid who was quickly dubbed "Big Bones." The smallest of them all, Irving, became "Little Bones." When his brothers were just teenagers, Floyd left Montana and went to Hollywood, where he became an actor, starring in B westerns under the name Wally Wales and later Hal Taliaferro.

Big Bones and Little Bones went to work at Eatons' dude ranch in 1920, and in 1923 they returned to Montana and the financially strapped ranch owned by their aunt and uncle, Z. T. and Mary Cox. It had been hit hard by drought and the depression that set in shortly after World War I, so the brothers put a proposal before the Coxes: turn the place into a dude ranch. The older couple loved the idea, and by 1924 a main lodge and a sprinkling of cabins were ready to receive the first guests.

One of them was dude ranch aficionado Mary Roberts Rinehart, who wrote about attending a roundup at the ranch in an article she published in the *Saturday Evening Post* in 1925. She also came up with the name. She'd met the two Alderson brothers at Eatons' and was so taken with the young men that she suggested they call their place Bones Brothers Ranch. By 1946 it was hugely popular, known as much for the cheerful personalities of its owners as its horses, wranglers, and the amenities in nearby Sheridan. Molly's parents thought she would enjoy a few weeks at a dude ranch and made a reservation for her starting on July 1.

Molly came from a family of prolific letter writers, and she wrote to her mother many times during her stay. She was pleased with her cabin and wasted no time jumping into the activities, going for a ride the very next day on a horse named Honey-Go that had ears like a bulldog. One Sunday morning she got up at five o'clock to help the wranglers bring in the horses for the day's ride. She went on a pack trip, attended a rodeo in Sheridan, and rode every day, sometimes for six hours straight. She begged her mother to send her some button-fly jeans, because the zipper versions just wore out. And she also asked for a few "glamour rags" because she had started going on dates with a cowboy who was six foot three.

Molly's letters home gave her mother the perfect picture of what it was like to be a dude ranch guest. She was a keen observer and had a flair for pulling comedy out of everyday situations. In her first letter home she wrote, "We had dinner in Sheridan last night and I met a man who payed $25 thousand for a quarter horse (I mean a whole horse, they call a quarter horse)." And when she and two other guests were filmed for a travel newsreel as they walked down the streets in Sheridan, she wrote, "Mommy! I've made the movies! You may see my little rear at your own local theater. Oh God!"

Molly also had an experience that a big, anonymous resort would never have given her: a surprise birthday party. She turned nineteen on August 4, and the Bones brothers presented her with a candle-covered angel food cake served with ice cream. Someone she called "Auntie Bones" (possibly Mary Cox) gave her a china horse, and that evening there were cocktail parties and presents of hard candy, peanuts, postcards, and cigarettes from the other guests. Molly told her mother, "Aren't people grand? I guess I'm just lucky."

Molly's letters are filled with the personal touches that made dude ranches unique, and the brothers were sincerely sorry when she had to go home the third week of August. As Allen "Big Bones" Alderson said in a letter to her mother, "Molly's a grand girl . . . we knew it right off the bat, but she is one to wear awfully well too."[4]

Other grand girls spent time on dude ranches, but not as guests. In 1946 *The Dude Rancher* profiled a college student named Patsy Whited, who worked as a wrangler on the Lazy F dude ranch in Ellensburg, Washington. She not only managed the horses but waited on tables, worked in the kitchen doing food prep, fruit canning, and washing up, greeted guests, and did some housekeeping. There was a good reason for this long résumé: her parents owned the Lazy F. Her father, Tom, was a cowboy singer, and Patsy and her mother also sang to entertain the guests. The writer of the article suggested that young girls should sign up to work on dude ranches, though the prospect of such work, if Patsy's accomplishments were an example of what it was like, probably did not appeal to most girls.

The article about Patsy included a photo in which she sits on a corral wearing cuffed jeans, a plaid shirt, and a cowboy hat tipped on the back of her head. Her clothes are utilitarian but are also a simpler version of what the dudes wanted to wear. By 1947 dude ranch clothing for women had become a staple of sportswear lines and was covered frequently in fashion columns. Designers didn't expect that their creations would be worn only on dude ranches, but they took their cues from what the dudines wore and came home with.

By the postwar period, western sportswear and dude ranch clothing was inspired mostly by the Southwest. Fay Foster was a print artist who especially loved southwestern designs, and she created dude ranch fashions that were carried by a number of stores in California, Arizona, Texas, Florida, and New York. For spring 1947 she created a "Dude Ranch midriff dress," a slightly scandalous design in which a small square of midriff peeked out from dress panels constructed at the waistline.

Jack Weil founded Rockmount Ranch Wear Mfg. Co. in Denver in 1946 to create a fashion identity for westerners. While they had jeans, hats, and boots, there were only limited offerings for shirts. He is credited with creating the iconic snap-front western shirt. His fabrics ranged from many solid colors to plaids, stripes, prints, and ornate embroideries that dominated designs in the decades to follow, through the present day.

However, some critics thought some western fashions went a little too far into musical comedy but said there was a place for more sophisticated clothing, even on a dude ranch. A fashion show in Dallas in the summer of 1947 featured colorful western wear that all on hand said was perfect for dude ranch wear. Travel and fashion columnists still warned people that a dude ranch vacation required something more than fancy gabardine pants and taffeta western shirts, especially on the Rocky Mountain ranches. There, guests would need wool socks, sweaters, and a warm jacket, even in summer. Arizona, New Mexico, and Southern California ranches were easier to pack for.

Dude ranchers wanted their guests to enjoy themselves, but they rolled their eyes when they saw what magazines recommended and what their visitors sometimes showed up wearing. In early 1949 a number of newspapers touted a western outfit for an Arizona dude ranch vacation, demonstrated by a photo of a slim young woman in linen shorts, cowboy boots, a buckskin vest, and a generous long-sleeved white shirt. Nervous dude ranchers would no doubt have discouraged her from getting on a horse.

A reader photo contest in the *Chicago Tribune* in 1949 featured a photo titled "Dude Ranch Vacationist." An attractive young woman sits on a fence with one leg draped over a saddle. She wears boot-cut, knee-reinforced riding pants, a Levi Strauss satin Rodeo Shirt with the popular "smile" pocket (a shallow pocket formed with two curved rows of piping), and a black cowboy hat. She cradles a shotgun uneasily on her lap as she smiles into the distance. She is clearly a dudine, but at least she could ride a horse in the clothes she wears.[5]

Movies continued to move fashion into western realms and sometimes explained how this happened. In *Two Guys from Texas*, a 1948 remake of *Cowboy from Brooklyn*, song-and-dance men Jack Carson and Dennis Morgan get stranded at a swank Texas dude ranch run by Dorothy Malone. The ranch's interiors are upscale but authentic, as the indoor scenes were filmed at the Thunderbird Dude Ranch in Palm Springs.

Before the men arrive, Malone has a chat with Pete, one of her hands, played by Monte Blue, who had actually cowboyed before starting his career in silents as a stunt man. The rodeo is coming soon to the nearby town, so more guests are arriving at the ranch. Pete says all the townspeople are tired of growing beards, wearing loud shirts, and acting like "sagebrush characters." Malone laughs and replies, "Well, that's what the dudes want and we've gotta give it to 'em."

Carson and Morgan, who made a number of similarly themed buddy movies together, are in complete dude getup in the film's trailer. Carson appears on screen first and, addressing the audience, says, "If you think I look silly wait until you see Dennis."[6]

Wild western clothing also appears in a unique 1947 film in homage to Murray's Negro Dude Ranch. The ranch, which still took in at-risk children in addition to being a vacation spot, had expanded its reach and clientele during

World War II. A Black National Guard unit was stationed in Victorville to protect the region's bridges, but they were not allowed into the whites-only local businesses or the USO. Lela Murray belonged to the city's chamber of commerce and objected to the practice. Someone set up a separate place for the Black soldiers to relax, but that wasn't good enough for Lela and Nolie. They started to welcome all soldiers to the ranch, regardless of color, and because they knew how to entertain, attendance at the USO began to dry up.

This was the first crack in the color barrier. A woman at one of the other dude ranches wrote an article for a union newspaper about seeing both Black and white children at Murray's. People began to write to the ranch to ask about staying, even if they were white, and over the next couple of years the ranch's guest list, as well as its staff, was fully integrated.[7]

Louis Jordan, "The Jukebox King," was a hugely popular saxophonist and bandleader who headed a group called the Tympany Five and recorded "Your Socks Don't Match" in 1944 with Bing Crosby, which cemented his place on the pop charts. He also broke into the movies, and in 1947 he starred in *Lookout Sister*, a hybrid film combining western comedy with a jazz soundtrack. Jordan must have known about Murray's or perhaps visited there, as so many other Black celebrities had done since the ranch opened. Although *Lookout Sister* wasn't filmed at Murray's, the core of its plot was all about Nolie and Lela.

Jordan plays himself as an exhausted bandleader who goes to a sanatorium for some much-needed rest and recuperation. He makes friends with his fellow patients, including a sick boy named Billy who wants to be a cowboy after he gets well. Jordan is moved by the boy's condition and his yearnings. That night, after taking his medication, he dreams that he and his band, now called Two-Gun Jordan & His Jivin' Cowhands, take a plane to Lookout, Arizona, where they go to the H&H dude ranch, which features amenities like a swimming pool and a nightclub.

The ranch's owners are a sister and brother who also take in poor city kids at their ranch for free so they can recover their health, and they can afford only it because of a few generous local donors. But the man who holds their mortgage is threatening to foreclose, so Jordan puts together a jamboree to raise funds for the ranch. After this story line is set up, the film mostly showcases Jordan's music, which threads some western swing melodies among the jazz standards.

Jordan saves both the ranch and Betty, the pretty ranch owner, and then wakes up to realize it had all been a dream. But the plight of the kids reminds him of Billy, so he decides to open his own ranch for boys and girls who need help and want the cowboy life. He calls his manager and tells him to gather up all the stars of radio, stage, and screen and invite them to the opening of his H&H Ranch. As he tells Billy, H&H stands for "Health and Happiness."

Lela and Nolie Murray could not have asked for a better tribute.

As America and the world recovered from the war, dude ranchers kept up with the usual tasks and faced the usual challenges: fixing fence, improving cabins and their plumbing, building new corrals, writing letters to former guests, and the perennial headache of finding good help and a good cook. Young people sent in letters to dude ranches about getting jobs leading trail rides, but no one offered to make beds. On the plus side, railroads asked ranchers to submit data about their guests so they could create better timetables and pricing. Big hotel and restaurant supply houses advertised in *The Dude Rancher* with zippy language about the crowds that would soon show up at dude ranches.

One of them was Carson's in Denver, whose 1947 ad read: "Yes, the DUDES are here. They're expecting the biggest, real, good old-fashioned WESTERN WELCOME they have received since before the war.... You will want, as always, to give them such a royal good time that they and all their potential 'dudes' and 'dudesses' from back East will hot-foot it to your corral next year—and the next." Apparently, the folks at Carson's were not completely up on the lingo, as they did not use the correct term for a female dude.[8]

Sugar and flour rationing finally ended in 1947, and some ranchers used up all their remaining wartime coupons before meager supplies were snatched up by desperate bakers and hungry housewives. Prices rose as foods came off ration, which Mary Shawver noticed with irritation in 1948. She told the readers of *The Dude Rancher* that she had written to some of her old guests, warning them they might have to bring their own beef.

Costs aside, ranchers were no doubt pleased to see that dude ranch culinary specialties had started to move out of the ranch kitchen and into American homes. In December 1947 California newspapers carried a big ad from the Sperry division of General Mills, which made flours under a variety of names. The company ran a photograph of a Mrs. Mathiot, of the Rancho Carmelo dude ranch in California's Carmel Valley, touting the excellence of Sperry Drifted Snow enriched flour for the baked goods she served to her guests. K. D. and Louise Mathiot ran Rancho Carmelo, and Louise was described as the ranch's "hostess" in the ad, whose guests eagerly passed their plates when she brought out the desserts. The ad was headed "Horse Sense Wins Success for Mrs. Mathiot," and this nod to the West gave her credit for both her good judgment in using Sperry Drifted Snow and her stable of prize-winning palominos. Just in time for Christmas, the ad also contained the image of a recipe card with instructions for making "Silver Fruit Pudding," which was a steamed pudding just like "Cowboy in a Sack."

Two years later, a report about the bumper crop of iceberg lettuce in Arizona also prompted some reporters to visit the state's dude ranches, which were open for weary snowbirds who wanted a vacation in the sun. Menus at these places were planned for the easy serving of appetizing foods, including dude ranch mulligan, apparently a favorite at local ranches.

Mulligan stew was a well-known hodgepodge of meat and vegetables whose origin, like that of so many foods, is a little hard to pin down. The most accepted story is that it originated in hobo camps in the early 1900s when the men threw whatever they had into a pot. "Mulligan" might be a nickname for Irish, and the concoction is also sometimes called Irish stew. A reporter who went to Arizona found a recipe at a dude ranch that used the popular name but instead of cut-up pieces of meat, this version was made with meatballs. Served with rice, corn muffins, and iceberg lettuce salad with French dressing, dude ranch mulligan would please the guests in anyone's home.[9]

Pleasing guests in *their* home was always the dude ranchers' way, and as the 1940s came to a close many were pleased to see regulars returning again. Even more delightful were the grown-up children of former guests, who now brought their own kids to stay on the ranch. One tradition from the past also remained, in a quiet way.

Jews were not denied reservations at ranches in the numbers they had been in previous years, and the practice had largely gone away by the late 1940s. But the unwritten rule against Jews at dude ranches did surface occasionally. In January 1947 a group of nine friends placed a "Situation Wanted" ad in the Tucson *Arizona Daily Star*. They desired to work at one of the West's "finer dude ranches" and provided a list of their employment qualifications: riding, singing, dancing, net games, archery, orchestra, billiards, office management, kitchen and dining room management. The most important qualification, which they gave in the ad's first line, was "Gentile."[10]

Dude ranching was still newsworthy, for a variety of reasons. A man named A. H. Floyd placed an ad in the *Reno Gazette-Journal* that read: "Would you like an educated British couple to buttle and cook on your Dude Ranch for six weeks?" Whoever they were, this couple obviously understood that a six-week stretch would just cover the waiting period for a quickie Nevada divorce.

Dudes staying at a ranch near Nogales, Arizona, packed a Geiger counter to take with them on trail rides into the mountains of the former mining town of Washington Camp, where there were rumored deposits of uranium. And Carol Ann Freeman wrote a letter to Santa Claus in December 1949, asking for a "dude ranch suit, size 8, cowboy boots and hat."[11]

Despite this unexpected but welcome publicity, Larry Larom was pessimistic about the business as 1950 opened. Even though he was no longer president of the Dude Ranchers' Association, people still sought his opinion, and he gave an interview in Billings in December 1949. He said he was discouraged by the way the government was encouraging Americans to travel to Europe again. Congress had appropriated $750,000 to advertise overseas travel by plane and ocean liner and had eliminated much of the funding for the Department of the Interior's publicity campaigns about visiting the national parks. Larom was never one to look at the bright side, but his pessimism was unfounded, mostly because the dude ranchers just chose to ignore it.

Faye Snyder and her husband, Don, ran the Sunlight dude ranch outside Cody. In early 1950, as they prepared their place for the summer season, Faye wrote to *The Dude Rancher* about their recent winter vacation and her own hopes for the future. "In spite of comments to the contrary, we are looking for a big year and all indications at the present point to the fact that we are going to have it."[12]

Chapter 13

Faye Snyder's faith in her guests was rewarded as the 1950s got underway. Ranchers continued to host 12,000 to 15,000 dudes each season, even with a rush of tourist trade back to Europe after the war ended. By 1952 the Dude Ranchers' Association estimated that their holdings were valued at $15 million, bringing in annual receipts of approximately $2.5 million. States like Colorado boomed with new industry and new residents after the war, and dude ranches contributed to the rise in tourist dollars.[1]

Americans bought more cars and drove on the ever-expanding interstate highway system during this decade, which was a boon to the motel and auto court business but a headache to dude ranchers. Tourists continued to book shorter stays, and because they saw a lot of scenery on their way to the ranch, they didn't feel they needed to spend weeks in one place to see the mountains or vistas of cacti they had already seen from the road. What had been a guaranteed two-to-three-month visit at a dude ranch during the 1930s now shrank to one or two weeks. Ranchers didn't like it, but they had no choice but to bow to the inevitable, though they still insisted that potential guests make reservations and not just show up expecting to stay in a cabin.

Railroads, dude ranching's partner for decades, also fought the automobile's increasing domination. They supported ranches by offering frequent service and printing up attractive brochures filled with the work of professional photographers. The Chicago, Burlington & Quincy Railroad spent about $50,000 on summer tourist advertising in 1950, and 20 percent of it was about dude ranching. Ranch owners met their guests at train stations and, when available, nearby airports, as airlines like TWA, Northwest Orient, and Western started to fly short hops to popular vacation destinations, and they also advertised in *The Dude Rancher*.[2]

The relationship between dude ranches and trains had gone both ways for decades. Not only did rail lines make visiting ranches easier, but the spread of dude ranching also helped railroads increase their business. Better train service into more locations brought more people to the West. Larry Larom believed that dude ranches were money makers for their counties and states. In a speech to the Billings, Montana, Rotary Club in 1952, he said he knew of 364 prominent and wealthy men who had settled in Montana and Wyoming after spending time on a dude ranch.[3]

But many ranchers relied too much on others to advertise their places, expecting that the old model of personal contacts back East would keep the dudes coming. But these efforts did not reach people who planned their trips with a road map and not a train schedule. Enthusiastic new westerners also tried their hand at running dude ranches, starting up businesses that quickly failed, and some old-timers also shut their doors. But the ranches that did more than just survive found that, as usual, the only way to keep going was to adapt.

A new generation of tourists wanted the real western experience that dude ranches promised, but they did not want to be uncomfortable in the process. They demanded amenities that would have brought out a horse laugh from dude ranchers of an earlier era. Walter Nye had predicted this back in 1947, when he was quoted in a newspaper article titled "Roughing It De Luxe." Tourists wanted to have all the conveniences of modern life and the luxuries they had come to expect at hotels. And while Nye didn't mention this, the reporter who interviewed him said that he no doubt thought dude ranch proprietors should have cold cream for sunburn, and "various soothing ointments for some muscles and those certain patches of epidermis which come in the most violent contact with a cowboy saddle."[4]

Horseback riding, the backbone of dude ranching, was also evolving. Trail rides used to take all day, so that the dudes could see the diversity of landscape and wildlife that surrounded the ranch. The newer riders of the 1950s were from the booming middle class, and unlike the monied classes who made up the bulk of dude ranch guests over the previous decades, not all of them grew up knowing how to ride. Spending all day on a horse did not always convince them to repeat the activity (and they certainly needed the soothing ointments). Pack trips, once a staple at Rocky Mountain ranches, were also shortened for people unused to camping.

Larry Larom saw another side of the trail ride. In his Rotary Club speech, he blamed western movies and rodeo as the "two curses" of dude ranchers because they gave people the impression that all travel by horseback was done at a dead run. He told his audience, no doubt made up of men used to riding at all kinds of speeds, that one of the most disastrous things ranchers were facing was dudes who wanted to forgo loping for galloping. His complaint was about the new versus the experienced rider, whose view of the West had been shaped by popular culture and not training.

One dude ranch near Encampment, Wyoming, bought a fleet of Jeeps for its guests to use. They weren't a replacement for horses but a way for fishermen to get to rivers and streams over roads that were too rough for their own car. The assumption was that these men were not comfortable taking a horse into a wilderness area for their day's fishing. Guests could also take the Jeeps to nearby scenic vistas or historic sites. And in 1958 the owner of the Falconberry Ranch, on Idaho's Loon Creek in the Salmon-Challis National Forest, bought a Cessna 180 plane to bring guests and supplies to his inaccessible dude/cattle ranch.[5]

These offerings were rare. For the most part, dude ranchers kept up with what had always worked and made some inevitable improvements, such as private bathrooms, swimming pools, and carpeting, irritating the old-time guests who decried these "dude" comforts. But successful ranchers kept their focus on guests and their needs. Margaret and Richard Hickey managed Rancho Linda Vista in Oracle, Arizona, in the winter, while their summer dude ranch was the Diamond L Bar near Missoula, and Margaret wrote to *The Dude Rancher* about her experiences with dudes in both places. "When one is a Dude Rancher his life is pretty much devoted to seeing that his guests have the best time possible. Our ranches may vary as to locale, size, accommodations, activities, and so forth, but there is no difference when it comes to giving service and seeing that each guest does the things he wants to do and is made happy, so that he will want to come back year after year."[6]

Dude ranchers worried about competition, about the crisis of the car trip, and other issues, but they were cheered by how dude ranching continued to play out in the larger culture. Some ranches had started to offer square dancing as the occasional evening entertainment, and musicians took note. Texan Adolph Hofner was a pioneer of western swing in the 1930s and led bands with a variety of names, until hitting on San Antonians. In 1950 the group recorded an album titled *Dude Ranch Dances*, which included standards such as "Cotton Eyed Joe" and "Little Brown Jug." The notes on the back of the album cover credit dude ranches with the new popularity of country dancing at parties in city living rooms.

The tourists now taking to the road bought a lot of postcards at gas stations, motels, and drugstores to send to friends and to keep as souvenirs. One of the most popular, and most imitated today, is the famous "Greetings From" series of linen postcards featuring large 3D letters spelling out the names of America's states. These were created in 1931 by German-born printer Curt Teich, who capitalized on the already-solid popularity of postcards and was inspired by similar cards he had seen in his native Germany.

In the 1950s he made a series of ten "Dude Ranch Comics" postcards, which were sold in towns and sometimes at the ranches themselves. These cards were edgier than the cheery "Greetings" postcards, featuring the foibles of dudes, or the potential for romance at a ranch. Women were usually the focus of the cards, and not always in a flattering way. In one card a woman dressed in a diaphanous lounging outfit and peekaboo sandals reclines on a bed, reading a magazine titled *Western Stories* while snacking from a box of chocolates. Outside her window, two smiling cowboys lean on a corral and watch the woman at her task.

Another shows a cute young woman in a short, fringed skirt, cowboy boots, cowhide vest, and leather gauntlets sitting on a very spiny cactus with a pained look on her face. Off in the distance is a bull with something red caught on one of its horns. The card is captioned, "The cactus looked so pretty / The bull appeared so tame / But since I met the both of them / I'll never be the same." Other cards show women in equally precarious situations, including being manhandled by a cowboy and being the focus of howls of cowboy laughter for wearing chaps with no pants underneath.[7] Dude ranchers, especially women, did not record how they felt about these cards, but their popularity during this decade means that some dudes, at least, thought they were funny and perhaps even true to their own experience.

Ranchers had to accept that attitudes toward vacations and toward dudes themselves were shifting, but there was no question that the dude ranch was still relevant. During the 1950s leisure locations with no relation to dude ranches at all started using the term to describe their businesses. One was the Singing Spur Ranch, a "dude ranch for trailers" that opened in Phoenix in 1950. Travel trailers were another popular form of on-the-road tourism during this decade. Snowbirds who brought their trailers to the Singing Spur in the winter could also bring their horses, though there were also horses on hand to rent. The owners hired wranglers to teach rope tricks to the part-time residents.

The Burnt Mountain–Circle 8 Dude Ranch in California's Yucca Valley was actually a motel with room for travel trailers. The owners of the San Bernardino County desert locale also cashed in on its tenuous western theme with a small stable of horses that people could rent and ride on nearby trails. They also offered special themed rides and, in 1958, a gymkhana, which was held the day after its Halloween party. Later that year Burnt Mountain started holding waltz contests on its large patio and awarded a special breakfast ride to the winning couple.

The promotions these places used to drum up business inspired real dude ranches to do the same thing, and ranchers all over the West partnered with local and national companies to offer vacations as promotional prizes. The company that made the popular kids' sneakers Red Ball Jets, for example, ran a jingle contest in 1952, and the five girls and five boys who wrote the winning tunes won a two-week stay at the Shadow Mountain dude ranch in Colorado.

The Dixie Dude Ranch in Bandera, Texas, offered a honeymoon stay for the winners of a local "Hillbilly Wedding" contest. And Wylie's Dude Ranch near Lewisville, Texas, hosted students from Boyd High School for their Senior Day celebration, where they swam, played ball, went horseback riding, and danced into the evening.[8]

Successful dude ranches looked at these marketing efforts and began to rethink how they got the word out, but they didn't jettison what still worked. Advertising in newspapers and magazines was expensive, but a strong relationship with a travel agent in a nearby town or the largest city in the region went a long way toward finding potential guests. Personal letters and chatty newsletters to former guests fell into the "personal contact" category, which remained a cost-effective method of booking repeat business and increasing word of mouth. But there was always room for new ideas.

Northern ranches closed during the winters and owners took their own vacations, often to warm locales in Southern California, Texas, and Arizona. Nan and Harry Hart, who owned the Dot Lazy S Dot dude ranch in Melville, Montana, spent the winter of 1952 at a golf resort in La Jolla, California. Nan Hart wrote a letter to the renamed "Women's Division" page of *The Dude Rancher* and told a story about helping her fellow guests understand what a dude ranch was.

During conversations at cocktail hour and other leisure activities at the club, Hart and her husband mentioned that they ran a dude ranch in Montana. They were always surprised to see looks of incredulity on people's faces, and as Hart put it, it was as though she'd told them they raised baby pandas in their spare time. Apparently, people in La Jolla did not know that dude ranches existed in the far north, as they'd come across only the sunnier places in Southern California and the Southwest. So, Hart went to work to change their minds.

She had a bandanna with a lively print of cattle brands all over it, and one afternoon as the couple were entertaining guests in their living room, Hart picked up a needle and thread and began to casually repair the scarf's frayed hem. One of the visitors asked her what the design was and Hart said the individual marks were cattle brands from Montana and Wyoming. She was flabbergasted when the woman said she didn't know what a cattle brand was. The Harts happened to have a copy of *Montana Stockgrower* on their coffee table, which listed all the registered brands in the state. Hart showed the book to her visitors and their education began.[9]

As they increased the volume and type of their advertising efforts in the 1950s, dude ranchers got a boost from new currents in American culture. One of them was television.

TV was a primitive and scarce form of entertainment in the 1940s but began its commercial rise and spread into the mainstream by the end of the decade. News and entertainment filled airwaves for those who were able to afford a set and lived near enough to stations that broadcast early shows. At first, TV series reflected popular radio dramas, as well as their formats, and many of the earliest programs were westerns.

Shows starring Hopalong Cassidy, the Lone Ranger, Gene Autry, and Roy Rogers debuted between 1949 and 1951. Television executives aimed these entertainments at juvenile audiences, but it was soon clear that grown-ups were also tuning in. Fledgling networks developed other series with adult-oriented plots, and from 1951 to 1959 western titles filled the airwaves. Among the most popular were *Sky King, Death Valley Days, Annie Oakley, Fury, The Life and Legend of Wyatt Earp, Cheyenne, Gunsmoke, Tombstone Territory, Wanted: Dead or Alive, Bat Masterson, Bronco, Lawman, The Rifleman, Laramie,*

Rawhide, and *Bonanza*. In its March 30, 1959, issue *Time* magazine reported that eight of the top ten shows on television were "horse operas."[10]

Dude ranching rarely if ever showed up in these shows. One of them was featured in a 1952 episode of *Death Valley Days* called "The Lost Pegleg Mine." A dude at the DeCourcey Guest Ranch tries to find a rumored gold mine discovered by a DeCourcey ancestor and in the process romances and wins the owner's daughter. The tenderfoot dude, who dubs his saddle a "chafing dish," is transformed into a man who matches the West.

These popular series featured cowboys, ranchers, marshals, gunfights on dusty streets, cattle drives, schoolmarms, saloon girls, bank robbers, and chases on fast horses. Their classic themes strengthened the pull of the western in American culture, and this reinforced the value of the dude ranch experience without mentioning dude ranches at all. However, Hopalong Cassidy himself touted the dude ranch in an interview in 1950 when he was making an appearance in New York. "Vacations at a dude ranch, with their modern conveniences, still give dudes all the pleasure of comfort plus the attraction of the healthiest outdoor sport—horseback riding."

Celebrity publicity was helpful, but sometimes new visitors to dude ranches were a little disappointed that they didn't experience the West they saw on the small screen. They did not expect to see gunfights or saloons but hoped to see vast herds of cattle and hear the jangling of spurs. Unless they booked a stay at a working cattle ranch, they were out of luck. But this attitude was rare, because dude ranchers strove to maintain the western flair they lived with every day.

Western ranchers fumed at the growing list of dude ranches in eastern states, especially in New York and Pennsylvania, which they saw as a threat to the authenticity of the original dude ranch. The DRA and regional organizations fired up their publicity machines and placed articles in newspapers and magazines, in addition to sponsoring more promotions. One article in the *Chicago Tribune* summed up their efforts, stating that there was no fakery about *western* dude ranches, because the setting and activities were real, and they even had real Indians to entertain guests, a practice that had not died out in the 1930s. In 1958, the Colorado Dude Ranch Association put out a press release to papers all over the United States, and the opening paragraph summed up its entire argument: "East is East, but only the West can offer an authentic dude ranch vacation."[11]

One rarely tapped market was children. Parents had brought their kids to dude ranches for decades, but the activities on offer were geared mostly toward adults. This was not a problem because horseback riding was a thrill for children and they were usually exhausted at the end of the day and didn't need much more stimulation. In the 1950s, however, more middle-class families could afford to take dude ranch vacations, which meant more kids on hand. Ranchers who either hosted children, or wanted to, made adjustments to their structures and their schedules, which also benefited the adults. Swimming pools were a big draw, and a few ranches even relaxed their rules against alcohol, hosting happy hours in rooms with colorful names like "The Saloon." There, they instructed their bartenders to learn how to make the two most popular children's drinks: the Shirley Temple and the Roy Rogers.

Television shows like *Spin and Marty* were one of the reasons that kids were more interested in dude ranching. This series ran from 1955 to 1957 as part of the popular *Mickey Mouse Club*. The story was set on the Triple R Ranch, a hybrid dude ranch and summer camp for boys, and the adventures of the main characters, as well as visitors from other ranches, reflected the wholesome western themes that also filled the scripts of Hopalong Cassidy's TV show.

The company that made the popular Madame Alexander dolls also got into the act. In 1955 it introduced a doll dressed for a visit to a dude ranch in denim pants, plaid shirt, cowboy boots, and a straw hat. And continuing a tradition that started in the 1940s, companies that made paper dolls regularly released books of dude ranch designs, with classic western dresses, shirts, pants, and accessories for cutouts of both boys and girls.

Ranchers also took the opportunity to interest kids in dude ranching with their promotions. The North Hollywood, California, newspaper *Valley Times* regularly ran a subscription contest for its paperboys and in 1954 started offering a stay at the Ride-N-Rock Ranch in Scottsdale, Arizona, as one of the rewards. In 1956 the paper added an exciting new prize for the boy who sold the most subscriptions: a trip to Disneyland.

Walt Disney's Magic Kingdom opened in 1955 and recalled both the simplicity of Disney's hometown of Marceline, Missouri, and the splash of the world's fairs of the early twentieth century. He wanted his visitors to have an immersive experience, so he envisioned a collection of "lands" that would plunge them into unique worlds. He was very attuned to currents in culture, and one of his themed attractions was "Frontierland." However, Disney was not the first to use this concept in an amusement park.

In the 1940s clever entrepreneurs started opening western-themed resorts or re-created frontier towns in scattered places around the country. Walter and Cordelia Knott opened a roadside berry stand in the 1920s in Buena Park, just five miles from Disneyland's future home, Anaheim. They started serving fried chicken, biscuits, and pie in their tearoom, which was so popular the couple decided to build an additional tourist attraction nearby. In 1940 they opened the Ghost Town. People kept coming, and Walter renamed the entire site Knott's Berry Farm in 1947, adding a railroad, a saloon, a schoolhouse, and a vaudeville theater.

The Last Frontier Hotel opened just outside Las Vegas in 1942, and in 1947 the developers built the nearby Last Frontier Village, where hotel visitors could wander the streets of a town that looked like the setting for an episode of *Gunsmoke*. In 1952 Frontier Town opened in North Hudson, New York, about one hundred miles north of Albany.

All these places tapped into the fascination for the West that also fueled the work of movie and television producers. And while there are no available statistics about how Disneyland and other parks added to the lure of the dude ranch, their success reflects the fact that cowboys, Indians, and gunfights were still a cultural force. These trends, shows, and tourist experiences became popular just as the West was becoming tamer, less mysterious, and more traveled, mirroring the expansion of dude ranching in the early twentieth century as the truly wild West had started to fade.

Costume designers for television shows took cues from the increasingly elaborate western wear sported by entertainers, and how it continued to be associated with dudes. Stores on the larger ranches and shops in nearby towns still stocked satin shirts, side-zip gabardine pants, and plaids for both men and women. But the 1950s saw the rise of new patterns and the use of metallic threads for sparkly accents on basic western shirts, which also showed up on store shelves. Designers made similar styles for both men and women, adding darts to women's shirts to make them more feminine. Dudines and the women who ran dude ranches also started wearing a dress that had been popular in New Mexico and Arizona since the 1920s and had been influenced by both Mexican and Native American styles.

It went by a variety of names, such as fiesta dress or patio dress, but it was more commonly known as a "squaw" dress. It had a full, crinkly skirt and a cinched waist and often featured rickrack in contrasting colors sewn in horizontal lines. Designers and marketing executives latched on to the design because it fed into the popularity of southwestern Indian jewelry and rugs. They then gave it a name that also came from portrayals of Indians in film and on television. The squaw dress was one of the western-wear designs that also migrated home from the dude ranch and into suburban backyard patio parties.

Fewer films were made about dude ranching during the 1950s. When a movie took place on a dude ranch it was usually because the filmmaker just needed somewhere for the action to happen, much like the films of the 1920s and early 1930s. The people on these ranches, even the dudes, wore less gaudy clothing, which signaled to viewers that their dude activities were not central to the plot.

One of these was *Lightning Strikes Twice*, from 1951, starring Ruth Roman, Mercedes McCambridge, and Richard Todd. It's a romance/film noir in jeans and snap-front shirts, and the dude ranch setting is faithful to the original novel, *A Man without Friends*, written by Margaret Echard. But all the story needed was an isolated location, so choosing a dude ranch was a nod, at least, to the book and to ranching's usefulness in moving a story forward.

Foxfire, from 1955, starred Jane Russell and Jeff Chandler and was based on the novel by popular novelist Anya Seton. Though the book's original southwestern mining town locale also made it into the film, the dude ranch scenes at the beginning and end of the movie were new to the script. They serve as a backstory for the main female character, a wealthy easterner who is traveling with her mother out West. They stay at the fictional La Paz Guest Ranch in Arizona, which is actually the Apple Valley Inn in Victorville.

The women in these films were not the spunky dude ranch daughters or western gals who had roles in *The Dude Ranger*, *Out West with the Hardys*, or *Cowboy from Brooklyn*. This reflects a larger trend in moviemaking in the years after the war, when an emphasis on domesticity and rebuilding families transformed the way women were portrayed on-screen as well as at home.

While the women of the Dude Ranchers' Association had always embraced their role as the mistress of the ranch, or sometimes the hostess, they knew it was not a subordinate one. Their own family life was one of the reasons the dudes felt at home during their stays. The tone of the Women's Division section of *The Dude Rancher* shifted in the 1950s, however. It began to resemble the pages of national women's magazines, with chatty articles about great vacation spots, family news, and more recipes.

Some of these were updated meals from the past. The recipe for "Cowboy in a Sack," first published in 1943, appeared again in the July 1955 issue. It still had suet and was baked in a coffee can, but dates and chopped citron were added to the fruit mix. The biggest change from the previous decade was the accompanying sauce. In 1943, ranch cooks recommended hard sauce, made with whiskey. Now, the recommendation was to serve it with nonalcoholic lemon sauce. Perhaps this was a nod to the children who now sat at their dinner tables.[12]

Some ranches started to offer special outdoor meals served from a chuck wagon, especially on Saturday nights. This mobile kitchen, familiar to any viewer of western films and TV shows, dated back over a century to the days of the early cattle drives. Ranch owners outfitted wagons and hitched up horses for excursions into the desert or to flat riverside plains, where dudes would eat outdoors like cowboys. The concept became very popular in the 1950s, and diners and restaurants all over the country were named or renamed the Chuck Wagon. In 1956 the Burlington Northern Railroad added a "Vista-Dome" to its Denver Zephyr passenger train and installed a café called the Chuck Wagon. Its glass serving plates featured a print of a chuck wagon and a cattle brand with the letters *DZ* (for Denver Zephyr), and the brands of Colorado dude ranches along the rim.

But even with the more domestic tone of *The Dude Rancher*, women could still come to dude ranches and enjoy a rugged vacation. There was no change in the way ranchers treated their female guests, and any woman who wanted to take a multiday pack trip, help the wranglers bring in the horses for the day's ride, or practice roping was welcome to do so. Women ranchers had always been able to navigate how their guests wanted to experience a dude ranch vacation and never thought that dudines needed to be treated any differently from dudes.

There was no shortage of sprightly women on dude ranches in print, however. One was nurse Cherry Ames, who was featured in a series of twenty-seven novels between the 1940s and the 1960s. Cherry is Nancy Drew in a white uniform and cap, and she meets with mystery and danger everywhere she takes on a nursing job. In 1953 author Julie Tatham published *Cherry Ames: Dude Ranch Nurse* and placed her protagonist at the Twin Mounds Ranch near Tucson, where she takes care of cranky asthmatic dudes and helps the owner's daughter find a lost fortune.

A younger dudine is Trixie Belden, heroine of another series of novels in which she also solves mysteries. In *Trixie Belden and Mystery in Arizona*, she and her friends vacation at a dude ranch and end up having to take over the cooking and cleaning when the staff mysteriously disappears. This book is nearly unreadable today for its racist and sexist language, but the dude ranch details come through.

In 1953 Bill and Barbara Hooton took a vacation out West and decided to throw away their comfortable life in Manhattan and buy a dude ranch near Santa Fe, New Mexico. Barbara Hooton collaborated with Patrick Dennis, author of *Auntie Mame*, to write up their misadventures and growing love for ranching in the book *Guestward Ho!*, which was published in 1956. The book was a hit, and Hollywood took note in 1959, optioning the story for a new TV series to run during the 1960–61 season. Vivian Vance, who had played Ethel Mertz on *I Love Lucy*, was considered for the lead role, but that fell through, and the ABC network hired Joanne Dru and Mark Miller to play Barbara and Bill Hooton.

The show debuted in September 1960, and though it ran only one season, its gentle comedy gave a big boost to the image of dude ranching. Ranchers entered the 1960s with enthusiasm, watching their guests enjoy activities both traditional and new.

Most of dude ranching's founders had passed away by the time the new decade opened, but their ranches lived on. Willis and Alden Eaton died in 1929 and 1937, respectively. Dick Randall retired and sold the OTO to a new owner in 1934 and passed away in 1957. Struthers Burt sold his shares in the Bar B C in 1937 and died in 1954. Mary Shawver, who finally retired from Holm Lodge but continued to be a force for women in dude ranching, died in 1958. The indomitable Larry Larom was still firmly in charge of Valley Ranch, but he would sell his place to a former guest in 1969 and die in 1973.

Dude ranchers felt these losses deeply, but the ranching business itself was on solid ground.

Chapter 14

The 1958 season was the most profitable on record, and in the spring of 1960 the Dude Ranchers' Association reported that bookings for the summer were up 15 to 25 percent over the 1958 numbers. Ranchers needed to keep advertising for the employees they needed and didn't have too much trouble finding them.

One man placed an ad in the Palm Springs *Desert Sun* in 1960 claiming to be an expert chef in both continental and American cuisine, with forty-five years of experience behind him. He hoped to find a job in an exclusive club, resort, hotel, or dude ranch. Kenneth Johnson, a thirty-four-year-old unmarried cowboy, advertised for a full-time dude ranch job in the *Jackson Hole Courier* in 1965. He lived in Amarillo but would travel anywhere for work, and his experience included wrangling cattle at summer camps, working in riding stables, and a lifetime with cattle and horses. And the Idaho Department of Employment consistently had jobs on its books for dude ranch cooks.[1]

Ranch popularity got a boost from a few movies, but it was nothing like the number of films released in previous decades. In the early spring of 1962 Warner Bros. shot portions of the film *Spencer's Mountain* on and around the Turner family's Triangle X dude ranch near Moose, Wyoming. The movie told the story of a family and its patriarch, set against the Tetons, and was based on the novel by Earl Hamner Jr., who went on to write the classic 1970s television series *The Waltons*. The premiere was held in Jackson Hole in May 1963 and was covered with glee in the pages of *The Dude Rancher*.

Two years later the dude ranch got a makeover for Elvis Presley. In *Tickle Me*, he plays a singing rodeo star who takes a wrangler job at what he thinks is a dude ranch called the Circle Z, but it is really a "fat farm" where beautiful young women go to get in shape. Advertising copy read: "Elvis Presley as a singing, swinging wrangler on a Dude Ranch For Girls!" And in that same year, Harve Presnell and Connie Francis starred in *When the Boys Meet the Girls*, a remake of the 1943 film *Girl Crazy* but with the dude ranch details of the original Broadway play.

Dude ranches would not be a major plot point in film for another thirty years, but this did not mean they disappeared from the entertainment world. Television had started to build stories around dude ranching in the late 1950s, before *Guestward Ho!* hit TV screens in 1960.

A TV series based on *The Thin Man* films from the 1930s and 1940s debuted in 1957 and starred Peter Lawford and Phyllis Kirk as the famous Nick and Nora Charles. In 1958 an episode titled "The Departed Doctor" saw the duo traveling to a dude ranch to solve the mystery of a missing doctor. In 1956 viewers watched the first season of *Sheriff of Cochise*. Though it sounds like a western, this was actually a contemporary crime drama about a sheriff in Cochise County, Arizona. The character was later promoted and the series title changed to *U.S. Marshal*.

In December 1960 two episodes featured dude ranch themes. In the first, a reporter accuses the owner of a dude ranch of being a dope smuggler. And in the second, the sheriff investigates crooked card games at a dude ranch. Whether they knew it or not, television producers and scriptwriters were following in the film tradition of using dude ranches as sites where crimes and criminals are hidden and then discovered, and where law and order prevail, just as in the Old West. Tom Mix, Hoot Gibson, and Gene Autry would recognize these themes anywhere.

The word "dude," in its original definition as someone from back East who isn't quite tough enough for the West, appeared in the 1962 film *The Man Who Shot Liberty Valance*. Lee Marvin's evil character Liberty Valance taunts eastern lawyer Ransom Stoddard throughout the film by calling him "dude." When they face off in a classic western shoot-out in the town of Shinbone, "dude" is one of the last words Valance says before he's shot dead.

Dude ranching met contemporary culture in 1963 with an episode of *The Jetsons* titled "Dude Planet." The futuristic animated series was a typical drama about a nuclear family, but with space-age furnishings and transportation. In this story, homemaker Jane Jetson is feeling run down, so her doctor tells her to take a relaxing vacation at a dude ranch. She goes by herself to the Beta Bar Ranch on planet Beta III, leaving her husband to run the house and manage the children, which is the main focus of the story. But this plot has some interesting elements.

Jane had to leave Earth to find a dude ranch, which echoes how far people still had to travel to take their ranching vacations in real life. The fact that the Beta Bar is on a different planet means that a dude ranch, at least as understood by the writers and animators, was such a unique place that Jane had to get into a spaceship to find one. Dude ranchers always emphasized that their ranches were worlds of their own. Jane Jetson discovered that time was different at the Beta Bar Ranch, and the past was a place to be.

The women's page of *The Dude Rancher* was renamed "Mrs. Dude Rancher" in the mid-1960s. Its articles about women's lives always emphasized that it was the wife, working behind the scenes, who kept the ranch's wheels spinning. Dolly Turner was one of them.

She was a widow raising her children in Arizona, and in 1966 she married a handsome cowboy from Durango who had started up a dude ranch nearby. Dolly and her kids moved to the ranch and she jumped into the life without any training or even any idea of what the challenges would be.

As her predecessors had long ago discovered, good cooks were well worth their salary, despite their frequent personality quirks. Dolly hired one cook who turned out to be a big drinker, and she had to frequently reprimand him for using foul language around the girls who worked in the kitchen and served at table. One night during an after-dinner game of charades in the main lodge, he came into the room and told Dolly he needed to talk to her. She followed him into the kitchen, and he said he was quitting because someone had used his towel. She said, "Frank, the clean towels are downstairs in the linen closet, go help yourself." He replied, "I warned them to not touch my towel and they did, and I told them if they ever did it again, I was out of here." The staff was so relieved when he left that they offered to fill in with all his duties until Dolly found a replacement.

Music was a big part of life at the ranch, and after lunch and dinner Dolly's husband played the guitar while everyone sang, and on Friday nights the staff put on a variety show. The ranch also hired a square dance caller for regular dance nights.

Dolly's life as a Mrs. Dude Rancher mirrored the lives of so many other ranching women. The visiting couples and families were mostly delightful, sometimes a waitress or housekeeper fell in love with a wrangler, and the only horses Dolly rode were the ones they couldn't put the guests on. She and everyone she knew who owned a dude ranch "worked their butt off," and she made this clear one day to a man who asked for her advice.

He had purchased a piece of property in another part of Colorado and wanted to start a dude ranch. From the beginning of their conversation, Dolly knew he was in trouble. She asked him why he wanted to run a ranch, and he said it was because he had always wanted to be a cowboy. Then she asked him what he would do if the sewer backed up or the well went dry, and he said he had plenty of money and would hire people to solve any problems. Dolly wished him luck and knew he wouldn't make it.

He didn't. His ranch lasted barely three months, his marriage fell apart, and Dolly wasn't surprised. "You don't just dress up with pleats down the middle of your pockets and clean Levi's on and become a successful dude rancher. You've got to get your hands dirty, or you have no business being there."

Dolly and her husband eventually divorced and she left Colorado. But she never forgot the other ranchers she met and made friends with. To her, they were the "cream of the crop."[2]

Some long-lived ranches were still doing well, but a few closed in the 1960s because their founders died, their families couldn't keep them going, or the original vision for the place had been lost. The Double Diamond Ranch in Wyoming and the Rancho Linda Vista and Monte Vista dude ranches in Arizona were among the casualties. The "For Sale" columns in newspapers all over the West ran many ads for dude ranches, with language such as: "It's small but it's good. 160 acre mountain dude ranch, ¼ mile wide by 1 mile long. With good fishing stream and . . . six bedroom modern cabin with large fireplace in lobby."[3]

When the tumultuous year of 1968 opened and unfolded, institutions all over the country found themselves unable to resist the forces of change. But dude ranches still lived in a bubble of popularity thanks in great part to the efforts of the Dude Ranchers' Association to keep on top of trends and world events, and individual ranches' outreach to former guests for the all-important word-of-mouth advertising.

In April of that year, students protesting racism at Columbia University, as well as its support of the war in Vietnam, garnered international headlines when they occupied the campus. In May, similar protests erupted in Paris. On top of this generational and political turbulence came the assassinations of

Martin Luther King Jr. and Robert Kennedy, and the uproar at the Democratic National Convention in Chicago.

Dude ranchers took note but for the most part felt insulated from the conflict. Conna May, now the executive secretary of the DRA, thought that if unrest escalated in Paris, people might be willing to leave the country for an American vacation. And predictions of a very hot summer could also send vacationers out to a cool Rocky Mountain dude ranch. Grayson Kirk, president of Columbia University, had spent time at Larry Larom's Valley Ranch, and Larom wrote to him in April, sending sympathies for the continuing struggles at the university. Kirk replied that the situation was fluid and he couldn't make any summer plans, but it was helpful to remember the healthy, restful climate of Wyoming.[4]

Larom and other dude ranchers realized that they had to change some of their long-established policies about accepting Jews and racial minorities. Stricter government regulation of the hospitality industry meant that overt racism, at least, was no longer acceptable. Cultural taboos were slowly changing, too. In August 1968 the Single Adult Club of Victoria, Texas, booked a weekend stay at the Dixie Dude Ranch in Bandera. Hosting individuals or groups for just a weekend was unthinkable just a couple of decades earlier, but ranchers were also facing competition from airlines. Middle-class families who were finally able to pay for a dude ranch vacation could now afford the airfare to exciting places like Disneyland and Hawaii.

Changing their business model was now old hat for dude ranchers and paid off for many of them. The Colorado Dude and Guest Ranch Association reported that 1968 was the most successful year in its history, in both tourist numbers and revenue. The average stay was about a week, which was now the norm for most dude ranches, the exception being wealthy dudes who still made a multiweek ranch vacation part of their yearly plans. In addition, the children of longtime guests now brought their own families to the dude ranches they had visited decades earlier. Repeat business was still one of the backbones of dude ranching.[5]

Journalists took note of how ranches were adjusting to changes in American leisure activities. One writer thought the true dude ranch was long gone because the owners had succumbed to their guests' desires for swimming pools, tennis courts, and golf courses. At these places, horses and cowboys were incidental and mostly for atmosphere. Dude ranchers begged to disagree. Just because guests stayed for only a week didn't mean that their business was any less authentic. No one booked a vacation at a dude ranch just to go swimming.

Journalists may have felt that the classic dude ranch was becoming obsolete because interest in the West itself was fading into the sunset, especially on television. By the mid-1960s most of the western TV series such as *The Life and Legend of Wyatt Earp, Bat Masterson,* and *Rawhide* were no longer on the air. Viewers wanted to see more family dramas and shows featuring teenagers, the new driver of American culture. Cowboys and Indians couldn't compete with *Gidget* or *American Bandstand*. The film *When the Boys Meet the Girls* was shown frequently on TV in the 1960s and 1970s, not because of its dude ranch subplot, but because it featured music by the British duo Herman's Hermits. Hollywood took note and began to film westerns that featured families and their stories, such as *The Big Valley, The High Chaparral,* and *Daniel Boone.* Some people objected to westerns because of their violence, and these softer series tried to address the problem.

America's acceptance of the simple black-and-white morality of the traditional western crumbled as the Vietnam War dragged on. Many young people viewed men like John Wayne and the cowboy characters he and others portrayed as destructive forces. Two series, *Gunsmoke* and *Bonanza,* survived into the 1970s because they already had a deep viewer base, but they went off the air as shows with urban settings took over in popularity and numbers.

What did this mean for dude ranching? The industry and the individual ranchers resisted the temptation to de-emphasize the western aspects of their enterprises. Even with swimming pools and tennis courts on their properties, dude ranchers dug in and continued to advertise their cowboys, horses, cattle herds, and classic western decor. But it wasn't for show. Ranchers really lived the life the dudes paid to participate in. Derogatory stories about dude ranching's irrelevance just rolled off their collective backs, no matter how strange they were.

In 1972, for example, Mao Zedong's Communist government in China opened special schools where cadres of elite young people performed hard manual labor, so they would not be tempted to form a leadership class and eventually challenge Mao's authority. American reporters who talked to these cadres and watched them work and study reported that "the six-month term is something like a long stay at a dude ranch for some of them." The idea was that spending time on a dude ranch, while a break away from real life, was neither strenuous nor unpleasant.[6]

Ranchers took advantage of advertising opportunities during the bicentennial in 1976. The National Park Service commissioned a play called *Our Living History*, which was performed at Grand Teton National Park that summer. The performance showcased characters from Wyoming history speaking about their lives, one of whom was a dude rancher.

Dude ranchers also piggybacked on tourism promotion in general. An advertisement titled "77 Great Things to See and Do in Colorado This Year," which ran in papers all over the West, included "Be tall in the saddle at a dude ranch." And Jackson Hole's Pioneer Days celebration featured the return of dude ranch events at the annual rodeo, which included calf riding for kids aged ten and under, and musical chairs with horses for teens.[7]

Dude ranching picked up steam as a television plot device as the end of the 1970s drew near. In 1977 *Charlie's Angels* traveled to the Sunwest Dude Ranch to find out whether one of the guests was a killer. The sixth season opener of *Happy Days* in September 1978 was a three-part story set on a Colorado dude ranch owned by Marion Cunningham's uncle. A more dubious distinction arrived with the debut of the adult film *Love Ranch* in 1978, described as a movie about a western dude ranch for women who "engage in activities more than riding horses."[8]

Celebrities had always taken vacations at dude ranches and usually asked the owners to keep their visits quiet so they could enjoy their time. Barbara Stanwyck and Robert Taylor, Cary Grant, and Clark Gable had stayed at ranches as far back as the 1940s. This flurry of interest had died down by the 1970s, but a few big names still made their way West. One of them was Alice Roosevelt Longworth, Theodore Roosevelt's oldest daughter.

Longworth was an outspoken, conservative, and somewhat controversial figure, and like her father, she enjoyed spending time in the Rockies. In August 1969, at the age of eighty-five, she arrived in Cody for her fourth Wyoming vacation, staying at Faye and Don Snyder's Sunlight Ranch about forty-five miles from town. Faye Snyder remembered her as quite a character. In an oral history, Snyder recalled the day her daughter answered the office phone. "Sally came running up and she said, 'Mom, the president wants to talk to Mrs. Longworth, where is she?' And so she went down and got her, and sure enough on the kitchen telephone in the help's dining room . . . she talked to the president. 'Oh, hi Dick! How are you? What do you want?'"

Dick, of course, was Richard Nixon.[9]

A more relevant star for the 1970s was Paul McCartney. He and his wife, Linda, took a vacation at the Tanque Verde Guest Ranch outside Tucson in December 1978, where they mingled easily with guests, didn't mind posing for photographs, and enjoyed their horseback rides.

Ranches loped along comfortably in the 1970s. Some of them had been selling souvenirs to their dudes for many years, and other ranch owners saw how successful they were and added items like ashtrays, glasses, trays, and matchbooks to the shelves of their small shops. However, some older ranchers sold their properties when they couldn't operate them anymore. Alice and Ken Gleason, who had opened the Circle 8 Guest Ranch in Choteau, Montana, in 1930, sold their place to the Nature Conservancy in 1978.

In that same year, *Esquire* magazine published an article that introduced Americans to a concept and a catchphrase that would sweep the country and give a big boost to dude ranching: the urban cowboy.

Aaron Latham wrote a story titled "The Ballad of the Urban Cowboy: America's Search for True Grit," which *Esquire* published in its September 1978 issue. Latham had observed city people flocking to country music clubs wearing jeans, boots, and cowboy hats with fancy hatbands, and he dug deep into this phenomenon to understand why. Simply put, the United States was still finding its way and redefining itself after the upheavals of the Vietnam War, which had ended only three years earlier. In answer to the question "Now, what?" Americans turned to the symbol that had always provided comfort in turbulent times: the cowboy.

Paramount Pictures saw the movie potential in the story and released *Urban Cowboy* in June 1980. It starred John Travolta and Debra Winger, and some critics called it a country version of *Saturday Night Fever*. The movie resonated with people across the social spectrum, and sales of western wear went through the roof. The soundtrack went triple platinum. And people risked injury to ride mechanical bulls in cowboy-themed bars. But beyond commerce, the movie's popularity spoke to a need for something intangible that could be filled only with the West.

Some filmmakers had started showing the darker side of western history in previous decades with movies such as *Little Big Man*, *The Wild Bunch*, and *Buffalo Bill and the Indians*. These stories told Americans some uncomfortable and badly needed truths. But by 1980 filmgoers wanted to feel good again, and *Urban Cowboy* was the right prescription. Journalists took note. And so did dude ranchers.

A year after the film opened, the director of the chamber of commerce in Wickenburg, Arizona, Buck Wayne, reported that dude ranches all over the country were seeing record business, which he said was a result of the urban cowboy craze. "People are now looking for more than a mechanical bull in the city. They say, 'Let's get out where it really happens.'"[10]

Ranchers were happy with the surge in visitors but told reporters that their places had always been popular, and interest in dude ranching wasn't new. They emphasized their century-old authenticity in advertising and interviews but also realized that dude ranches had finally become a mainstream vacation destination. In addition, the jeans-and-boots *Urban Cowboy* fad echoed something that had already happened on dude ranches. By the 1970s no one bought a special wardrobe for a ranch vacation. Jeans and chambray or cotton shirts were common casual clothing for both men and women, and that's what dudes packed for their trips. Adding a cotton western shirt and a cowboy hat was just common sense, and no longer a costume.

Expanding urban development and the lure of big money to be made in western property led to more ranch closures during the 1980s, though. Some of them were absorbed by government agencies: Grand Teton National Park took over management of the former Bar B C, and the Forest Service bought the old OTO place in Montana. Murray's Negro Dude Ranch in California was long gone. Nolie and Lela Murray had sold off parcels in 1955 and 1970, and by the late 1980s the entire property was in receivership. The crumbling buildings were burned by the local fire department in a training exercise, and the Mojave slowly took over.

In the 1980s lesbian and gay Americans who wanted a dude ranch vacation could now visit without hiding their orientation or their partners. A 1986 film took up this story but set it in the past. In *Desert Hearts*, an eastern woman stays at a Reno divorce ranch in 1959 and begins a passionate affair with a younger woman. Since the film is set in the 1950s, their relationship has to be secret. Based on a 1964 novel, the movie appealed to members of the gay community already interested in country music and the urban cowboy lifestyle, thanks to the films *Urban Cowboy* and *Coal Miner's Daughter*. LGBTQ people would have to wait about another twenty years before dude ranches would host special gay weeks or weekends, but it was a start.

A 1991 movie sparked an uptick in dude ranch reservations, even though it wasn't about dude ranching at all. *City Slickers* told the story of three men in the midst of midlife crises who decided to join a cattle drive, with the action focused on the Billy Crystal role. The ranch's owner told the men they were at a real working ranch, not a dude ranch where things were "pretend." Pretend or not, the film touched a nerve and dude ranch occupancy rates went up to 84 percent from 64 percent the previous year.[11]

By the late 1990s and early 2000s dude ranching was old enough to be the topic of museum exhibits, doctoral dissertations, and books about the history of individual ranches. And when ranches had to close, their demise was covered with sorrow in local papers. But the ranch buildings themselves didn't always go away or crumble into the sagebrush. Dude ranches were set up to serve large groups of people, and many of them went on to new and interesting lives. In the first fifteen years of the 2000s former dude ranches were turned into artist communes, addiction treatment centers, spas, golf courses, wineries, day-care centers, nonprofits, and even private homes.

Dude ranching continues to show up in entertainment and literature today. In 2002 *The Simpsons* aired an episode called "Dude, Where's My Ranch?" *Modern Family* featured a dude ranch theme in 2011, and a 2015 episode of HBO's *Veep* included a scene in which the main character and some college friends briefly reminisce about their dude ranch vacation. Movies on the Hallmark Channel occasionally feature dude ranch locales.

The 2010s also saw a surge of cowboy-themed romance novels set on dude ranches, including stories about LGBTQ relationships. Writers looked around for places where romance could thrive and tapped into the dude ranch story potential that novelists like Caroline Lockhart had seen nearly a century earlier. These works range from sweet to steamy, and publishers continue to release dude ranch–themed books that meet the need for both romantic wish fulfillment and the enduring masculine appeal of the cowboy.

An enterprise so dependent on the changeable winds of popular culture, vacation habits, and interest in the West could easily have passed into obscurity or turned into something it didn't want to be. But an interesting thing happened in the early twenty-first century: young people got into the business.

Bryce Albright, executive director of the Dude Ranchers' Association, has ranching in her blood. Her parents met at the Triangle X dude ranch near Jackson Hole, and Bryce grew up helping her aunt and uncle, who were the managers of Wyoming's CM Ranch. She did every job from housekeeping to wrangling to leading trail rides, which she especially loved. A business degree led to a job at the DRA in 2018 and eventually the executive director position. She saw dude ranches from the inside at an early age, so she knows how they have to adapt in order to not only stay in business but stay relevant.

She says that one obvious change has happened at the dinner table. Most ranches still lean toward serving western food, but food preferences and special diets have evolved, and a meal of meat and potatoes isn't always about a hamburger anymore. Some ranches have Cordon Bleu–trained chefs and farm-to-table programs. Many ranches have kept the tradition of the Saturday night cookout, and although steak is still the focus of this special meal, ranches also offer salmon as an option. But dudes still expect baked beans, biscuits, corn, and cobbler, and they're even better when they're cooked in a Dutch oven, because that was "the way of the cowboy."[12]

In dude ranching's early decades, young women were steered into the kitchen and housekeeping jobs and were not allowed near the corrals, unless they were the daughter of the owners. Today, young women like Bryce are wranglers alongside the young men; another is Iowa-born Colleen Chisman.

Colleen earned degrees in biology and natural history interpretation and worked for many years in immunochemistry research. When her company had to lay off employees, she took the severance package and decided to do something different with her life. In 2015 she started working on a yacht owned by a wealthy corporate titan. Stuck on a boat in the middle of the ocean with "grumpy people" was not how she envisioned her future, especially as a midwestern girl who liked trees. She then heard about a job as a housekeeper/server at a Wyoming dude ranch and jumped ship to take it.

She had learned to love horses and riding when she was a child at summer camp and had always been intrigued by the idea of a dude ranch. Since that first experience, she has worked at five ranches as a server, wrangler, bike and ATV tour guide, and bartender and especially enjoys the perk of being able to ride every day.[13]

Many ranches are still managed by the descendants of their founders, with younger generations bringing their perspective to what twenty-first-century dude ranches should look like. The children and grandchildren of longtime guests continue to go to those same ranches. Some kids are reluctant to give up their electronic devices when they first arrive, but once they're put on a horse, take a dip in a pool, or work with an archery instructor, they discover they would much rather be outside.

Bryce Albright saw this for herself when she worked at the CM dude ranch as a teenager, because these guest experiences were, and still are, fueled by the dedication of the owners and staff members. When she cleaned a family's cabin, she tried to make it feel like home. And when she led a trail ride or served dinner, she knew she was giving visitors more than just a horseback ride or a meal. She was giving them an experience they could not get anywhere else.

Colleen feels the same. As a server, she is the first face guests see at breakfast, and the last one they see at dinner. The dudes love to tell her about their day, and how excited they are for the one to come.

Bryce formed lifelong relationships with people she got to know as a teenager at the CM, and many of them attended her wedding in 2020. Colleen also stays in touch with many people she got to know at the ranches where she worked, including the author, who met her in 2015 at the Flying E Dude Ranch in Wickenburg, Arizona.

These connections, so embedded in the dude ranch experience, were challenged in ways ranchers never faced before in 2020. The COVID-19 pandemic, as well as explosive western wildfires, created stress and anxiety across the tourism industry. Member ranches of the DRA alone saw their visitor numbers plummet by 50 percent from 2019, and some ranches couldn't find a way to take in guests. Owners of the ranches that could open their doors put protocols in place that kept the dudes safe. Shorter guest lists were not always bad news, though. Many people were new to dude ranching and had booked their trips because cruises and international travel were no longer possible, which recalls dude ranching's rise in popularity during World War I.

Success had a different face in 2020. Ranchers did what had always worked for them: they adapted, they cooperated, they looked to their own history of resilience for guidance. And it paid off. Many first-time guests in 2020 rebooked for 2021 and told their friends and neighbors about their extraordinary vacation when they got home. Even more importantly, they told their hosts how grateful they were for their time on the ranch. Being outdoors, even having physically distanced meals with other people, felt normal in an abnormal time.

Ranchers were also grateful for their dudes and dudines, and not just because of the slim profits they were able to make, as Bryce Albright explains. "One of the things that makes dude ranching so special is the authenticity and the magic that happens on dude ranches... all of our ranches talk about the magic. The ranches that decided to close for the year said it was a very different feeling on the ranch. The people were not there and the magic never did appear." The magic isn't just for the dudes.

Dude ranchers are a hopeful bunch and have every reason to believe that their industry will survive and thrive, even as it faces inevitable cultural and natural obstacles. Dude ranching is the most repeated vacation in the United States, for the simple reason that, as Bryce puts it, "the public needs our places."[14]

Epilogue

In September 2019 I flew to Laramie, Wyoming, to do research for this book at the American Heritage Center (AHC), housed at the University of Wyoming. The AHC had given me a travel grant, but I thought I would save some money by not renting a car. In a university town like Laramie, I thought it would be easy to get around in cabs or with a car service like Uber.

My connecting flight from Denver landed around 9:00 P.M. I joined the small group of passengers that walked into the tiny airport, and we milled around in a room with a metal roll-up door, waiting for our luggage. I asked someone whether cabs regularly came by the airport, and she said no, I would have to call. Two people standing nearby recommended one particular service, so I stepped away and called them, asking for a ride to the AmericInn on East Grand Avenue.

"It's a forty-five-minute wait," the dispatcher told me. I tried the other company and got the same answer. I looked around; people carrying bags were leaving the airport, and I could see no staff or personnel anywhere, including at the car rental desk. A quick view out the front door revealed darkness and a near-empty parking lot, and I realized that by the time the cab showed up, I would be completely alone in the airport, which was likely nowhere near town.

As I stood there contemplating my fate, a woman who had sat in front of me on the plane walked up and said, "Hi, I couldn't help overhearing your conversation. Your motel is on the way to my house. My husband is picking me up. Could we give you a ride?"

With a sigh of relief, I said yes and thanked the woman, whose name was Kori Wilkinson. Her husband, Mark Jones, came into the airport a few minutes later, and I followed them to their truck. As we drove, I introduced myself and my purpose for coming to Laramie, and about fifteen minutes later they dropped me at my motel, giving me a cheery wave as they headed out.

The next day was Sunday, which I had reserved for seeing Laramie's historic sites. I had not done my due diligence, however, and the only place on my list that was open on Sundays was the Wyoming Territorial Prison. I had breakfast and then called both of the city's cab companies to get out there. No one at either place answered the phone.

OK, plan B: Uber or Lyft. No cars, no drivers available.

Well, plan C then: walk to the American Heritage Center to see how far it was in case I had to trek there for the five days I would be doing research. It was a beautiful morning and I enjoyed the two-mile stroll, but I knew I couldn't do that twice a day. I thought about renting a car after all, but I would have to take time away from my research to go out to the airport to do the paperwork, and I had only five days to get everything done.

I had passed a small strip mall on my walk and noticed that it had a movie theater. With everything closed and downtown Laramie many miles away, I threw in the towel and went to the 10:30 showing of *Downton Abbey*.

I was hungry when I left the theater, so I walked across the parking lot to a restaurant called the Rib and Chop. I had a book with me, *Dude Ranching in Yellowstone Country*, and once I was seated and ordered something to drink, I pulled it out and started to read.

A young waitress whose name tag read "Amanda" came by to take my order, glanced at my book, and asked what it was about. I told her, and she seemed so interested I mentioned that I was in town to do research about dude ranching. "Are you a professor?" she asked me. I replied, "I'm a writer, and my next book will be about dude ranches." She then told me about her own university studies in business management, and her desire to get into agribusiness. We chatted for longer than a waitress should, and then she took off to put in my order.

After Amanda left, I had a brainstorm. When she walked by again and refilled my water glass, I asked her a question.

"Would you or any of your friends like to make a little money this week? I need someone to pick me up at my motel and take me to the American Heritage Center in the mornings, and then take me back in the evening, for the next five days. Do you know anyone who might be interested?"

Amanda thought for a second, then said she would see what she could do. A few minutes later she stopped at my table and told me, "I posted your request on my sorority's Facebook page, and I'm sure someone will want the job."

I was thrilled and said so. We exchanged phone numbers and she told me her full name was Amanda Smith. After I finished my lunch, I got her attention, said goodbye, and walked out of the restaurant. I took a chance and opened the Uber app again, and this time I found a driver. He was about my age and said he wasn't available that morning because he was in church. He also said there were very few Uber or Lyft drivers in town, so I was especially grateful I'd found Amanda.

By the time I finished my pizza delivery dinner at the motel that night, Amanda had solved my problem. Her sorority sister Jenne Lee Sanford would pick me up at 8:30 the next morning and we would work out the details for the balance of the week.

She was waiting for me outside the motel front entrance the next day. Jenne Lee was a communications student and happy to take care of me. I asked her whether she was also available to drive me to the airport on Friday afternoon, and she said yes. With transportation no longer a worry, I could concentrate on my research.

I spent evenings downloading my notes in my motel room, but on Tuesday night I took Amanda out to dinner as a thank-you. I let her pick the restaurant, and the native Californian in me laughed when she chose a sushi place. Sushi in Wyoming? Well, I was there for adventure, of a sort. I mentally chastened myself for my snobbery when the food turned out to be really good, and I applauded Amanda's good taste.

I found an email from Kori when I got back to the motel. She was just checking in with me to see whether everything was going all right. She gave me her phone number and said to call if I needed a ride or anything else.

I'm one of those people who have to get to an airport well before their flight, just in case there's any traffic or weirdness on the roadways. I didn't think that would happen in Laramie, but I asked Jenne Lee to get me there early enough for my comfort, even though it was not our regular drive time. She was prompt, as always, and I was happy to pay her more than what Uber would have charged me.

I thought a lot about my trip on the flight home. I had a blast doing my research, but what stayed with me, and still does to this day, was how four people saw that I needed help and gave it to me without hesitation. I was a stranger when I landed in Laramie. By the time I left, I was part of it.

What does this have to do with dude ranching? Well, everything. One of the many mythologies about the West is its reputation for hospitality. If someone showed up at a ranch and needed food or a bed for the night, the rancher was obligated—and sometimes honored—to provide it. Or so the legend goes. This story line is baked into movies, books, and television shows. When James Stewart is ambushed by Lee Marvin in *The Man Who Shot Liberty Valance*, John Wayne and Vera Miles tend to his wounds and give him a place to stay, though they don't even know who he is.

Of course, the opposite also shows up as an occasional plot point in western films and books: a man nobody knows rides into town and until proved otherwise, he is a potential threat. That's the start of a good tale, but deeper stories emerge from the West's openhanded acceptance of the newcomer, a match for the vast spaces in which they travel.

This attitude, whether myth or not, lies at the root of dude ranching. On the ranch, strangers become friends, and some friends become family. Hospitality is not a theory or a business practice. It's a way of life and has been since the Eaton brothers set out their first guest book in 1882.

In a memoir published after her death, the Circle 8's Alice Gleason wrote about seeing the dude ranchers come into Billings for the first meeting of the Dude Ranchers' Association in 1926. They inspired her and her husband to open a place of their own, with sentiments that ranchers would recognize today.

"They had a friendly, relaxed attitude toward life. They were beautiful people in our eyes. To us, who loved the land, the outdoor life and Montana, it looked like the kind of life we wanted to live and share with others."[1]

Appendix
The Dude Ranchers' Association

The Dude Ranchers' Association
P.O. Box 2307
Cody, WY 82414
www.duderanch.org

Current members of the Dude Ranchers' Association, March 2021
4UR Ranch, Creede, CO
7D Ranch, Cody, WY
A Bar A Ranch, Encampment, WY
Absaroka Ranch, Dubois, WY
Alisal Guest Ranch & Resort, Solvang, CA
Allen's Diamond 4 Ranch, Lander, WY
Averill's Flathead Lake Ranch, Bigfork, MT
Bar Lazy J Guest Ranch, Parshall, CO
Bar W Guest Ranch, Whitefish, MT
Black Mountain Ranch, McCoy, CO
Blacktail Ranch, Wolf Creek, MT
Bonanza Creek Guest Ranch, Martinsdale, MT
Broken Arrow Lodge, Alder, MT
Bull Hill Guest Ranch, Kettle Falls, WA
Cherokee Park Ranch, Livermore, CO
Circle Bar Ranch, Hobson, MT
Circle Z Ranch, Patagonia, AZ
C Lazy U Ranch, Granby, CO
CM Ranch, Dubois, WY
Colorado Trails Ranch, Durango, CO
Covered Wagon Ranch, Gallatin Gateway, MT
Crossed Sabres Ranch, Cody, WY
Diamond D Ranch, Boise, ID

Drowsy Water Ranch, Granby, CO
Eatons' Ranch, Wolf, WY
Elkhorn Ranch, Gallatin Gateway, MT
Elkhorn Ranch, Tucson, AZ
Elk Mountain Ranch, Buena Vista, CO
Flat Creek Ranch, Jackson, WY
Geronimo Trail Guest Ranch, Winston, NM
Goosewing Ranch, Jackson, WY
Greenhorn Ranch, Quincy, CA
Gros Ventre River Ranch, Moose, WY
Hawley Mountain Guest Ranch, McLeod, MT
Hidden Hollow Hideaway Cattle & Guest Ranch, Townsend, MT
Horseshoe Canyon Ranch, Jasper, AR
Hubbard's Six Quarter Circle Ranch, Emigrant, MT
Hunewill Circle "H" Guest Ranch, Bridgeport, CA
JJJ Wilderness Ranch, Augusta, MT
Kara Creek Ranch, Sundance, WY
Kay El Bar Guest Ranch, Wickenburg, AZ
K Diamond K Guest Ranch, Republic, WA
Klondike Ranch, Buffalo, WY
Latigo Ranch, Kremmling, CO
Lazy L & B Ranch, Dubois, WY
Lone Mountain Ranch, Big Sky, MT
Long Hollow Ranch, Sisters, OR
Lost Creek Ranch, Moose, WY
Lost Valley Ranch, Sedalia, CO
Majestic Dude Ranch, Mancos, CO
Marble Mountain Ranch, Somes Bar, CA
McGarry Ranches, Rexburg, ID
McGinnis Meadows Cattle & Guest Ranch, Libby, MT
Medicine Bow Lodge Adventure Guest Ranch, Saratoga, WY
Moose Head Ranch, Moose, WY
Mountain Sky Guest Ranch, Emigrant, MT
Nine Quarter Circle Ranch, Gallatin Gateway, MT
Parade Rest Guest Ranch, West Yellowstone, MT
Paradise Guest Ranch, Buffalo, WY
Rainbow Trout Ranch, Antonito, CO

Rancho de la Osa, Sasabe, AZ
Rancho de los Caballeros, Wickenburg, AZ
Rankin Ranch, Caliente, CA
Rawah Ranch, Glendevey, CO
Red Horse Mountain Ranch, Harrison, ID
Red Reflet Guest Ranch, Ten Sleep, WY
Rich Ranch, Seeley Lake, MT
Rimrock Ranch, Cody, WY
R Lazy S Ranch, Teton Village, WY
Rocking Z Guest Ranch, Wolf Creek, MT
Spotted Horse Ranch, Jackson Hole, WY
Sprucedale Guest Ranch, Eagar, AZ
Stagecoach Trails Guest Ranch, Yucca, AZ
Sundance Guest Ranch, Ashcroft, British Columbia
Sundance Trail Guest Ranch, Red Feather Lakes, CO
Sweet Grass Ranch, Big Timber, MT
Sylvan Dale Guest Ranch, Loveland, CO
Tanque Verde Guest Ranch, Tucson, AZ
The Broadmoor's Ranch at Emerald Valley, Colorado Springs, CO
The Hideout Lodge & Guest Ranch, Shell, WY
The Red Rock Ranch, Kelly, WY
Three Bars Cattle & Guest Ranch, Cranbrook, British Columbia
Tombstone Monument Ranch, Tombstone, AZ
Triangle C Ranch, Dubois, WY
Triangle X Ranch, Moose, WY
Tumbling River Ranch, Grant, CO
Upper Canyon Outfitters & Guest Ranch, Alder, MT
V6 Ranch, Parkfield, CA
Vee Bar Guest Ranch, Laramie, WY
Vista Verde Ranch, Steamboat Springs, CO
Western Pleasure Guest Ranch, Sandpoint, ID
White Stallion Ranch, Tucson, AZ
Wind River Christian Dude Ranch, Estes Park, CO

Notes

Chapter 1
1. *Brooklyn Daily Eagle*, August 27, 1883.
2. Borne, *Dude Ranching*, 21, 22.
3. *Nebraska State Journal* (Lincoln), June 24, 1883.
4. This comment was later printed in the *Chronicle-Express* (Penn Yan, NY), June 20, 1883.
5. *Times-Democrat* (Lima, OH), February 10, 1881.
6. *Lincoln County Leader* (White Oaks, NM), December 1, 1883.
7. *New York Times*, May 27, 1883.
8. Twain, *Connecticut Yankee*, 66, 95.
9. *Wahpeton (ND) Times*, June 24, 1886.
10. DiSilvestro, *Theodore Roosevelt*, 93.
11. Ringley, *Wranglin' Notes!*, 38.
12. Cheney and Erskine, *Music, Saddles & Flapjacks*, 14.
13. *Bismarck (ND) Tribune*, June 12, 1899.
14. Ringley, *Wranglin' Notes!*, 69.
15. *Bismarck (ND) Tribune*, December 17, 1903; *Morning News* (Wilmington, DE), January 23, 1904.

Chapter 2
1. Burt, *Diary of a Dude-Wrangler*, 30.
2. *East Oregonian* (Pendleton, OR), August 8, 1912.
3. Shaffer, "See America First," 571.
4. Nicholas, *Becoming Western*, 68–69.
5. Kensel, *Dude Ranching*, 60.
6. *New York Times*, May 4, 1919; *Nebraska State Journal* (Lincoln), June 29, 1919; *Brooklyn Daily Eagle*, June 8, 1919.
7. *Buffalo Sunday Morning News*, June 23, 1912.

Chapter 3
1. *Kansas City Times*, December 26, 1919.
2. *Champion* (Norton, KS), March 8, 1900.
3. Evarts, "Dude Wranglers," 182.

4. Borne, *Dude Ranching*, 57.
5. *New York Herald*, February 19, 1922.
6. Borne, *Dude Ranching*, 52.

Chapter 4

1. Borne, *Dude Ranching*, 47, 51; *San Francisco Examiner*, May 3, 1929.
2. Walter H. James Papers, untitled manuscript, SC 1953, Montana Historical Society, Helena.
3. Kahn, *Jewish Life*, 13.
4. Eatons' Ranch brochure, January 1, 1913, McCracken Research Library, Buffalo Bill Center of the West, Cody, WY.
5. Elizabeth Phillips to Larry Larom, March 29, 1923; Larry Larom to Elizabeth Phillips, April 4, 1923; Larry Larom to Elizabeth Phillips, July 21, 1923; Irving H. "Larry" Larom Collection, 1906–1981, MS 014, McCracken Research Library, Buffalo Bill Center of the West, Cody, WY.
6. *Great Falls (MT) Tribune*, November 28, 1929.
7. Rinehart, "What Is a Dude Ranch?," 128.
8. Larry Larom to Winthrop Brooks, December 10, 1923, Irving H. "Larry" Larom Collection, 1906–1981, MS 014, McCracken Research Library, Buffalo Bill Center of the West, Cody, WY.
9. *Indianapolis News*, January 17, 1928.
10. *El Paso Herald*, July 25, 1928.
11. Lew Freedman, "Hemingway in Wyoming: Writer Fished Clarks Fork, Stayed in Cody," *Cody Enterprise*, January 28, 2019.
12. Lee Alan Gutkind, "Hemingway's Wyoming," *Casper Star-Tribune*, October 19, 1970.

Chapter 5

1. *Boston Globe*, April 25, 1931; *Arizona Daily Star* (Tucson), April 26, 1931.
2. *Alton (IL) Evening Telegraph*, February 20, 1936.
3. *Emporia (KS) Gazette*, November 7, 1936.
4. Krims, *Dude Ranch*, 37.
5. *Albuquerque Journal*, June 8, 1930; *New York Daily News*, April 25, 1931; *Salt Lake Telegram*, October 11, 1934.
6. Emmons, review of *The Mythic West*, 122.
7. *Oakland Tribune*, May 31, 1936.
8. *Santa Ana Register*, July 4, 1936.
9. Smith, *Dude Ranches and Ponies*, 235.
10. *Lead (SD) Daily Call*, February 12, 1935; *Billings (MT) Gazette*, August 8, 1935; *Santa Fe New Mexican*, June 14, 1935.
11. Smith, *Dude Ranches and Ponies*, 243.
12. *The Women*, directed by George Cukor (1939; Burbank, CA: Warner Archive Collection, 2018), DVD.

13. Burt, "Boccaccio in Chaps," 73.
14. *St. Louis Star and Times*, June 27, 1934.

Chapter 6

1. Bernstein, *Families That Take in Friends*, 93.
2. *Natrona County Tribune* (Casper, WY), August 3, 1910; Federal Highway Administration, "State Motor Vehicle Registrations, by Years, 1900–1995," https://www.fhwa.dot.gov/ohim/summary95/mv200.pdf.
3. "House Management Department," *The Dude Rancher*, December 1932, 10.
4. *Arizona Daily Star* (Tucson), July 8, 1930.
5. Shawver, *Sincerely, Mary S.*, 36, 48.
6. Helen B. Herford to Levi Strauss & Co., undated, Helen Brooke Herford Papers, 1886–1957, Collection 2019, Merrill G. Burlingame Special Collections, Montana State University, Bozeman.
7. *Great Falls (MT) Tribune*, February 18, 1930.
8. Young and Mathis, "Remounts," 28–29.
9. Rinehart, "What Is a Dude Ranch?," 128.
10. *The Women*, directed by George Cukor (1939; Burbank, CA: Warner Archive Collection, 2018), DVD.
11. Shawver, *Sincerely, Mary S.*, 60.
12. *Arizona Republic* (Phoenix), February 12, 1935.
13. Fielding, *French Heels to Spurs*, 68.
14. J. Walter Thompson Agency to Larry Larom, June 21, 1939, Irving H. "Larry" Larom Collection, 1906–1981, MS 014, McCracken Research Library, Buffalo Bill Center of the West, Cody, WY.

Chapter 7

1. Copeland, "Dude-Puncher Steve," 343, 346.
2. *Sunset Trail*, Censorship Dialogue Script, October 24, 1938, William Boyd Papers, 1911–1955, Scripts, 1935–1955, Collection 08038, American Heritage Center, University of Wyoming, Laramie.
3. *Gallup (NM) Independent*, June 17, 1939.
4. "Monkey Ward" was the nickname for the now-defunct mail order and department store business called Montgomery Ward, where men could buy clothes for their dude ranch vacations.
5. Lynne Lugosi Sparks, email to author, December 7, 2020.
6. Cooper, "To the Dude Rancher," 12.
7. *Albuquerque Journal*, September 15, 1932; *Ottawa Journal* (Ontario, Canada), March 6, 1935; Borne, *Dude Ranching*, 62, 176; *Independent-Record* (Helena, MT), November 9, 1935; *Billings Gazette*, January 23, 1935; *Billings Gazette*, March 4, 1930; *Santa Fe New Mexican*, August 30, 1932; *Daily Sentinel* (Grand Junction, CO), March 4, 1931; Ryan Summerlin, "Black Market Booze, Gangsters in Glenwood's '20s," *Post Independent* (Glenwood Springs, CO), April 8, 2017,

https://www.postindependent.com/news/local/black-market-booze-gangsters-in-gwoods-20s/; *Daily Sentinel* (Grand Junction, CO), April 12, 1955.
8. *Star-Tribune* (Casper, WY), July 22, 1935.

Chapter 8

1. Kensel, *Dude Ranching in Yellowstone Country*, 127–30.
2. Larry Larom to Julian Bryan, May 26, 1932, Irving H. "Larry" Larom Collection, 1906–1981, MS 014, McCracken Research Library, Buffalo Bill Center of the West, Cody, WY.
3. Diary of Philip H. Cummings, September 29, 1932, Estate of Philip Cummings, courtesy of Patricia A. Billingsley.
4. Patricia A. Billingsley, email to author, November 8, 2020.
5. Burke, "'Worry, U.S.A.,'" 19–20.
6. Helen Howe, "Manana," MS Thr 1027, Box 1, Helen Howe Papers, Houghton Library, Harvard University; *Albuquerque Journal*, April 16, 1937.
7. *Longview (TX) News-Journal*, May 31, 1936; *Brooklyn Times Union*, July 29, 1936; *Evening News* (Harrisburg, PA), July 30, 1936.
8. Lora Hale, "My Impression of a Dude Ranch," *The Dude Rancher*, October 1937, 3, 31.
9. "Young Woman Wants Job on Dude Ranch," *The Dude Rancher*, April 1936, 22.
10. *Press Democrat* (Santa Rosa, CA), July 9, 1939.

Chapter 9

1. *San Francisco Examiner*, March 3, 1875; *Weekly Journal-Miner* (Prescott, AZ), November 2, 1887.
2. *Muncie (IN) Evening Press*, October 9, 1922; *Billings Gazette*, May 21, 1929; *Fresno Bee*, June 4, 1933; *San Bernardino County Sun* (San Bernardino, CA), March 24, 1939.
3. Patton and Schedlock, "Let's Go," 510.
4. *Nevada State Journal* (Reno), March 29, 1938.
5. Sorin, *Driving while Black*, 61, 79, 153, 181–82, 184–85.
6. "Negro Dude Ranch Opens in California: World's Heavyweight Champion Is a Guest There," *Life* 3, no. 20 (November 15, 1937): 116; *San Bernardino County Sun* (San Bernardino, CA), October 8, 1939; March 9, 1939; July 17, 1939.
7. Meares, "1930s California Dude Ranch."
8. Beck, *Beckoning Frontiers*, 57, 215–16.
9. "New Deal Programs," The Living New Deal, https://livingnewdeal.org/what-was-the-new-deal/programs/.
10. Federal Writers' Project, *Montana*, 6.
11. Federal Writers' Project, *New York*, 629.
12. Bernstein, *Families That Take in Friends*, 95, 100.
13. *The Dude Rancher*, July 1941, 5.
14. *The Dude Rancher*, January 1940, 8.

Chapter 10

1. White, *Git Along, Little Dogies*, 46.
2. Priestley, *Midnight on the Desert*, 95.
3. *Minneapolis Star*, February 9, 1935.
4. *Courier-Post* (Camden, NJ), January 24, 1936; *Visalia (CA) Times-Delta*, August 9, 1939; *Bakersfield Californian*, August 10, 1939; *Billings Gazette*, November 3, 1933.
5. *Oakland Tribune*, October 27, 1936; *Decatur (IL) Herald*, January 2, 1938; *Long Beach (CA) Independent*, July 24, 1939.
6. White, *Git Along, Little Dogies*, 2.
7. *St. Louis Post-Dispatch*, July 5, 1931.
8. *Oakland Tribune*, January 31, 1939.
9. *Oakland Tribune*, April 4, 1940; April 8, 1940; *Minneapolis Star*, April 7, 1940; *Salt Lake Tribune*, April 22, 1940.
10. Bernstein, *Families That Take in Friends*, 96; *Harrisburg (PA) Sunday Courier*, September 1, 1940.
11. Kyne, *Dude Woman*, 26.

Chapter 11

1. *Jackson (TN) Sun*, December 25, 1941; *Circleville (OH) Herald*, April 12, 1944.
2. Borne, *Dude Ranching*, 175; Kensel, *Dude Ranching in Yellowstone Country*, 125.
3. *The Dude Rancher*, July 1942, 5, 28.
4. *Billings Gazette*, February 20, 1943.
5. *The Dude Rancher*, October 1943, 5; *Arizona Daily Star* (Tucson), January 2, 1944.
6. *The Dude Rancher*, July 1942, 5; April 1943, 5, 15; July 1943, 5.
7. *San Bernardino County Sun* (San Bernardino, CA), February 4, 1942; *Brooklyn Daily Eagle*, January 3, 1943; *Albuquerque Journal*, July 17, 1944.
8. *Billings Gazette*, January 26, 1945; April 19, 1945.
9. *Billings Gazette*, November 4, 1945; *Cincinnati Enquirer*, August 13, 1944.
10. *The Dude Rancher*, April 1945, 5; July 1945, 5.

Chapter 12

1. Borne, *Dude Ranching*, 180, 181, 187.
2. *Fort Worth Star-Telegram*, June 20, 1945; *Democrat and Chronicle* (Rochester, NY), October 1, 1945; *Santa Fe New Mexican*, December 1, 1948; *The Grizzly* (Big Bear Lake, CA), August 13, 1948.
3. *The Dude Rancher*, April 1946, 5.
4. Molly Wilson to Mother, July 2, 5, 21, August 7, 1946; Allen R. Alderson to Mrs. Wilson, August 5, 1946. The author is grateful to Lucy Murphy, Molly Wilson's daughter, for her kind permission to reproduce excerpts from her mother's letters. Copies of the letters are in the Molly Wilson Magee papers, 1946, SC 2492, Montana Historical Society Research Center Archives, Helena.

5. *Los Angeles Times*, January 6, 1947; *Daily Oklahoman* (Oklahoma City), June 4, 1947; *Brooklyn Daily Eagle*, June 8, 1947; *San Saba (TX) News and Star*, February 3, 1949; *Chicago Tribune*, February 27, 1949.
6. *Two Guys from Texas*, directed by David Butler (1948; Burbank, CA: Warner Archive Collection, 2016), DVD.
7. Thompson, "Murray's Ranch."
8. *The Dude Rancher*, July 1947, 34.
9. *Bakersfield Californian*, December 1, 1947; *Press Democrat* (Santa Rosa, CA), December 9, 1949.
10. *Arizona Daily Star* (Tucson), January 5, 1947.
11. *Reno Gazette-Journal*, February 22, 1949; *Arizona Republic* (Phoenix), December 9, 1949; *Dawson Springs (KY) Progress*, December 16, 1949.
12. *The Dude Rancher*, April 1950, 7.

Chapter 13

1. *Billings Gazette*, November 16, 1952; Bernstein, *Families That Take in Friends*, 145.
2. Borne, *Dude Ranching*, 189.
3. *Billings Gazette*, November 18, 1952.
4. *Billings Gazette*, December 4, 1947.
5. *Billings Gazette*, November 18, 1952; *San Francisco Examiner*, May 25, 1952; *Times-News* (Twin Falls, ID), February 19, 1958.
6. *The Dude Rancher*, January 1953, 7.
7. Postcard, "Dude Ranch Comics," Curt Teich & Co., no. C-194, ca. 1950, author's collection.
8. *Arizona Republic* (Phoenix), January 5, 1950; *Hi-Desert Star* (Yucca Valley, CA), October 30, 1958; November 13, 1958; *Mansfield (PA) Advertiser*, May 7, 1952; *Monroe (LA) News-Star*, May 1, 1952; *Courier-Gazette* (McKinney, TX), May 3, 1952.
9. *The Dude Rancher*, April 1952, 7.
10. Paul Waldman, "Country Strong," *The American Prospect*, August 23, 2011, https://prospect.org/article/country-strong/.
11. *Chicago Tribune*, August 13, 1950; *Los Angeles Times*, April 20, 1958.
12. *The Dude Rancher*, July 1955, 36–37.

Chapter 14

1. *Desert Sun* (Palm Springs, CA), December 17, 1960; *Jackson Hole Courier* (Jackson, WY), May 13, 1965; *Idaho State Journal* (Pocatello), July 4, 1965.
2. Dolly Turner, interview by the author, Wickenburg, AZ, November 24, 2019.
3. *Lubbock (TX) Avalanche-Journal*, July 25, 1968.
4. Grayson Kirk to Larry Larom, May 10, 1968, Irving H. "Larry" Larom Collection, McCracken Research Library, Buffalo Bill Center of the West, Cody, WY.
5. *Fort Collins Coloradoan*, November 14, 1968; *Miami Herald*, June 28, 1970.

6. *Sentinel* (Carlisle, PA), December 6, 1972.
7. *Jackson Hole Guide*, July 1, 1976; *Arizona Republic* (Phoenix), June 19, 1977; *Jackson Hole News*, July 20, 1977.
8. *New Mexican* (Santa Fe), May 2, 1978.
9. Faye Snyder, oral history interview, Oral History Collection, 1998–2012, MS 201, box 5, folder 30, McCracken Research Library, Buffalo Bill Center of the West, Cody, WY.
10. *Charlotte (NC) News*, June 13, 1981.
11. *Daily Sentinel* (Grand Junction, CO), July 15, 1991.
12. Bryce Albright, Zoom interview by the author, October 29, 2020.
13. Colleen Chisman, email interview by the author, October 8, 2020.
14. Bryce Albright, interview.

Epilogue

1. Barhaugh and Guthrie, *Starting from Scratch*, 115.

Bibliography

Manuscript Collections

Bones Brothers Ranch records. Montana Historical Society, Helena.
Charles Belden Collection. McCracken Research Library, Buffalo Bill Center of the West, Cody, WY.
Dr. Caroline McGill Collection. Merrill G. Burlingame Special Collections, Montana State University, Bozeman.
Dude Ranchers' Association Records. American Heritage Center, University of Wyoming, Laramie.
Dude Ranches Photograph Albums, 1931–1935. American Heritage Center, University of Wyoming, Laramie.
Dude Ranch Histories of Charles Roundy. McCracken Research Library, Buffalo Bill Center of the West, Cody, WY.
Eatons' Ranch Records. American Heritage Center, University of Wyoming, Laramie.
Elsa Spear Papers. American Heritage Center, University of Wyoming, Laramie.
Helen Brooke Herford Papers. Merrill G. Burlingame Special Collections, Montana State University, Bozeman.
Helen Howe Papers. Houghton Library, Harvard University, Cambridge, MA.
Irving H. "Larry" Larom Collection. McCracken Research Library, Buffalo Bill Center of the West, Cody, WY.
L. A. Huffman Collection. McCracken Research Library, Buffalo Bill Center of the West, Cody, WY.
Molly Wilson Magee Papers. 1946, SC 2492, Montana Historical Society, Helena.
Peter B. Kyne Papers. Special Collections and University Archives, University of Oregon, Eugene.
Walter H. James Papers. Montana Historical Society, Helena.
Western Filmscript Collection. Yale Collection of Western Americana, Beinecke Rare Book and Manuscript Library, Yale University, New Haven, CT.
William Boyd Papers. American Heritage Center, University of Wyoming, Laramie.

Oral History Interviews

Albright, Bryce. Zoom interview by the author. October 29, 2020.
Chisman, Colleen. Email interview by the author. October 8, 2020.
Turner, Dolly. Wickenburg, AZ, November 24, 2019.

Books and Articles

"1935: A Short-Lived Crest." *The Bela Lugosi Blog.* https://beladraculalugosi.com/1935-2/.

Athearn, Robert G. *The Mythic West in Twentieth-Century America.* Lawrence: University Press of Kansas, 1986.

Barhaugh, Genny, and Carol Guthrie, eds. *Starting from Scratch: The Adventures of a Lady Dude Rancher.* Choteau, MT: Star Route Publishing, 2001.

Beck, George W. T. *Beckoning Frontiers: The Memoir of a Wyoming Entrepreneur.* Edited by Lynn J. Houze and Jeremy M. Johnston. Lincoln: University of Nebraska Press, 2020.

Bernstein, Joel H. *Families That Take in Friends: An Informal History of Dude Ranching.* Stevensville, MT: Stoneydale Press, 1982.

Bold, Christine. *Selling the Wild West: Popular Western Fiction, 1869–1960.* Bloomington: Indiana University Press, 1987.

Bommersbach, Jana. "Homos on the Range." *True West,* November/December 2005. https://truewestmagazine.com/article/homos-on-the-range/.

Bonnamy, Francis. *Death on a Dude Ranch.* New York: Caxton House, 1939.

Borne, Lawrence R. *Dude Ranching: A Complete History.* Albuquerque: University of New Mexico Press, 1923.

Burke, Flannery. "'Worry U.S.A.': Dude Ranch Advertising Looks East, 1915–1945." *Montana: The Magazine of Western History* 69, no. 2 (Summer 2019): 3–20.

Burt, Struthers. "Boccaccio in Chaps." *Vogue* 85, no. 10 (May 1935).

———. *The Diary of a Dude-Wrangler.* Jackson, WY: Sastrugi Press Classics, 2019.

Carhart, Arthur. *Hi, Stranger! The Complete Guide to Dude Ranches.* Chicago: Ziff-Davis, 1949.

Cheney, Roberta, and Clyde Erskine. *Music, Saddles & Flapjacks: Dudes at the OTO Ranch.* Missoula, MT: Mountain Press, 2000.

Clayton, John. *The Cowboy Girl: The Life of Caroline Lockhart.* Lincoln: University of Nebraska Press, 2007.

Cooper, Gary. "To the Dude Rancher." *The Dude Rancher,* January 1937.

Copeland, Fred. "Dude-Puncher Steve." *Scribner's* 69, no. 3 (March 1921): 343–52.

Corkill, Gail Waechter. *Circle Z Guest Ranch.* Charleston, SC: Arcadia Publishing, 2016.

DiSilvestro, Roger L. *Theodore Roosevelt in the Badlands: A Young Politician's Quest for Recovery in the American West.* New York: Walker, 2011.

Emmons, David M. Review of *The Mythic West in Twentieth-Century America. Journal of the Southwest* 30, no. 1 (Spring 1988): 121–24.

Evarts, Hal G. "Dude Wranglers." *Saturday Evening Post* 192 no. 44 (May 1, 1920).

Federal Highway Administration. "State Motor Vehicle Registrations, by Years, 1900–1995." https://www.fhwa.dot.gov/ohim/summary95/mv200.pdf.

Federal Writers' Project of the Works Progress Administration for the State of Montana. *Montana: A State Guide Book.* New York: Viking Press, 1939.

Federal Writers' Project of the Works Progress Administration in the State of New York. *New York: A Guide to the Empire State.* New York: Oxford University Press, ca. 1940.

Fielding, Loraine Hornaday. *French Heels to Spurs*. New York: Century, 1930.
George-Warren, Holly, and Michelle Freedman. *How the West Was Worn: A History of Western Wear*. New York: Abrams, 2001.
Green, Douglas B. *Singing in the Saddle: The History of the Singing Cowboy*. Nashville: Country Music Foundation Press, 2002.
Greubel, Curtis. "Tim McCoy: Wyoming Cowboy, Military Officer, Politician and Movie Star." *Wyoming Postscripts*, March 24, 2016. https://wyostatearchives.wordpress.com/2016/03/24/tim-mccoy-wyoming-cowboy-military-officer-politician-and-movie-star/.
Grey, Zane. *The Dude Ranger*. New York: Skyhorse Publishing, 2017.
Hagedorn, Hermann. *Roosevelt in the Bad Lands*. Boston: Houghton Mifflin, 1921.
Harris, Richard E. *The First 100 Years: A History of Arizona Blacks*. Apache Junction, AZ: Relmo, 1983.
Hmura, Merideth A. *Mountain View Ranch: 1915–1945*. Lockport, IL: Leaning Pine, 1996.
Hooton, Barbara C. *Guestward Ho!* New York: Vanguard Press, 1956.
Kahn, Ava F., ed. *Jewish Life in the American West*. Los Angeles: Autry Museum of Western Heritage, 2002.
Keen, Rusti Leigh. "'Look West,' Says the *Post*: The Promotion of the American Far West in the 1920s *Saturday Evening Post*." Master's thesis, Indiana University, 2012. https://pdfs.semanticscholar.org/97b6/48f4d627c08794a7b78740c2ad33772f8f57.pdf.
Kensel, W. Hudson. *Dude Ranching in Yellowstone Country: Larry Larom and Valley Ranch, 1915–1969*. Norman, OK: Arthur H. Clark, 2010.
Krims, Milton. *Dude Ranch*. New York: Macaulay, 1930.
Kyne, Peter B. *Dude Woman*. New York: H. C. Kinsey, 1940.
"A Lady on a Dude Ranch." *Literary Digest* 85 (June 27, 1925): 48–50.
Lamont, Victoria. *Westerns: A Women's History*. Lincoln: University of Nebraska Press, 2016.
LeCompte, Mary Lou. "The Hispanic Influence on the History of Rodeo, 1823–1922. *Journal of Sport History* 12, no. 1 (Spring 1985): 21–38.
Lockhart, Caroline. *The Dude Wrangler*. New York: Doubleday, Page, 1921.
———. "Jim's Dude." *McClure's Magazine* 32, no. 4 (February 1909): 389–95.
Meares, Hadley. "The 1930s California Dude Ranch That Broke Racial Barriers." *Curbed Los Angeles*, May 27, 2015. https://la.curbed.com/2015/5/27/9956904/murrays-dude-ranch.
McGee, William, and Sandra McGee. *The Divorce Seekers: A Photo Memoir of a Nevada Dude Wrangler*. St. Helena, CA: BMC Publications, 2004.
Mitchell, Clarence. *Montana Montage: Memoir of a Dude Wrangler*. Lincoln, NE: iUniverse, 2006.
Moore, Jacqueline M. *Cow Boys and Cattle Men: Class and Masculinities on the Texas Frontier, 1865–1900*. New York: New York University Press, 2009.
Morsman, Edgar M., Jr. *The Postmistress of Saddlestring, Wyoming*. Deephaven, MN: Edgar M. Morsman Jr. Publications, 1998.

Nicholas, Liza J. *Becoming Western: Stories of Culture and Identity in the Cowboy State.* Lincoln: University of Nebraska Press, 2006.

Patton, Tracy Owens, and Sally M. Schedlock. "Let's Go, Let's Show, Let's Rodeo: African Americans and the History of Rodeo." *Journal of African American History* 96, no. 4 (Fall 2011): 503–21.

Poling-Kempes, Lesley. *Ladies of the Canyons: A League of Extraordinary Women and Their Adventures in the American Southwest.* Tucson: University of Arizona Press, 2015.

Pomeroy, Earl. *In Search of the Golden West: The Tourist in Western America.* Lincoln: University of Nebraska Press, 1957.

Priestley, J. B. *Midnight on the Desert: A Chapter of Autobiography.* London: William Heinemann, 1937.

Rinehart, Mary Roberts. *The Out Trail.* Garden City, NY: Garden City Publishing, 1923.

———. "What Is a Dude Ranch?" *Harper's Bazaar* 155 (August 1927).

Ringley, Tom. *Wranglin' Notes! A Chronicle of Eatons' Ranch, 1879–2010.* Greybull, WY: Pronghorn Press, 2010.

Rothman, Hal K. *Devil's Bargains: Tourism in the Twentieth-Century American West.* Lawrence: University Press of Kansas, 1998.

Shaffer, Marguerite S. "'See America First': Re-envisioning Nation and Region through Western Tourism." *Pacific Historical Review* 65, no. 4 (November 1996): 559–81.

Shawver, Mary. *Sincerely, Mary S.* Casper, WY: Prairie Publishing, 1953.

Simmon, Scott. *The Invention of the Western Film: A Cultural History of the Genre's First Half-Century.* Cambridge: Cambridge University Press, 2003.

Smith, Lawrence B. *Dude Ranches and Ponies.* New York: Coward-McCann, 1936.

Sorin, Gretchen. *Driving while Black: African American Travel and the Road to Civil Rights.* New York: Liveright Publishing, 2020.

Springate, Megan E., ed. *LGBTQ America: A Theme Study of Lesbian, Gay, Bisexual, Transgender and Queer History.* Washington, DC: National Park Foundation, 2016.

Staudohar, Connie. "The 320 Ranch." *Montana: The Magazine of Western History* 55, no. 2 (Summer 2005): 75–77.

Tatham, Julie. *Cherry Ames: Dude Ranch Nurse.* New York: Grosset & Dunlap, 1953.

Taylor, Candacy. *Overground Railroad: The Green Book and the Roots of Black Travel in America.* New York: Abrams Press, 2020.

Taylor, Rosemary. *Bar Nothing Ranch.* New York: McGraw-Hill, 1947.

Thompson, Richard D. "Murray's Ranch: Apple Valley's African-American Dude Ranch." MojaveHistory.com. http://mojavehistory.com/murray1.html.

True, Russell. *Dude Ranching in Arizona.* Charleston, SC: Arcadia Publishing, 2016.

Twain, Mark. *A Connecticut Yankee in King Arthur's Court.* New York: Harper & Brothers, 1899.

Waldman, Paul. "Country Strong." *American Prospect*, August 23, 2011. https://prospect.org/article/country-strong/.

Wegman-French, Lysa. "Faraway Ranch Special History Study: Chiricahua National Monument." Intermountain Cultural Resources Management Professional Paper no. 72. Santa Fe, NM: US Department of the Interior, Cultural Resources Division, 2006.

Weil, Steven E., and G. Daniel DeWeese. *Western Shirts: A Classic American Fashion.* Salt Lake City: Gibbs Smith, 2004.

White, John I. *Git Along, Little Dogies: Songs and Songmakers of the American West.* Urbana: University of Illinois Press, 1975.

Wolman, David, and Julian Smith. *Aloha Rodeo: Three Hawaiian Cowboys, the World's Greatest Rodeo, and a Hidden History of the American West.* New York: William Morrow, 2019.

Wrobel, David M., and Patrick T. Long, ed. *Seeing and Being Seen: Tourism in the American West.* Lawrence: University Press of Kansas, 2001.

Young, James A., and Dave Mathis. "Remounts." *Rangelands* 4, no. 1 (February 1982): 28–30.

Index

Page numbers in *italic* typeface indicate illustrations.

Aldrich Lodge, 16
Alterie, Diamond Jack, 78–79
American Guide, 131–32
automobiles, 59–60, 65, 78, 105, 128, 149, 161, 171, 173
Autry, Gene, 72, 142–44, 157, 176, 184

Bar B C dude ranch, 12, 17, 32, 56, 182
Belden, Charles, 86–87
Binko dude ranch, 36
Bird, Isabella, 2, 14
Black cowboys and tourists, 127–30, 144–45, 166–68, 191
Bower, Bertha Muzzy, 22
Bones Brothers Ranch, 163–64
Boyd, William ("Hopalong Cassidy"), 73, 129, 176–77
Brooks, Winthrop, 18–19, 37, 41, 83
Buck Benny Rides Again (film), 144–46
Buffalo Bill's Wild West, 6–7, 14, 21–22, 124
Burt, Struthers, 12–13, 18, 56, 60, 151, 182

Calamity Jane, 10
cattle industry, 2–3, 24, 50
Chip of the Flying U, 22
Circle 8 guest ranch, 190, 199
City Slickers (film), 192
CM Ranch, 61, 159, 193–94
Cody, William F. ("Buffalo Bill"), 2, 6–7, 12, 14, 19, 85, 131

Cody, Wyo., 16–20, 26–27, 34, 41, 44, 57, 62, 68, 85, *115*, 124, 131, 135, 170, 189
comic strips, 76
Cooper, Gary, 75
Cowboy and the Lady, The (film), 32
Cowboy Millionaire, The (film), 72–73
cowboys, 21–23, 41–43, 127–30, 135–36, 137–48, 156–58, 163–65, 167–68, 174, 177–79, 181, 183, 185–88, 190–93
crime, 78–79
Cummings, Philip H., 83–85
Custer Trail Ranch, 4, 10–11

Death on a Dude Ranch, 76
Deep Well guest ranch, 50, 139
Desert Hearts (film), 191
Devil Horse, The (film), *115*
DeYong, Joe, 37
Double Dee dude ranch, 86–87
dude, history and meaning, 4–8, 34
Dude Cowboy, The (film), 48
Dude Ranch (book and film), 46–48
Dude Rancher, The (magazine), 58–61, 75, 87–88, 90–91, 134–35, 146, 151–55, 159, 162, 164, 168, 170–71, 173–75, 180–81, 183, 185
Dude Ranchers' Association, 34–36, 40, 52–53, 58–61, 64–65, 77, 87–91, 133–35, 147, 149, 150–52, 156, 158, 161, 170–71, 180, 183, 186–87, 193–94, 199

dude ranches: advertising and promotion, 18, 24, 33–39, 46, 51–52, 58–60, 69, 87, 91–92, 93–94, 97–98, 100, 102–3, 109, 111–12, 120, 171, 174–76, 178–79, 186, 189, 191; clothing, 4–6, 26, 55–57, 59, 63–64, 70, 73–74, 87, 90–92, 95, 115, 122, 143, 145–47, 165–66, 179–80, 186, 191; divorce ranches, 53–55, 57, 67, 73, 89, 132, 144, 170, 191; films, 19–21, 24, 32–33, 46–49, 54–55, 67, 72–74, 115, 142–46, 157–58, 166–68, 180, 183, 184, 191–92; food and cooking, 26, 30, 40, 61, 65, 67, 77–78, 106, 132–33, 135, 153–55, 168–70, 180–81, 185; railroads, history, 2, 10, 14, 35–37, 39, 52–53, 59–60, 65, 72, 85, 87, 90, 93, 103, 110, 150, 159, 168, 171–72, 181; rodeo, 46, 48, 51, 57, 71, 91, 123–29, 164, 166, 172, 183, 189; television, influence of, 176–78, 180, 182, 184–85, 188–89, 192, 199; tourism, 1–2, 13–15, 53, 55–56, 20, 24–26, 28–30, 35, 40, 64, 68, 72, 78, 87, 93, 128, 132, 150, 156–58, 161, 171–74, 179, 187; women, 6, 16–17, 30–32, 36, 46–48, 54, 56–57, 61–65, 76, 82–83, 86, 90–92, 117, 126, 145–47, 152, 155, 158–59, 162–65, 174–75, 179–82, 185–86, 189, 191, 193; World War I, 1, 14, 19, 24–25, 27–28, 35, 38, 66, 149, 153, 163, 194; World War II, 77, 81, 87, 106, 121, 148–58, 160, 167; wranglers, 21–23, 25–26, 40–43, 46, 55, 62, 66, 70, 90–92, 126–27, 135–40, 150, 158–59, 162, 164, 175, 181, 193. *See also* individual dude ranches; films by title
Dude Ranger, The (book and film), 46, 48–49
Dudes Are Pretty People (film), 157
Dude Woman, 147–48
Dude Wrangler, The (book and film), 27–28, 48

Earhart, Amelia, 86–87
Eaton, Alden, 3–4, 11, 182
Eaton, Howard, 1, 3–4, 6, 9, 11, 13, 22, 24, 31
Eaton, Willis, 3–4, 11, 182
Eatons' dude ranch, 1, 7–11, 17, 21, 37, 39–41, 59, 70, 86, 91, 97, 163

Fielding, Loraine Hornaday, 69
Flyin' Cowboy, The (film), 33
Foxfire (film), 180
Frazer, Elizabeth, 24–25
French Heels to Spurs, 69

Galloping Dude, The (film), 32
Garlow, Irma, 19
Gibson, Hoot, 33, 184
Girl Crazy (film), 142, 184
Gleason, Alice, 190, 199
Grey, Zane, 22, 27, 46–49
Guestward Ho! (book and television series), 182, 184

Hard-Boiled (film), 33
Hearst, Phoebe Apperson, 101, 131
Heart of the Rio Grande (film), 157
Hell Cat, The (film), 19–20
Hemingway, Ernest, 43–45
Herford, Helen Brooke, 63–64
horses, 65–67, 172–73
Hough, Emerson, 22
Howe, Helen, 88–89

In Old Santa Fe (film), 72, 143–44, 157
Indians, 18, 22, 26, 47, 70–72, 88, 177, 179, 188

Jack & Jill Ranch, 102
Jack London Ranch, 51–53, 121
Jeffries, Herb, 144
Jews, and anti-Semitism, 37–40, 128, 169, 187

Jordan, Louis, 167–68
JY dude ranch, 12, 32

Krims, Milton, 46
Kyne, Peter, 147–48

Larom, Irma Dew, 41
Larom, Irving ("Larry"), 17–19, 22, 33–34, 37–41, 60, 69, 70–71, 83–85, 87, 90, *114*, 138–39, 149–51, 158, 170, 172–73, 182, 187
Latinx, history, 28, 50, 124, 149–50, 179
Lazy K Bar dude ranch, 17, 23, 61
Lee, H. D., 146
Levi Strauss & Co., 56–57, 63–64, 122, 146, 166, 186
LGBTQ history, 82–86, *117*, 191–92
Lightning Strikes Twice (film), 180
Lockhart, Caroline, 26–28, 57, 192
London, Charmian, 51–53, *121*
Longworth, Alice Roosevelt, 189
Lookout Sister (film), 167–68
Louis, Joe, 129–30
Lowdermilk, Romaine H., 140–42
Lugosi, Bela, 74–75

Maisie (film), 73–74
Majo Ranch, 39
Maynard, Ken, 72, 143
McConnell, Gladys, *115*
McGill, Caroline, 64
McLaughlin, Jim, 18
Medora, N.Dak., 3–4, 6, 8, 11
Mix, Tom, 33, 43, 48, 76, 79, 184
Moore, Marion, 61, 159
Morris Ranch, *115*
Murray, Lela and Nolie, 128–30, 167–68, 191
Murray's dude ranch, 129–30, 144–45, 166–68, 191
music, 40, 99, 137–45, 147, 173–74, 185

O'Brien, George, 49, 72, 74
OTO dude ranch, 12–13, 17, 21, 34, 37, 44, 91, 133, 182, 191
Out West with the Hardys (film), 74
Ox Yoke Ranch, 17, 91

Phillips, Elizabeth, 39, 139
Pierson, George Weston, 51, 107
Pierson dude ranch, 51, 107, 125–26
Pitchfork Ranch, 86–87, *116*, 154

Racketeer Roundup (film), 49
Rand, Sally, 79–82
Randall, Dora Roseborough, 10, 17, 133
Randall, James ("Dick"), 9–11, 13, 22, 34, 87, 182
Randall, Lesley ("Gay"), 10
Rawhide Romance (film), 49
Reno, Nev., 54–55, 57, 67, 73, 89, 169, 191
Ride 'Em Cowboy (film), 157
Riding High (film), 158
Rinehart, Mary Roberts, 1, 16, 31, 40–41, 67, 163
Road to Reno, The (film), 73
Rockmount Ranch Wear Mfg. Co., 165
Roosevelt, Theodore, 8–10, 189
Russell, Charles M., 1, 31, 37

Sally Rand's Nude Ranch, 80–81, *108*, 146
Shawver, Mary, 62–63, 134–35, 153, 155, 162, 168, 182
Sheridan, Wyo., 11, 31, 44, 57, 59, 70, 78, 91, 164
Shipman, Gladys, dude ranch for dogs, 51, 155–56
singing cowboys, 137–45
Snyder, Faye, 170–71, 189
Sunlight Ranch, 44–46, 86, 170, 189
Sunset Trail (film), 73

Take It Big (film), 158
Teich, Curt, 98, 174

Thayer, Peggy, 31–32
Tickle Me (film), 183
Triangle X dude ranch, 183
Two Guys from Texas (film), 166

Valley Ranch, Cody, Wyo., 18–20, 33, 37–40, 44, 57, 69, 70–71, 83, 85–86, 91, *114*, *117*, 138–39, 150, 182, 187
Valley Ranch, Pecos, N.Mex., 68
Valley Ranch School, Cody, Wyo., 83–85

Weil, Jack, 165
When the Boys Meet the Girls (film), 184
Wickenburg, Ariz., 29, 57, *111*, 138, 140–41, 148, 161, 191, 194
Wilson, Molly, 163–64
Wister, Owen, 10, 22, 27, 44
Women, The (film), 54–55, 67
Wrangling Dudes (film), 20–21, 24

Yellowstone National Park, 2, 9–12, 27–28, 32, 59, 62, 86

www.ingramcontent.com/pod-product-compliance
Lightning Source LLC
Chambersburg PA
CBHW031434160426
43195CB00010BB/731